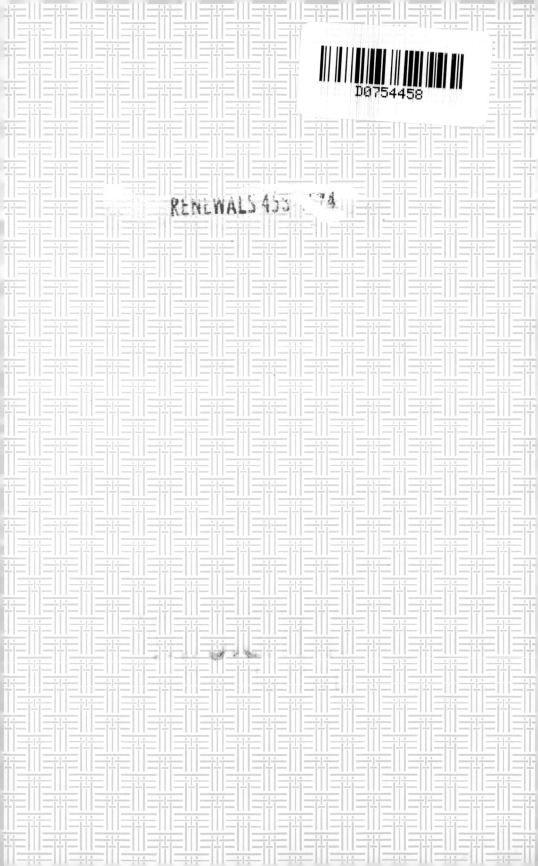

D0754458

# Price Trends

# &

# Investment Probabilities

## Thomas L. Dussault

**THOMSON**

Australia · Brazil · Canada · Mexico · Singapore · Spain · United Kingdom · United States

# THOMSON

™

# PRICE TRENDS & INVESTMENT PROBABILITIES
## Thomas L. Dussault

Library of Congress Cataloging in Publication Number is available. See page 303 for details.

For more information about our products, contact us at:

Thomson Learning
Academic Resource Center
1-800-423-0563

**Thomson Higher Education**
5191 Natorp Boulevard
Mason, Ohio 45040
USA

ii

# Table of Contents

# Dedication

*To the recent passing of my mother whose gift of passionate concern I never felt in kind from anyone else and thus who held riches far more fulfilling than money. It is our parents to whom we are ever indebted and to whom the label "hero" should apply. For whatever accomplishments we might ultimately enjoy can largely be traced to them having sacrificed so much of themselves throughout their lives for us. We can only feebly ever return that aspect of their genuine love.*

*To one very special ex, Joyce, who along with the woman above meant more to me than any other I ever knew. And from whom I learned that the very "sweet roses" only get dropped in our laps so many times in life; best we keep them safe in our arms and never let them go...*

*They were each the bouquet of my life.*

# *Prologue*

*Twenty-two times, 18 times, 16 times on an initial investment! No you haven't chosen a book on astral projection. These numbers reflect the actual and the extraordinary magnitude of returns any investor would have savored in Microsoft (MSFT), America On Line (AOL) and even more conservative Merrill Lynch (MER). Terrific returns—no question, but these numbers were achieved in just 64 trading days!! (October '98—December '98.)*

*Welcome to the savvy investment world of the followers of price trend. Those experienced few that recognize the <u>randomness</u> of short-term movement; who accept regression to the norm for long-term return; and who have the willingness to allow price momentum to become the dominant element for the ultimate fate of investment strategies. Investors who may deploy willing segments of their portfolio's asset base to an idealized investment duration of several directionally trending months and advance their opportunities by the judicious use of leverage. For whoever coined the financial phrase "The trend is your friend" was being lighthearted. The price trend, for investment purposes, is near God-like.*

*In these chapters, the reader/investor can be expected to learn a proper blueprint to exploit—and reap—vast investment potential, not even measured on Wall Street—and rarer still, practiced. To remove the tendency to be a <u>predictor</u> of Wall Street's price action and to permit Nostradamus to rest peacefully, you will instead become more of a savvy observer than reactor to its price message. While very strong trends are few per annum, their leveraged results can be breathtaking! They can play out to grand wealth when allowing them to run to their full extent.*

*This book is the end result of having written and judged hundreds and hundreds of* investment ideas, tips and strategies, resulting from continued learned experiences over nearly a quarter of a century, two decades of professional experience within the securities industry, and researching nearly two hundred investment texts which inevitably imprint one's views. This prompted the decision to collate all of it into a workable on-going investment ideology which could be utilized daily and modified as necessary; thus, the present written expression.

Note: The author was one of the very few, who having created relevant <u>fundamental</u> analysis models, captured Cisco Systems as an investment choice in 1991/1992, <u>years</u> before the mainstream investment community. To prove that model's value early after its inception, in 1981, the best investment return on the New York Stock Exchange belonged to Prime Computer, then PRM, one of the mini computer industry's leading companies. The very same stock was selected by the same fundamental model and which yours truly certainly never allowed the clientele to forget quickly! The mention of which is to merely cite that fundamental analysis didn't escape this author's usage. Yet in retrospect, the study of price movement and of trend focus would have yielded far greater return than the current emphasis on strictly fundamental analysis with an almost non-usage of the technician's proficiency. It was a very expensive tutoring.

The work was designed to provide the reader with a consecutive investment approach. Part One reviews the basic premise of the power of price trend and 'the whys' are explained. Part Two implements in a logical, virtually precise manner, the preferable steps in taking investment action for either long or short investment goals.

Readers expecting a precise sequential pathway to guaranteed riches need to be awakened. Our securities markets are neither exploited by intellectuals, scientists or crap shooters. It is best to align with the best of probabilities that are conceived from repeated successful results. Investment in our markets is not as deductively precise as we might wish it to be. Hence, jettison the explanation that investment actions will work based on a latest or oldest theory, "new" intellectual software, or in-vogue emphasis on something. Or, that securities investment can be channeled into a type of repetitive based logical continuum, not unlike the engineer who designs the girder to support the load and expects it to—every time. The investment domain isn't one of similar scientific expertise nor deductive scrutiny that plays out always as promised. It is probabilistic forecasting of events and it might be more art than science. It is, at minimum, an ever-changing hybrid of each.

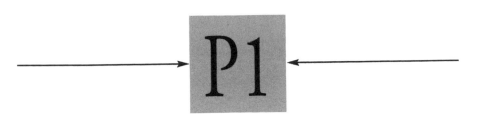

# Part One:
# Planning & Education

# Investment Returns— Fact & Myth

## What's a "Normal" Investment Return Really Telling Us?

Choose almost any investment text and there will be continued mention of the historical long-term return attributable to equity investment (since the early part of the twentieth century) at about a 10 percent per annum compounded clip (albeit even a shade higher over the stellar 1982 to 2000 period.) Most would agree equity investment is the preeminent long-term investment alternative when compared with bonds, real estate, collectible coins and art, etc., despite greater risks associated with equities. What does the 10 percent really tell us?

Equity returns are usually understood as an *absolute* increase in value, annually, on one's equity portfolio assets. However, this isn't completely accurate since the effects of inflation for the duration need to be subtracted out, as would any federal/state income tax liability due, if the asset was a non-qualified investment such as a personal investment portfolio. In addition, some comparative provision—at least some thought—needs to be given to what might have been earned in "riskless" assets, such as U.S. Treasury Obligations as one option. For example:

If a 12-month Treasury Note, yielding 4.5 percent was an alternative option, as well as the simple passbook savings account, then an equity portfolio return inferior to these (at 3 percent) meant the "risk" of holding equity assets was not compensated for. Although this portfolio return may have been senior to a few assets, in our comparison, its return was still inferior to that of riskless Treasury obligations.

Assuming a second portfolio earned the "normal" long-term 10 percent return, and same as above, a 12-month 4.5 percent riskless asset was available, then the investor may have been said to have actually earned only the difference, 5.5 percent (10 percent less 4.5 percent), as the fair compensation for assuming investment risk (asset depreciation). The 5.5 percent figure would be labeled the "excess return."

## How Does Risk Play into Returns?

To make the problem more intricate, there are those who claim that a treasury security is not a "risk" type of asset. That assumption might prove to be misleading because while there are no instances of a U.S. debt obligation defaulting (not paying expected interest and principal) there is always "market risk"—the risk of price decline. Don't think so? Ask someone who purchased a mid- to long-term bond in 1994 and then watched interest rates rise. A 15 to 20 percent depreciation in bond pricing does occur and if a sale were necessary during that period…well, even market losses in Treasury obligations aren't unthinkable.

There can also be risk affecting returns by doing nothing, remaining stagnant in safe bank account assets with little protection from the risk of "asset inflation," the erosion of value over the years from all forms of inflation. To wit: a safe 5 percent bank return lessened each year by a net 1 to 2 percent tax liability and further weakened by 2 to 3 percent inflation, results in zero asset growth—perhaps a rude price for safety? But this monetary reality affects all of us, whether we are investors or not.

There is certainly risk, or an opportunity cost, in remaining buried in declining assets of any type.

There is profound risk, although not directly affecting an asset in place by being unprepared to invest, in not educating oneself long prior to action, or in allowing emotion to dominate once-reasoned planning during difficult periods.

And there is ceaseless risk in refusing to learn from prior mistakes and in an inability to apply sound investment discipline after learned investment experiences—whether the investment is successful or not.

Once again, investment risk comes in many forms.

## Measuring Return—It Should Be Relative First

Rather than getting too academic regarding all the dynamics of what constitutes a normal equity return, the analytical investor, will take note that measuring investment performance correctly on a relative asset basis is a bit involved. Nonetheless, a 10 percent gross, historical normal return—sans any tax consequence in an IRA or 401 qualified plan and compounding over 20 years results in a near eightfold increase or 700 percent. Pretty good, or is it?

The rule of 72 can be helpful: Dividing 72 by any assumed, constant, annual expected return yields the time in years for an investment dollar amount to double in value. Example: 72/10 percent = 7.2 or the number of years it takes for a block of money to double at 10 percent; $1,000 becoming $2,000 in 7.2 years, the $2,000 becoming $4,000 in about 14, and $4,000 totaling approximately $8,000+ around the 21st year.

Investors who are timid regarding equities and want to shun frequent up and down valuation levels, will typically invest in more sanguine alternatives such as bonds, preferred stock, or even cash. For the investors' predisposition to slight risk or simple want for immediate return, measuring performance for their portfolio style might only ask if they outperformed the average cash or income return. Yet with multiple investment inclusions, it's not quite that easy to measure.

An authentic picture of investment skill can be best gauged by a pro rata comparison to these many alternatives. If real estate is very strong, a 10 percent equity return might not be viewed as good on that relative basis. If an investor was only interested in small company U.S. stocks and over-diversified into that sector, then perhaps a 15 percent return on bonds wouldn't be that appealing if the average returns of their small stocks equaled 25 percent. If the S&P 500 returned 5 percent, investors garnering a 10 percent performance in foreign equities, might feel they had outperformed the "market." In esoteric wording, in order to attain a "pure" measure of return, we need to compare broad average asset class returns to the investor's individual asset class returns. The following simple illustration provides an example.

| Percent Weight | $$$ Investment Portfolio (investor) | Reference Indexes (unmanaged) |
|---|---|---|
| 10 | 10,000 Cash | Money Market Returns |
| 20 | 20,000 Large Cap Stocks | S&P 500 Index |
| 15 | 15,000 Small Stock Mutual Funds | Russell 2000 Index |
| 30 | 30,000 Long-term Treasury Bonds | Goldman Sach Long-term Bond Index |
| 25 | 25,000 Real Estate Limited Partnerships | Real Estate Investment Index |

| Asset Class | Annual Returns: Portfolio | Indexes | Superior? |
|---|---|---|---|
| Cash | 4.25 % | 4.86 % | Index |
| Stocks | 10.57 % | 21.64 % | Index |
| Small Stocks | 17.12 % | 4.25 % | Investor |
| LT Bonds | 8.27 % | 9.13 % | Index |
| Real Estate | 12.11 % | 19.00 % | Investor |
| Total Avg. Percent Return: | 10.62 % | 12.97 % | Index |

In this academic example, the indexes did better than the investor's portfolio. This investor's return of 10.62 percent is less than the index's *12.97 percent* simply earned by investing in the respective indexes for the same various asset classes, with almost no effort. (No time is being accounted for shuffling between selections.)

Now let's suppose the investor shunned the idea of spreading his assets <u>between</u> sectors and instead placed the entire portfolio into small cap mutual funds. The 17.2 percent example return, while senior to the 10 percent long-term equity historical return, is still inferior to a return which could have been earned by simply investing in an S&P 500 type index—with no research, no timing, and no effort! This example is hardly fictitious, since "professional" money managers surpass the S&P 500's unmanaged index performance only once in about every five years (that's a paltry 20 percent of the time.) What a case for long-term indexing! Buying the market then falling asleep.

In another strange way, Wall Street sets the cruel paradox of luring investors who are trying to seek superior performance, yet fully aware investment professionals are challenged just trying to match market averages. Try and imagine an advisor noting his profession's dismal on-average track record, then adding, "For historical returns such as this, we additionally charge 1 to 3 percent ongoing annual fees."

There seems to be many reasons why investment professionals do not match S&P 500 long-term performance. One being they must always be invested—even in falling markets—since who is willing to pay management fees if investments are held 100 percent in cash or equivalents? Would you?

Another reason is that money managers can rarely choose the crème de la crème of investment securities as it would mean they would be too heavily concentrated in too few issues, not to mention being adverse to SEC regulations. Thus, too many second-choice securities populate their holdings. And with more than 3,500 mutual funds trading, up a robust 10 times factor since 1982, be assured there are many,

many, second choices populating mutual fund portfolios.

An additional reason is that advisors naturally charge fees, usually in the rage of 1 to 2 percent, for their attempt at making money and for their never-ending quest at matching S&P 500 performance, so an investor's net return is smaller still. These fees are about the negative extent of the difference between their matching S&P performance and not. Were they charging no fee, their performance would almost exactly match that of the S&P 500. And if you think about it, it should, since most of the S&P 500 components are constantly bought by the pros managing mutual funds and pensions.

One further point regarding returns: participation in common mutual funds is "public" investment management. This is when monies are pooled together with an accumulated value and the fund's concept is managed for a preset annual recurring fee.

There is another alternative known as a "private" investment management. In a private investment relationship, the investment objective is given unique priority. And again, the advisor is usually paid a flat percentage fee, normally 1 to 3 percent, based on the continuing valuation of the account's assets. Conceptually, this latter relationship has many pluses. The most material being, by the contract nature of the relationship, the advisor must hold the objectives and results as a main priority. Yet it makes sense to explore some type of added incentive or penalty payment if the advisor performs superior or inferior to the markets or sectors in general, especially when a 2 percent fee only means a $50 to $1 effect upon the advisor's own fee income. Do you think at this rate of "incremental effect" any advisor is losing precious sleep researching investment strategies in the investor's behalf? You would be correct in stating that advisors' management performance suffers because their wallets are so slightly influenced by their performance.

There are also questions pertaining to the accuracy of so-called average equity historical returns, which usually produce a 10 percent return per annum…regardless of how inaccurately we measure available information. Since the measurement for results (academic and news-reported) is always based on reporting entities to the SEC, the NASD, or public shareholders (mutual funds and banks as two examples) and not based on non-reporting groups, private investment management firms, small pension groups, individual accounts and the like, it is a possibility that we have little idea of knowing what the true average investment return across all investors really is.

How do we know if private money managers don't return significantly more than reporting public funds, etc? Factually, we don't. The only common denominator to whom almost everyone reports to is the IRS. This reporting unknown opens an intriguing number of possibilities as to what constitutes investment acumen on an objective scale and questions long held ideas regarding investment models and concepts we have all accepted without review.

If an investor's portfolio did not have a planned asset allocation strategy, unlike as in our prior example, and if the investor decided to concentrate on just domestic markets based on overwhelming evidence of professionals consistently under-performing the market averages meant any attempt "to beat the averages" might prove useless, they might opt for "indexing"—in whole or part.

Indexing is buying an equity position in an investment that tracks a broad market. One such example of trading on the American Stock Exchange, is the S&P 500 "Spiders," which represent 1/10 of the Standard & Poor's 500 index. Another example includes buying shares in another "index type of mutual fund," such as the "Diamonds," which tracks the Dow Jones 30 Industrials. In either case, our investor will earn what the respective indexes return, since those investments are designed to replicate the indices they represent nearly perfectly. *(When a stock is added to, or deleted from, the S&P 500, index funds set buy and sell criteria to immediately replicate those changes—if you are savvy and quick enough, so should you.)* The investor is assured of obtaining the same actual returns—good and bad—from "indexing." This simple approach assures a near 100 percent correlation with the index applicable to whatever proportion of the total account that might be invested therein. With no continuing investor effort, no brainwork, or minimal fees, and performance superior to only a handful of advisors, it's hardly any wonder why these indices have emerged as investor favorites during bullish times!

And if an investor attempted to enhance the portfolio value even more, he or she could invest less than 100 percent in these index types of investments and try to secure superior choices with the balance. Or the investor may attempt to "market time" the indexing, entering (buying the index fund) and exiting (selling the index fund) at the presumed opportune time. It's not easy, but at times it can add to portfolio value compared to sitting through a three to four month decline is no joy. Remember, public companies — *nor in actual practice, investment managers*—cannot go on "investment vacations." "Their" shares trade every day so they participate in everything…and everything isn't always good.

However, few investors have to be invested, every week, of every month, of every year, despite the studies that ascertain being out of the market for even a few select bullish periods can play havoc with returns. Because, doesn't the corollary follow? Being 100 percent present during severe sell-offs certainly can't be lining one's pocket, nor, calming the digestive process, especially where qualified money, IRAs, and 401ks, are involved. Thirty percent industry hits, and times worse, now happen with regularity. Passively hoping, as a substitute for action as money evaporates, isn't a sensible plan for wealth preservation. (It is puzzling as to why an investor in any type of qualified retirement plan would ever sit passively through an evident market or sector correction since there isn't an immediate taxable consequence and the Internet on-line brokers have helped make commission transactions throughout Wall Street incidental. Why risk so much potential downside? If you are remaining in investments only to lose the least…rework the process. Enron debacles are rare but their lessons aren't:

Always mind your money from the perspective of price!)

A parting word for all the perpetual bullish pundit's who didn't and won't alter their dogged perceptions and hence dragged their "blind" followers through 30 to 50 percent short-term price carnage, yet feel vindicated at market's end in some distant month/year as prices ultimately fend higher. That measure for ultimate "acquittal" would never be wrong except for the rare bankruptcy filing, since stock prices (and other items) have a long-term upward tilt to price anyway.

It equally reasons that coming to the press to defend a stock or a market that had been unmercifully pummeled and pronouncing its undervalue is no hard sell. Were the newly bullish proponents just as convinced when issues were 30, 40, and 50 percent higher? Did they warn of impending downside? That posture would have been difficult and placed them out on a reporting limb, or on the "record"…thus they often remain silent and singularly viewed and/or blinded, refusing to accede with actual real event price action, often waiting to opinionate only until probabilities then overwhelm their chance of being wrong—e.g., at very, very, overdue bottoms and tops.

**You can lose a lot of profit during fabulous bull markets through inevitable nasty corrections—a "bull market" label doesn't insulate entirely—nor forever.**

Ultimately, irrespective of the specific magnitude of an investment return, the investor will determine his or her personal satisfaction with performance, yet each would be well-advised to remember that investments do not resolve in a vacuum; performance should always be compared to investment alternatives.

Earning 28 percent in risky biotech mutual funds, when their average returns in some years are 45 percent, should be a large disappointment on a relative basis. A 28 percent return would thrill most of us despite under-performing in the average sector return we had chosen to invest in.

Yet despite academic methodology, a simple objective return can rarely measure complete satisfaction from non-objective, non-measurable effects: fear and worry is almost non-existent in fixed income investments like CDs, money markets, etc. But, of course, there is a price paid for sound sleep.

## Who Do You Trust When Analyzing Returns?

*It is far more than a rhetorical question.*

When trying to assess a good rate of return, too often comparison is made to other indices as measurement for how everyone else is doing. Wall Street's method for tallying returns is to compare a return to major indices during similar periods of time. Yet unfortunately it's fixation in computing indexes—the measuring barometer—on the basis of market capitalization (current market price times number of shares outstanding.) This means the largest companies within the respective indexes will dispro-

9

portionately affect that index level, and investors' perception of how they are supposed to be doing is affected in an equally erroneous manner. The resulting returns from this flawed formula finds its way into the business and Wall Street press, so the percentage returns illusion created by the biggest companies' price movements gets assumed as a proxy for the average returns being earned by all investors. This is sheer lunacy being played illogically through. *(Were this computation rationale a method to estimate profits within an industry, the industry's "health," say in software, then using its largest component, currently Microsoft, might then make practical sense.)*

In April 1998, Microsoft, Intel, Dell and Cisco Systems, the backbone NASDAQ foursome, represented about 25 percent of NASDAQ's market value (Cisco singularly represented about 7 percent of the entire NASDAQ as of November 2000.) If this foursome continued to display greater relative price appreciation, their overweighting in the NASDAQ, NASDAQ 100, and S&P 100 index(s), would only get larger—the bigger feeding upon itself to obtain a greater and more distorting share of any other index they may be part of.

In a year when those four stocks advance 40 percent, as in 1998, and the balance of NASDAQ (both the National and their Small Cap Market portion) totaling 5,600 issues drops five percent, the announced return throughout the investment community would be an approximate *positive 6.3 percent.* Yet in real terms, the average NASDAQ issue across all other company shareholders (99.93 percent) lost money! The horse and buggy era has passed. Data processing is with us and the computation of authentic returns is no longer a puzzle.

In 2000, the press touted how NASDAQ had undergone the year as the "Worst in history." However, if results are measured on an un-weighted average basis with small cap issues carrying the same weight (or importance) as any of the large, the average NASDAQ stock actually advanced almost 28 percent. Yes, 28 percent! Just as in 1999 when the NASDAQ reported the large capitalization stocks were up 80 percent but down a recorded 40 percent in 2002, they then erroneously attributed the decline to all NASDAQ stocks. In truth, for the year 2000, actual NYSE and ASE averaged un-weighted returns were about 11 and 17 percent respectively and did not, as reported throughout the business press, constitute a blanket losing year. And, assuming the "average" investor had a diverse mix of equities with no over-weighting in large cap technology, which very much did get pummeled, they did very well in the year 2000.

Fast forward to early 2001 and in the midst of another NASDAQ technology laden sell off: the average NASDAQ issue was significantly up, approximately 18 percent, through the week ending March 16 and 54 percent in the week ending May 18. Yet, there is nothing in the Wall Street press to cite this fact, nor to limit the pervasive public opinion as to the perception of how the OTC's markets were truly fairing! Provided the average investor was in a diverse mix of equities, they were doing splendidly—even being solely in NASDAQ non-tech stocks! It is in its absence, shameful and misleading, as it is irresponsible for the "Street" to perpetuate the illusion by its silent focus solely on cap weighted results.

2003? The press reported NASDAQ as gaining approximately 50 percent. However investors measuring returns on an <u>un-weighted</u> basis saw the average issue almost double in percent returns. A scant 50 point percentage error between (un-weighted) fact and (capitalization) fiction.

Once again we see just how skewed cap-weighted indices really are in reporting actual, real world, results. And how Wall Street's reliance upon its past and provincial ways does not do justice to informing investors as to what is really going on.

The improper report of what percentage mathematics suggests, can distort: the weighted NASDAQ 50 percent increase would lead many to believe they enjoyed 50 percent increases in their portfolios and they are now 50 percent richer. This presumes they all bought—their original cost basis was one year prior and close to the bottom. If normal investors watch their holdings dwindle during the bear market, their portfolio valuation net results, even after a "50 percent increase," would be murderously beneath peak valuation. Factually NASDAQ had fallen about 70 percent at its trough. *The 50 percent gain actually equates to an estimated 15 percent recovery of lost portfolio valuation.* One more way to more thoroughly view return.

Unfortunately, improper reporting isn't limited to just the OTC market. The Dow Jones 30 Industrials are a price-weighted index. The Dow's overall market value, based on market capitalization, is approximately 90 percent of the S&P 500, and whenever the Dow is up for the year, automatic headlines circulate the positive number so all investors presumably have much to cheer about? Do they really?

A single $200 Dow stock carries as much weight in the Dow's computation as any other four Dow stocks that add up to its $200 price level. In this example, four out of five Dow stocks could be down yet the index might be higher.

Of the many industry sectors within the S&P 500 in the very late 1990s, technology alone accounted for a little more than 24 percent of the entire S&P 500 value. If the tech stocks in that index rose in a proportionately greater percentage amount, then the balance of the index would be further skewed, reflecting more disproportionate results.

The vaunted S&P 500 is universally perceived as the 500 largest public companies by market cap throughout the domestic United States. It is, however, the 500 "largest" by way of the committee that oversees changes in the Standard and Poor's index. Inclusion might mean one of the 500 largest by way of capitalization, or it might be by the committee's choice to include or remove companies, in an effort to balance the many industries within the 500. The result? The S&P 500 index isn't as pure as investors have been led to believe.

In this advanced age of information processing we can, and should, compute the average stock price change across all stocks on an un-weighted—non-capitalized basis—to obtain the true average percentage change of all stocks. All stocks would be given equal weight. When a $10 stock advances 1 point or 10 percent it would be accorded the same meaning as a $70 holding, moving 7 points, a $20 company advancing 2 and so forth. Only in this manner can we know how the average investor, or the average industry sector, is performing in real investment percentage return terms irrespective of the "investment size" of the company. Daily un-weighted percentage figures are available in the market laboratory section of Barrons, the Dow Jones financial weekly, as well as on several quote machines like Quotron. Evidently, Wall Street's conservative past continues to have its way and it's a fair criticism that the Street doesn't report what the average equity in its own profession is accurately returning on a percentage basis. *Plus, to make an historic comparison of weighted versus un-weighted figures, over perhaps the past century or so, would involve an inordinate amount of computational effort for the near 250 daily price changes each year.*

**Weighted price indices, price or capitalization biased, favors no one. They drastically misinform and disproportion performance figures as to how most investors are fairing. This causes professional money managers to make changes and advance more risk in order to "keep up" with the presumed averages that they rightly know are very biased and flawed.**

The purpose of computing the average of anything, is to find out how the presumed majority—the average in-mass—is fairing, not the select few, or, as in these cases, the very biggest companies. A true average return, "the silent market," provides an accurate insight as to how investors are fairing across all equity issues. This is hardly useless information.

Even more alarming is Wall Street's reliance on but a few stocks within industry sectors as an investment proxy for their entirety—sheer nonsense. In most instances, only four to six companies are judged per their collective investment performance, as an accurate representation of their entire industry average, often within industries that contain hundreds of public companies. It is like suggesting an investment in a small semiconductor company should be less important in investment performance than if alternatively having been placed in Intel, the industry's largest. Or insinuating select "large by investment size" drug companies are the "benchmark" for the hundreds of other public pharmaceutical firms, large and small, in the same industry, yet whose overall average investment return apparently is less noteworthy than that of the few chosen? Absolutely senseless and ultimately useless to investors.

On 10/14/2002, with the Dow rocketing upward 4.8 percent, Microsoft then represented 49 percent of the value of the Dow Jones Software Index alone! But…this index comprises 74 *other* software companies whose performance presumably was worth only half of the index's valuation. Seventy-three software investment returns were no greater in importance than one Microsoft? Puzzling…

# *Measuring/Enhancing Investment Performance*

## Demystifying Diversification: Safety, but at What Price?

How might diversification affect returns? It should be axiomatic that as more equities are added to a portfolio during an "active" investment management style with consistent adding and deleting of portfolio equities, there will come a point where the investor, perhaps unwittingly, has chosen to become average, to replicate the norm.

The NYSE had about 3,350 issues trading regularly. If an investor owned an equal proportion, of 100 shares of each company, then our performance would exactly mirror that index (if computation were un-weighted). This makes clear sense, but what it tells us conceptually at least, is that the greater number of unrelated positions an investor owns in an equity portfolio, the more probable the investment outcome will match the broad market from which those equities trade. When former Fidelity Magellan Fund manager, Peter Lynch, was at the helm in the early 1980s, the Magellan portfolio held over 2,300 companies, consisting of more than 70 banks alone. Magellan was almost <u>the</u> market by itself, yet Lynch and his staff still managed to <u>outperform</u> the indices year after year. Truly an amazing equity investment management performance!

Academic studies vary as to how many stocks, and choices, blended into a portfolio constitute the "ideal" number. Theoretically, the ideal number constitutes the fewest stocks that will provide an ample amount of diversification so that "market risk" is minimized. The statistical term "standard deviation," or the "bounce," and the volatility or range of a security's movement are all synonymous with Wall Street's definition of asset "market risk." Minimizing risk really means spreading assets across varying <u>unrelated</u> equities of different risk parameters.

For instance, we wouldn't choose all volatile, all industry similar, etc. (at least in theory.) Of course, explain this to the investor who plunked everything into Dell Computer during the 1997 to 1999 divine technology period and rode away into a southern France sunset with the blonde(s) in the new Ferrari! There are times when "putting all eggs into one's basket" will indeed cede better returns—just hope that lone choice is a front runner! And it naturally follows that if one is so inclined to invest in the "hottest" industry sectors by joining the short-term momentum crowd and be willing to enter and exit intra-week to intra-month, then diversification is automatically being applied by merely switching amongst hot sectors.

Bottom line: Diversification means spreading portfolio risk amongst many equities, so the risk of significant loss to the overall portfolio, in the event one area or stock should falter, is *minimized.* But—*and it's a huge but*—by definition it means subordinating the portfolio's edge if one company has <u>exceptional</u> investment return like the Dell Computer example above, since its grandiose performance would be averaged into the portfolio's presumed more normal returns. Too many equity choices approach the norm; too few add to risk, especially if amongst the few choices is a very inadequate performer. Therefore, an MIT education isn't necessary to understand this basic investment maxim: Too many securities can be just as harmful to potential overall portfolio returns as too few.

If called to task, an ideal number of securities in a personal investment portfolio might be between five to seven, utilizing equal dollar amounts, in different unrelated industries, providing some diversity so as to minimize overall portfolio price risk yet still allow for a few stellar returns to produce a meaningful impact to the overall portfolio investment return.

And the maximum might be simply the top two from each chosen industry, a portfolio total of 10 to 14. The point again: too many can be as harmful as too few. Err on the side of fewer, but choose very carefully. Be very demanding in your inclusion criteria. It is certainly a requirement for the long-term investor to adequately diversify across various unrelated investment choices, far less so for others investing over shorter time frames where profitability is sought in any manner.

## Answering the Question of Choice

In the most theoretical instance, the choice of which stocks might constitute an investor's portfolio should be based on the prospectively highest percentage potential return over your intended holding period (12 months), then resorted so as not to include too much risk from over-concentration in one sector or industry. This means that if you opt to sort or rank the best prospective securities on a percent basis, you would have to do so almost every day based on the universe of opportunities you chose to monitor. If your monitor criterion is 400, then 400 securities should be resorted after each market close. If that number is 4,000, still more computer crunching will be necessary—but this *is* ideologically correct. Why?

If one portfolio stock rose 40 percent in one day, its new percentage investment potential, measured over twelve months, would no doubt change. And if it was one of your original selections, an immediate sale of it, and a sorted replacement from elsewhere, might be warranted action.

Fortunately we live and endure in a more practical world and do not in practice, rebalance and modify our already existing portfolio this frequently. And we probably shouldn't, because stocks might flip-flop and our best today might, after your "downgrading," reemerge the following day as a worthy choice. The only entities making money from this practice would be your broker via commission transactions and your accountant through a UPS truckload of transactions slips.

Consequently, it is recommended that this shifting or re-balancing be done at minimum on a monthly basis, or at least quarterly for an existing portfolio. Of course if the portfolio review is not completed then our initial selection thesis of sorting all possibilities to find the current "best" is recommended at least when new inclusions are considered.

In modern research on equities, termed fundamental analysis with the proliferation of computers for information analysis, what once took hours, if not weeks, for wanted "search" criteria can be produced in seconds!! The author took about 40–45 minutes in the early 80s to completely research the financials of a single stock using annual, quarterly and 10K reports, then manually sorted each result. The point: today, everybody has access to almost instant fundamentals research. It's readily available for a retail price or, in some manner, free. Thus, any investment payoff is no longer attainable from hard numbers crunching which was once the case if you had the desire to put in long, long hours. Technology has removed that advantage and greatly leveled "the informational playing field."

## Measuring Individual Investment Performance Correctly

The percentage difference between net sales proceeds and net purchase cost constitutes the preferred measure of performance (return). Hence the "winner" isn't the one who makes the most, rather the one who achieves the greater percentage return.

| Investor A | | Investor B |
|---|---|---|
| Buy 500 shares of a $40 stock, stock, pay $25 in commission, later sell at $75 less the same $25 commission | | Buy 1000 shares of a $10 stock, sell at $20 with commissions |
| **Net Purchase Cost:** | | |
| 20,000 (500 @ $40) Principal | | 10,000 (1000 @ $10) |
| 25 | Commission | 25 |
| $20,025 | Total Net Purchase Cost | $10,025 |
| **Net Sales Proceeds:** | | |
| 38,500 (500 @$75) Principal | | 20,000 (1000 @ $20) |
| 25 | Commission | 25 |
| $38,475 | Total Net Sales Proceeds | $19,975 |
| **Absolute Return:** | | |
| 38,475—20,025 | | 19,975—10,025 |
| $18,450 | | $ 9,950 |
| **Percent Return:** | | |
| + 92 percent | | + 100 percent |

In our somewhat elementary example answers the question as to which investor did better this year if these transactions constituted their sole investments Investor B did better because of the superior percentage despite making far less absolute money. If Investor B had made the same investment(s) as Investor A, the proceeds would have grown to just below $40,000 which is slightly better than the $38,475 Investor A earned.

There are huge piles of investment dollars, college endowments, larger mutual funds, and sizeable pension funds that earn hundreds of millions of dollars per annum. These raw amounts mean very little unless their investment performance is judged in percentage return and then further compared to the amount of assumed risk undertaken to garner that return.

# Why the Brightest Minds on Wall Street...Still Fail— and Should Never Be Blindly Followed

One of the wonders regarding investment of any duration, especially long-term, is why the seemingly so financially unsophisticated (to Wall Street) terminology and structure can make money and sometimes acquire vast fortunes when the most conversant, most information-rich often don't. How the poorly educated, devoid of financial acumen, acquire great investment wealth while James Cramer, once editor of "the Street.com," and one of the brightest minds on Wall Street, has a mediocre annual 1998? After all, we aren't replacing someone's spleen! What did they all know that Cramer didn't? Maybe...probably...nothing.

This happens because investment returns are independent of investor efforts—clearly after purchase. In almost no other profession will hard effort have little—possibly zero—positive effect. Study, hard work, and preparation are all mainstays for the U.S. societal labor force and vocational successes in general but not necessarily for investment attainment on Wall Street. Very baffling, but very true. The sweet side is that all of us can garner the same percentage investment return as Microsoft's Chairman, Bill Gates, yet with nothing contributed! And that investment fact is extraordinary. With none of the concerns regarding competition, personnel, financing, technological might, knowledge, and a host of other factors, we all can earn the same percentage return as the CEO's of America's great companies. Capitalism at its very best.

The investment decision-making process, after thorough research, is a two-step event—knowing when to buy and when to sell. What occurs in-between is nothing the investor can alter. Corporate management, economic and national policy, world order and so on all have effects, while the investor adds nothing. And since a company's management almost always has a far more significant investment in their company's stock than most shareholders, they have far and away more incentive to affect in a positive manner a continuing stock performance. The investor is thus piggybacking on the efforts of the few who run the company on a daily basis and is really one of the greatest benefits of modern capitalism! Management efforts and an entire world of other events all contribute to the investor's ultimate return regardless of their being wide awake or in a financial coma. Wall Street doesn't pay up for the "intellectual baggage" any of us might have learned, only for the disparity between the price at purchase and the price at liquidation.

And if there were but one assurance, if one of Wall Street's best truly knew where price was headed, there is no way they would announce that fact before acting in their own behalf. And were they consistently prophetic they would undoubtedly command a following which would then make their predictions less potent since attendant masses would move and exit too quickly on their say-so. Robert Prechter and Joe Granville are two former gurus who for a few years held markets captive, and as is usual, they ultimately lost most of the followers.

## Can We Enhance Individual Investment Performance—or Is the Market's Price Trend Just Too Dominant and Neutralizing?

For most investors, their investment goal is to do better than the norm. And within reason, do whatever it might take to accomplish superior return. If an investor believes he or she cannot, or isn't willing to attempt to, acquire superior investment returns, they should merely index their monies. Indexing is simple and it provides a matching return from the results of its component companies.

Only a handful of people have sufficient wealth or clout to affect the companies that their investments are in, and thus most investors only observe results and the investment aftereffects. For those intent upon out-performance, let's discuss three primary methods to enhance investment return:

1. Enter and exit positions with better timing.

2. Learn the art and science of security price trend observation.

3. Choose better investment alternatives by some investment discipline.

Let's summarily observe each one.

### Entrance and Exit Timing

The timing of securities entrance and exit pricing is a matter of learning better execution periods but can never be perfect or consistently close. This is because the driving component of ideal price execution, the buyer/seller decision-making process, is in any instant an unknown to an investor. Pricing is dynamic in fact. A great price today can look awful in a few days. Obtaining consistently, near-ideal pricing, takes on the acquisition of more fortune than skill. And superior entrance and exit pricing still will account for generally a small portion of any excess return.

### Price Observation (Technical Analysis)

Attaining the discipline and savvy to be stock price observant, that is not too anticipatory as to where price may lead without pricing proof, allows us at least the chance to witness a price trend completely played out. Here is where big money is often made. It means capturing most of the available price movement in a price trend—up or down—by allowing investors to move price wherever logic (or not) takes it. *And naturally setting limits to minimize loss would follow as well, since while we might wisely witness price trend movement sans assumption as to duration and magnitude, we clearly don't control it.*

Unfortunately, price trend observation will have one substantial limitation—we cannot observe that which has not yet taken place. We must accept that if we follow price, we will miss some portion of its commencement. A pure fundamentalist, who is intent upon understanding the internal dynamics of the companies they select, can build a position in anticipation of being information accurate on the then price movement.

18

Let's say a company decides to align with China and contract to service that country's huge population. For the sake of example, they obtain exclusive rights to some type of service. And this is to go into effect in the year 2006, with an expected tripling of earnings as a result of the agreement.

If an investor is sufficiently prudent to determine this today, and his or her research proves accurate—the equities may in fact triple in earnings and the value placed on their respective industry's earnings. The standard P/E did not change, and the investor would appear to have reaped a 200 percent gain (the triple) in their future. Yet price valuation based upon fundamentals takes into account a company's industry P/E value, as well as the overall markets valuation upon earnings.

Accordingly, if the industry valuation as well as the broad market in 2005 does not change then a 3 times factor for earnings should result in the practicing fundamentalist investor becoming very handsomely rewarded. However, should any of those three affecting variables play out less than as expected, then our fundamentalist might become a bit poorer from the effort. Yet, they would arrive first whereas the pure technician cannot. But once price trend has begun, the price observer can then participate to the full extent of the duration of the trend—pure fundamentalist decision-making generally doesn't.

### *Making Superior Investment Choices*

Finally, the aspect of securities selection would appear to be another element where we might become more proficient and gain investment advantage. But let's see what that process might entail.

Peter Lynch reminds us that since World War II, corporate profits have risen near 250 fold and so too have securities prices. Hence the near one-to-one correlation… and we all know that stockholder equity translates into corporate worth and ultimately share price, and is best increased by earnings gains. We have also witnessed these facts in observing the long upward spiral of price over 60 years. Price reflected the fundamentals reality. Fortunately, price alone also reflects the market's estimation of value today, with or without earnings. Remaining sensitive to price, permitted investors to participate in the hot market sectors such as biotech, the internet, and the NASDAQ take-off in 2003, despite significant measures of profitability.

Basing participation upon solely a fundamentals approach—which many excellent investments didn't have—would have meant forgoing at least the possibility of great gains throughout the mid- to late-1990s and maybe even a sideline position since stocks sold at virtually historic valuation measures, EPS, book value, revenue to price, and so forth, throughout most of that decade.

The fact is that because earnings have risen and so too have securities prices, doesn't mean that they alone have driven price up. What it means is that solid earnings, in the right investment period, are <u>one</u> of many reasons that create buying interest in specific equities. The unfortunate fact is that earnings alone can't create a lasting edge in the buy and sell equation under bleak investment periods. Even in the absence of corporate profitability, stock prices have still soared in market sectors and no matter how temporary that may have been, remarkable returns have been realized. If earnings indeed were an independent variable as Mr. Lynch suggests, then ample returns should be evident regardless of market period. And without same, simply should not. Market history educates us otherwise.

If you chose investments on the basis of their fundamental qualities, the business model, actual earnings, product portfolio and so forth in a manner that an investor might seize upon "undiscovered" information and therefore acquire an investment edge, would they research in superior fashion? Maybe. Would they value the fundamentals they discover in a more acute manner than most? With financial information so readily available, that's a tough sell. Is there even a way to remove a 30 percent price advance, the proportion of that move based upon buyers and sellers making fundamental decisions alone? And if we can, can we know how we might perceive fundamentals repeatedly better than the next guy? The answer to each is a hearty not likely.

Wall Street security analysts get paid, on average, six figures to pour over company fundamentals, make periodic visits, gain inside access to information sources, and earn management's ear. Despite their inconsistent earnings prediction and incessant bullish preoccupation (since their company's future is always rosy) even their critics would probably agree, that they know their company inherently better than most investors could hope to. Then how do we as private investors amiss in fundamental review gain any advantage?

All brokerage research firms follow the largest companies first, typically the S&P 500. With that aspect of the marketplace so saturated with fundamentalist opinion, it would seem logical to research and focus upon areas where Main Street research chooses not to examine. This lands us in the areas of mid-cap and small-cap companies, those of generally less than one billion in market value. Since the "pros" don't research in these areas very often, the inefficiencies of a fertile, undiscovered market portion can be brought to advantage if done correctly and—almost as important—if that sector or section of the marketplace is then in vogue.

When this author "discovered" Cisco Systems (CSCO) in 1992, it was then a small–cap growth company with a fundamentals–only approach, with 30 percent pretax profit margins, earnings doubling each quarter, and a positioning in information processing. It became a stellar investment because the "small-cap sector" in general and technology in particular, was "in play." They were very hot. Otherwise, Cisco may have languished for years as did much of that market sector in the late 1990s, despite achieving an historic valuation advantage compared to their larger brethren.

What we may be left with if our only approach is that of pursuing the fundamentals of the largest companies in trying to capitalize on inefficiencies, yet knowing that is most unlikely, is the probability that superior performance will be fueled by market and/or industry impetus via price trends. Or, in simple English, you are unlikely to outperform selecting large companies on the basis of their fundamentals solely—professional competition is too keen. Your investment return is, more likely than not, going to match their overall performance.

If we correctly align with the types of securities that are trending in a definitive manner, and if we can position ourselves soon enough to capture most of their directional price nature, we are creating the probability of superior return on the basis of a price trend singularly. And not on how much we can understand about the companies we own a part of, as lone shareholders, or their earnings, internal expectations and the like. At best, most investors take a cursory view of what they own. Most of us could not possibly understand all the dynamics of our investment holdings, and in most instances, it wouldn't terribly matter. For it's one thing to totally comprehend a business model in concept; it's radically different trying to ascertain and predict its execution—the demand for its services and investor reaction.

It is questionable whether even a CEO can affect demand other then on a temporary basis. As investors, we control and affect virtually nothing within our investment portfolio. Our knowledge of what we believe is going on, is always subordinate to what mere price observation tells us. If management paints an exceptional picture—think of Enron for a moment—and price cascades down nonetheless, why remain trapped by the promise of fundamentals bailing you out? They might, but from what price level? And when? Yet intense price observation, with loss limitations, would surely have saved most of them!

### A Few Final Observations

If fundamental research has real meaning for you, try and confine the effort to those areas least followed. Trying to outguess what all the pros seek is tough and probably pointless. Discovery of an unknown company can have far greater favorable investment impact.

Only in the instance of the commencement of a price trend, would price observation not be superior to reliance upon fundamentals. As investors, we profit only from price. From buying low to selling high, it makes practical and realistic sense to be focused upon the price value of our investments. All else is, in reality, secondary.

What we see in price isn't expectation. Nor is it wordy opinion. What you witness in price trend is reality for as long as it endures and despite the reason behind it.

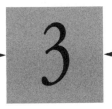

# Price Trend Formation

## True Story...Proving a Point

The time was the spring of 1980, I was four years removed from having gone off to law school (chose not to finish, so hold the hand clapping) and employed with the utmost patience at E.F. Hutton as a novice broker. And with seemingly at times, that gloried youthful opinion that suggested whatever I felt about our equity markets <u>would</u> be played out...of course exactly, and naturally, *when* I expected. But reality and the calendar would eventually bring about a harsh perspective. (With a prime rate of 16 percent, we were pitching stocks—hello in there! Of course, none of us had the simple insight to have captured the then-available, intermediate and long-term historic yields on any non-callable bonds.) Yet drifting aimlessly or not, about to invest in one of the most profitable investments in percentage terms that I would ever stumble into in my life, with both eyes wide open, I might have made a small fortune.

The price of oil that spring was rocketing with security analysts all advising of a soon-to-be $50 per barrel price tag. Every brokerage firm in the world was pushing oil and gas and real estate limited partnerships as "can't miss," "...they are all excellent" diversification type investment vehicles. (Years later, these same firms would be dodging an array of legal "bullets," for those recommendations having sadly tanked.) Houston was the hotbed. Oil drillers and rigs were everywhere and bellowing—and so was J.R. on "Dallas." It was the modern era of "Black Gold."

It reasoned that, if the price of oil were to continue skyward, and if an oil company engaged in pursuit of the crude, they would show fast and fat profits. Their stock price would probably sing skyward and investors would reap millions on the boiling energy boom. It made for economic persuasion and it sure appeared to make investment sense—at least it did on paper.

I decided, with research, some money in the bank, a secure and growing income stream, and with no urgency attached to the invested monies, to venture into an oil company, Superior Oil (SOC at the time), and purchase their call options. (Call options advance in value with a corresponding rise in the underlying stock price.) My "investment" now controlled the equivalent of 1,000 shares of a $200 plus stock, something I could never have afforded with cash or with margin (borrowed) buying. I had "leveraged" my investment dollars in the <u>right direction</u> of an <u>advancing intermediate trend</u>. My small dollar outlay "controlled" the equivalent of nearly a quarter of a million dollars worth of the common stock—I was ready for a very, very, sweet ride!

As the months went by, Superior Oil would run upward quickly at times, slightly pull back, make another advance, somewhat stall, but again move forward. Yet the stock would always make a "higher high," and when it declined a bit, the lower pricing would be higher than the prior correcting price lows. The classic "technical" uptrend bullish pricing pattern—*higher highs and higher lows.*

With the stock consistently trending higher with the underlying options following and with my not fearing losing any profits since there was no evidence of a near term decline in the price pattern and with no immediate need for the monies, I was allowing myself to view the stock play itself out completely. To witness the stocks total intermediate move minus any assumptions or forecast on my part. I was in control and was not using "scared money." Being both a fortunate holder than a lucrative participant and not just a mere sideline viewer bemoaning: "Why did I ever sell…"

The stock would ultimately begin to slow its ascent, then cease to advance at all, where I then felt it was time to exit. I had the absolute temerity with a cost basis of a shade above a buck ($1), to place a sell <u>limit</u> order at $20, on a portion of the option position, being too dim to sell it all. (The $20 limit order meant I had to receive at least $20 for each of those options…or no sale could take place! Apparently $19.50 wouldn't have been sufficient!!! Talk about impractical greed. And you can't wonder why some species eat their young.) Luckily I got the "fill." I was out with immediate plans for a second XKE. I then proceeded to watch, to sit and watch the remaining position fall about 70 percent before being sold—a real stroke of brilliance. This was a trend reversal in motion, from bullish to bearish…and I hadn't a clue. A -$5,600 profit pass. The price of extraordinary naiveté and classic evidence of any discipline or exit strategy or, bluntly, having not a hint as to what I was doing.

It was later asked why I hadn't purchased "puts" after the first sale at $20, since I had "called" the intermediate top. (Puts are an options investment which assumes a <u>falling</u> stock price.) Back then, I couldn't imagine investing in a reversing trend that quickly and risking large profits to potentially pocket more money from downside movement. The true "gift" for youth and ignorance.

The final outcome provided a <u>1,300 percent profit in about 76 days</u>—even having missed the full potential of a 20 times factor profit! (In bantering a "what if and perfect" scenario: Had $20,000 been invested...might $280,000 have been removed? And if total liquidation were at the top $20 price...perhaps $400,000? Those entire amount(s), invested near the bull markets August '82 bottom, would have had this author well into retirement by the mid-90s...from a one trade outcome!)

In retrospect, many years, and many, many, thousands of transactions later, an almost perfect lesson for a price trend following thesis. A style/technique that should have been theoretically replicated each time thereafter. The return wasn't earned over 15 years at a 10 percent long-term norm or over two weeks on a "hot tip," nor was it "day trading." Rather over a few short months, by merely following the directional intermediate trend in place to its own price conclusion, with a coincident strong market and industry/sector as a tailwind. When the Dow roamed in the 800 to 900 area and 35 Dow points was viewed as a buying panic.

## How Much Potential Is There in Enduring Intermediate-Term Trend Movement?

It is one thing to conjure up that a strategy for a market period that you think can be very profitable and yet quite another to actually find attainable results. After attempting to locate at least a formal study on options performance and having no luck, I completed a study in November 1998 (two years prior to the conventional acceptance of the market's peak) to ascertain what the average option would have returned compared to the average stock across many different industry sectors during five then-recent intermediate market periods—recent as to reflect what was the then current state of market condition and investor mindset, etc.

### The Study

The 1998 study sought to find out how much effect the broad markets intermediate trend movement might have on stocks and their respective options and to find out the magnitude of that effect. Historically, 80 to 90 percent of stocks will directionally trend—that is, follow the market's up or down direction over most short-term periods. Would merely being correct about the market's intermediate direction be profitable? An easy bet, but if so, by how much with both stock and options? The results were a stunner!

### *The Study's Design & Construction*

The Dow Jones 30 Industrials were used as the sample market index. (While the Dow is only 30 stocks and at times is at odds with the other indices in the short-term, reviewing the various historical chart patterns of the S&P 500, NASDAQ, Russell 1000, 2000 and 3000 etc., there is a very strong directional correlation and magnitude between all these indices and the Dow over periods other than the short-term.)

Yet, if desired, the S&P 500, the standard equities portfolio benchmark, could have been used virtually interchangeably; indubitably the results would not have been dissimilar.)

The selection of industries and securities therein was made across a broad sample so no concentration in one area would skew results. The hottest sector, the Internet, was not utilized since its results would have returned unrealistically high and unlikely-to-repeat figures. (Words written in 1998, how prophetic.)

The options exercise prices measured was set approximately 10 percent above/below (for respective calls and puts) the then underlying stock price, just slightly out-of-the-money, or the closest option strike price to the stock price in other cases.

The expiration period was set as close to 60 days out to provide the time to capture intermediate term trend price movement.

The measured performance for call options was from their respective options price at the beginning of the market's intermediate term move, or bottom, to their then options theoretical, or actual price, coincident with the markets later intermediate term ending, or top. And vice versa with put options.

The Black Scholes (Options Pricing) Model was used to estimate volatility and pricing where necessary.

*The Results*

| | | DOW JONES | | OUR SAMPLE | | |
|---|---|---|---|---|---|---|
| Intermediate Trend Periods | Direction | | Stocks: | Options: | Type: |
| 4/11/97–8/7/97   17 weeks | BULLISH | + 28% | + 23% | + 191% | Calls |
| 8/7/97–10/28/97 13 weeks | BEARISH | - 8% | - 5% | + 15% | Puts |
| 1/12/98–4/22/98 15 weeks | BULLISH | + 20% | + 25% | + 192% | Calls |
| 7/17/98–10/8/98 12 weeks | BEARISH | - 17% | - 27% | + 356% | Puts |
| 10/8/98–11/24/98 7 weeks | BULLISH | + 20% | + 32% | + 619% | Calls |

During the 1/12/98–4/22/98 bullish period, 91 percent of the sample stocks rose—in correct proportion to the historical norm. From 7/17/97–10/8/98, in a very difficult sell-off, 98 percent of the sample fell, and from the 10/8/98 bottom, during that marvelous bullish period, through the arbitrary sample end—not the price end—on 11/24/98, 90 percent of the sample stocks advanced.

View the 10/8/98 market intermediate term bottom and note the total return through 11/24/98 when the Dow mildly stalled and our study was prematurely completed. The average total return for the call options was a stunning 619 percent! Even missing 20 percent of the bottom and top, still resulted in a stellar 360+ percent return (619 percent -20 percent and -20 percent) compared to a shade above 18 percent for the sample stock return. 18 percent versus 360 percent; 20 times the difference between options and stocks! This was one startling effect in leveraging investment dollars—thoroughly appealing when it works. Again this study was completed months prior to the Dow's top in the Spring of 1999, and well before the late October through early January 2000 intermediate term advance when NASDAQ ran wild.

*Note the AMAT example below:*

Using Applied Materials (AMAT) a large semiconductor company as a proxy: In late October 1999 the stock sold for about $40. The then, February 2000, $45 call options would have sold for about 4 and the stock hit about $95 in February 2000. The same option would have then fetched about $52, a 13 times factor, 1,200 percent; $2,000 was then worth $26,000, and $5,000 increased to $65,000! We all know that NASDAQ advanced well into late March 2000...when the champagne indeed ran dry.

It is also worth mentioning that since there are far fewer intermediate-term trends than short-term, an investor need not be as continuously directed toward monitoring, or toward investment activity, to earn a handsome profit. This is a huge benefit in infrequent investing activity and needless to point out, fewer commissions get generated, less paperwork is written for the tax consequence, fewer strategies have to be examined, and less stress is felt.

An easy critique of the study is to argue that the resulting stocks and options implicit bullish returns, involved trade entry, for calls, coincident with the market's (the Dow's) intermediate low and an exit, coincident with its ensuing top–both admittedly near impossible. (And equally true for bearish trends.) Yet the option's ultimate pricing did not necessarily coincide with the markets, meaning there would have been a more-or-less, profitable picture depending on the investor's trading abilities. Presupposing that an investor missed the first 20 percent of an intermediate advance and sold 20 percent prior to the top, the resulting 60 percent "capture" would still be nearly attainable and in most instances that as well, was extraordinary! Again to emphasize, these are the average study returns. Average. How attractive might the results have been for an ability to have chosen the better within the sample, maybe the upper one-third? Or, even the top few!

**The dramatic inference from the study is that the simple magnitude of return using the leverage of options was so far in excess of what might have been assumed. These numbers invite a hard look. It should cast the intermediate option as a very viable investment tool.**

(Similar study results and conclusions are to be expected in future time periods and not just limited to the late 1990s, since option returns on lengthy trending equity positions are going to be very lucrative regardless of the calendar year.)

## What About the Other Trends: Long-Term, Short-Term

### *The Long-Term "Can't Miss," "Old Testament" Script*

The long-term investment dictum of "buy and hold" has been referred to as "can't miss" and "a sure thing" for so long (almost 20 years since the bull market's secular rise begun in August 1982) that it is the rarest of an increasing informed investment community that hasn't bought into the idea: Equity investment is essentially one direction—up—if one waits long enough.

During periods of Federal Reserve restraint, when long- and short-term interest rates—the competition for equities—are under an accommodative Fed policy (and thus have a downward bias) most investors know that equity prices have historically risen. Hence no "magic bullet" theory needs to be perpetuated to arrive at the conclusion that barring Fed intervention and an upward bias to interest rates, and that with rates low to moderate, equities are the place to be. They can only approach the sun over time (well not quite). This has been true for so long that arguing against long-term equity investment as a reasoned substitute for almost all savings, except a few months of emergency need, has been simply imprudent. It has flat out worked.

Keep in mind it's worked for as long as you have remained in a long-term bull market and when we haven't—or had consequential sector corrections—your portfolio would been very adequately diversified, and if a bad industry period or two was reported it would not create a significant negative impact. Without adequate diversity, the simple buy and hold can be <u>disastrous</u> during bleak market or industry sector periods.

### Never, never, believe buy and hold works long-term for any type of equity portfolio.

### It doesn't!

And in historical context, rising rates aren't always an impediment to advancing markets so long as their absolute rate is far below the long-term 10 percent equity return. The easy rationale as to why the U.S. markets have risen with corresponding rising interest rates, the alternative cash or "riskless" investment, wasn't appealing enough to draw money away. But it might well be, at 10 to 11 percent prime and corresponding 7 to 8 percent money market rates.

Corporate management, however prone to short-term mistakes, over the long haul will always try to isolate and remedy problems. There is, therefore, a natural bias for stock performance to be upward since management efforts (to get profits going) as well as their compensation (much of their remuneration is tied to common stock performance) are aimed at better—not worse. Investors too are always looking for stocks to own, to buy but rarely to sell and almost never short. Can you imagine someone thumbing through financial profiles eager to find stocks to short in their retirement accounts—assuming a maverick trustee would even allow the idea? The long-term bias is simply always rolling upward. And there is nothing to disagree with here.

In economics, the statistical term "regression to the norm" suggests that as results move too far in direction from their historical average, those out-of-the-ordinary figures are destined to regress to their more normal levels. This means that when equity returns advance well above their historical 10 percent norm, such as throughout the past two decades, they will have to revert to that more sanguine level.

This assumes that the historical 10 percent return is the "normal" and that a new lasting era hasn't begun which would change return expectations. Suffice to say, waiting for equities to do the "expected" can take many years and cause much frustration. It's sound and is far more lucrative to focus in the current investment climate rather than anticipate what the long-term might produce. The above suggestion would have kept investors in the markets during the late 1990s, despite the pessimists arguing that stocks were overvalued and due to collapse. The failure in the non-believers thesis was that they ignored a basic market axiom.

**The market dictates what is and isn't relevant through price revelation, not market pundits or the press. The flow of stock pricing is too obvious a final say to be ignored. Pricing at a moment in time is not illusory; quite the contrary, it is very stark reality.**

Despite the above warnings, there does appear to be statistical correlation to the continuing expectation of investment returns regressing to the norm over long duration even when banner market periods occur—the 1950s through the early-to mid-60s. The longer one measures returns, the more those returns approach the historical 10 percent norm—that is, they approach the average. If you take mutual fund returns, as one example, over a ten year period and then view the same investment group's results over 15 years, the latter returns will be lower—and lower still at 20 and still lower at 25 years. In other words, returns motion toward the markets 10 percent long-term norm, the longer the measuring period.

Using a more academic view, as equities age, their "differing" component (their Alpha) tends to approach zero or be a non-event or irrelevant. An equities Beta, which is sensitivity to overall broad stock market movement, tends to approach 1.00, a one-to-one correlation between the overall market and a stock's movement. Thus, if there is no Alpha effect and no differing Beta effect, then stocks over a period of decades will parallel the market as a whole and thusly return the market's normal 10 percent equities return. The explanation (and you are in bed with history as to why) is security performance tends to even out over multiple years and over decades. Generally, the best regress to normalcy is the inferior progress to an average.

29

An actual Dreyfus mutual fund ad from Barrons, April 5, 1999 issue, the "Lipper Mutual Funds Quarterly" summary, appears in Figure 3.10 attesting to this phenomenon. It shows the average Lipper Mutual Fund long-term returns for hundreds of types of mutual funds for growth and growth and income investment objectives. As expected, the longer the holding period, the more these fund's returns revert toward the historic 10 percent equities benchmark.

Figure 3.10

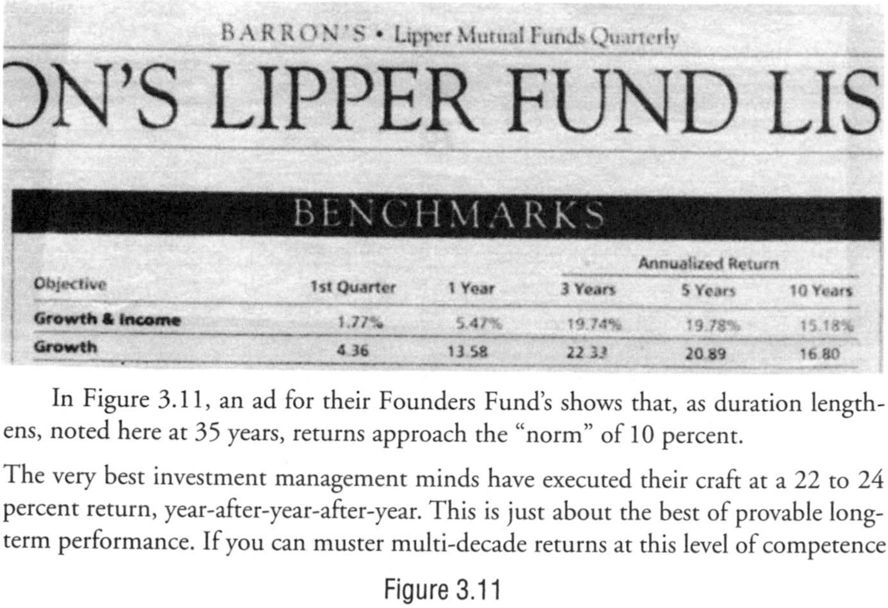

BARRON'S • Lipper Mutual Funds Quarterly

## ON'S LIPPER FUND LIS

### BENCHMARKS

| Objective | 1st Quarter | 1 Year | Annualized Return | | |
|---|---|---|---|---|---|
| | | | 3 Years | 5 Years | 10 Years |
| **Growth & Income** | 1.77% | 5.47% | 19.74% | 19.78% | 15.18% |
| **Growth** | 4.36 | 13.58 | 22.33 | 20.89 | 16.80 |

In Figure 3.11, an ad for their Founders Fund's shows that, as duration lengthens, noted here at 35 years, returns approach the "norm" of 10 percent.

The very best investment management minds have executed their craft at a 22 to 24 percent return, year-after-year-after-year. This is just about the best of provable long-term performance. If you can muster multi-decade returns at this level of competence

Figure 3.11

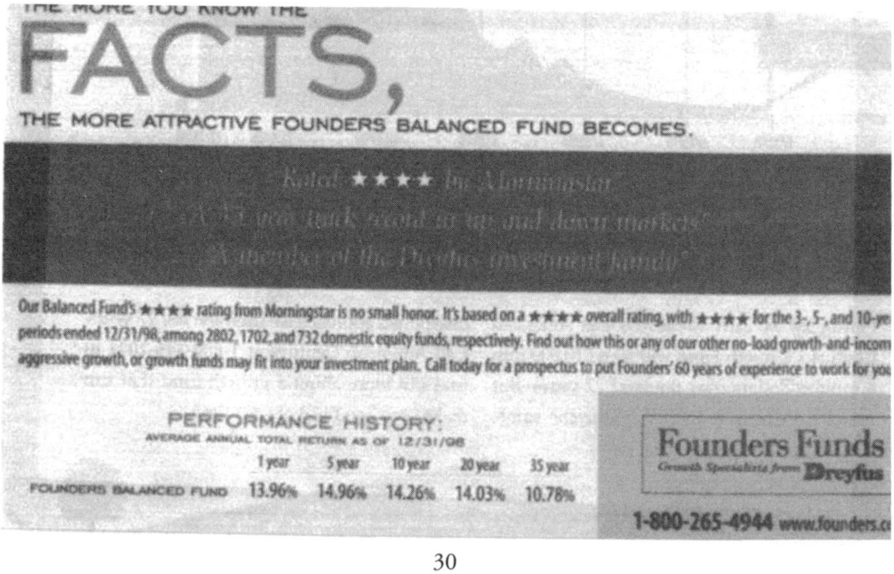

THE MORE YOU KNOW THE

## FACTS,

THE MORE ATTRACTIVE FOUNDERS' BALANCED FUND BECOMES.

Rated ★ ★ ★ ★ by Morningstar.

A 35 year track record in up and down markets.

A member of the Dreyfus investment family.

Our Balanced Fund's ★ ★ ★ ★ rating from Morningstar is no small honor. It's based on a ★ ★ ★ ★ overall rating, with ★ ★ ★ ★ for the 3-, 5-, and 10-ye periods ended 12/31/98, among 2802, 1702, and 732 domestic equity funds, respectively. Find out how this or any of our other no-load growth-and-incom aggressive growth, or growth funds may fit into your investment plan. Call today for a prospectus to put Founders' 60 years of experience to work for you

PERFORMANCE HISTORY:
AVERAGE ANNUAL TOTAL RETURN AS OF 12/31/98

| | 1 year | 5 year | 10 year | 20 year | 35 year |
|---|---|---|---|---|---|
| FOUNDERS BALANCED FUND | 13.96% | 14.96% | 14.26% | 14.03% | 10.78% |

Founders Funds
Growth Specialists from **Dreyfus**

1-800-265-4944 www.founders.c

you are one of the very best anywhere and very well paid—and deservedly so. Yet sitting on one's hands, to just buy and hold, during the duration of a long-term bull market isn't tasking, or a cerebral event. Watching valuations tilt up and down, and only measuring end result, takes zero talent. Nearly anyone can accomplish what three to four years of inactive un-involvement produces. The intent, and the goal, should be to attain *superior* relative period performance and not mere sleepwalk through significant price gyrations. Because the one time when an investor needs to completely remove monies for something very significant or permanently might not just coincide with an accommodating market climate.

### But over the Long-Term, Everything Rises Anyway

The astute reader also understands that although equities produce long-term <u>positive</u> returns there isn't anything unusual about most assets and goods in general <u>appreciating</u> over years and certainly over decades. It's cast from wages and inflation in a free economy. Because of the long-term equation of a buying and selling, forces on goods and services, tangibles and commodities etc, inflation and systematic upward pressure on pricing has always been somewhat prevalent. We have even heard there haven't been any rolling 20 year periods where the Dow hasn't been higher. Is this really unique?

In what other areas of commerce are prices less than 20 years prior! Where else? Housing? Whose residence is cheaper today then when Ronald Reagan took over? Education? You educate your college son and daughter for less today then when you went? Food? The family's food bills are dwindling? Health Care? Yes, of course, it's cheaper today, just as are health care premiums and hospital stays. With but few exceptions, everything rises over decades; it's hardly a wonder that equities would as well.

Most men can relate to changing their own car's oil—at least at some time. What was the price of a quart of oil 20 years ago? Maybe 30 to 40 cents. Today it's $1.50–$1.75. A $100,000 stockpile of motor oil, inventoried somewhere, and now put on the market suggests the owner has a potential 300+ percent profit upon sale. They enjoyed long-term appreciation as well.

Consequently, it isn't <u>unexpected</u> that equity prices would rise as well over decades. Can't it be argued that placing the same monies optioned for investment into a basket of commodities or household nondurable goods might rise in value, although perhaps not in exact equal manner? It certainly would seem so.

Yet another example: the Dow first broke the 1000 point level in 1966 but not again until August of 1982—a formidable 16 years later. Only in 1992, in inflation-adjusted terms, did it actually surpass the 1966 high! Yet in <u>constant</u> dollars, excepting the price of computer chips, or television sets, everything else seems to rise in price over time, equity prices being no exception.

Of course this isn't meant to suggest that the main fundamental variable affecting normal long-term stock performance—the internal earnings growth compounding over decades would equate, in total investment return, to that of hoarding a basket of commodities for later revival. The point however: the impact of inflation raises all boats–the prices of both General Electric's stock, as well as its light bulbs.

The reader should be cautioned to not presuppose that long-term equity strategies such as "dollar cost averaging," during continuing bull markets, and within adequately diverse portfolios, and the truly remarkable effect of compounding money over decades, each don't make an outstanding contribution to investment success with or without the effects of inflation. These are the benefits of long-term "true" investment and, where most American fortunes have been, and continue to be found.

Yet, <u>evident</u> bear market periods—certainly near their advent—should invite no "dollar cost averaging", since continually falling prices means shares will be capable of dropping lower and lower...and lower still. Contrasted with bull markets, where by definition buying the "dips" (the retracements against the primary upward trend) means buying more shares at lower prices, all the while knowing those shares are destined to be higher over time.

What once looks as easy and one-sided as to "how the long-term always wins," when judged today in <u>relative</u> terms—surely seems a bit less glowing.

### And to the Very Short-Term

Short-term trends can be defined as those from minute-to-minute, day-to-days, or anything from weeks to a month, maybe even two. One thing is a given: the shorter term, the focus, the more random the result and an overwhelming cessation of consistent investment advantage.

The gist of short-term investor thinking is that other investors will process information in the same manner and with the same sense of urgency as they do. For a given set of facts, others will see the investment in like manner, will parallel their thinking, and buy or sell accordingly. But what happens if they don't?

If you're convinced just-released bad news will hurt your holding and you rush to liquidate, but most of the other holders already felt, rightly or wrongly, that selling wasn't warranted at that time—such as: the news was "already in the stock"—you will have been price premature and probably poorer. If you are ultimately proven correct and the stock drops unmercifully, you will still wear the "having sold too soon" tag and with less than should-have-been proceeds. This example provides all the more reason why the short run is so rough.

When the focus is extremely short-term, at worst minute-to-minute, the basis for judgment can't be much. Therefore luck and fate play an increasing role. An example of this, in part, is any kind of day trading phenomenon. This is where an investor armed with an array of technological might has the edge of instant access to quotes from multiple competing electronic exchanges with <u>real</u> bids and offers for stocks displayed and attempts to buy and sell many hundreds, and frequently, thousands of shares. This is an almost instant process, and profit on the "spread" means the difference between buying and selling price. For some—and apparently very few—it works well. *At least it works well some times.* For the majority, it doesn't, nor should it—at least no more than one would expect when the defining element between success and failure must occur in perhaps minutes and often seconds! Any assumptive "skill level" pointing to why success is achieved is much in question.

*The following examples are illustrative:*

An investor watches a stock plunge along with the market and later watches an apparent rally beginning from a price level of 30. If this ultimate short-term advance (of course unknown before the fact) is going to be 7 and 37 points, and our investor simply watches the price advance to 32 before he or she is convinced the rally is a real one. The investor does the same thing at a potential exit price of 37 by witnessing a 35 price before pulling the trigger, to shrink a potential 7 point gain into one of three. Perhaps not bad, but less than 1/2 of what might have been. Pull out two commissions—however now insignificant—and a fat ordinary tax bite from the short-term gain plus, the transaction anxiety involved and it might not be a debate if even profitable short-term moves are worth the effort.

Assume another investor has to decide between buying stock outright at $50, or its options, with a strike price of $50 for $3, or $300 per contract. If the investor purchases 500 shares outright he or she advances $25,000 and each point upward means a $500 profit. The options purchase costs $1,500 and a 5 contract lot times $3, or $300 each. Assuming a purchase, the following might occur within 30 minutes and NO real "skill" has at any time to be deployed:

If the stock advances to $55 our stock buyer is $2,500 ahead (the five point advance times 500 shares.) The option buyer likely sees his or her price run to about 7. That's a 4 point profit times a $5 contract holding or $2,125, which is a slight difference from the stock purchase. If the stock drops two points from the initial price of $50, (-4 percent), the stock buyer's "paper" loss, yet unrealized, is $1,000. However, the option price might become 1, resulting in a smaller loss of $625, but with a -42 percent paper loss drubbing, all for being but four percent "wrong." (The worst is yet to come as the option's buyers ultimate total loss remains potentially $1,500 at expiration; this of course would result in a 100 percent <u>realized</u> loss.)

Therefore, for being only four percent "wrong," our options purchase has resulted in a 42 percent loss, with the time left to expiration to turn things around being of only slight consolation. Granted, the stock might still rise, or it might continue to fall. The point is you cannot know definitively in the short-term what will occur next. When trading stock options, we can see the almost perfection needed to not lose our investment capital is to develop a downside protective plan to limit large percentage losses. Blame it on the absence of time to deploy any expertise.

*Excellent Case in Point:*

During this writing, this author purchased a few call options on drug giant Pfizer at a $1 3/8 price. The stock was in a clear uptrend and closed to an all-time high, indicating that perhaps a price breakout, a further lasting immediate price advance, was imminent. The market <u>and</u> pharmaceuticals industry were advancing. The prior day the stock had been down, and on the day of purchase was down an additional -1 when the purchase execution was made. A "good" price was thought to being received, but from whose perspective! The following morning, a Wall Street firm—unannounced and uninvited—decided to opinion that the drugs might not be the place to be. All stocks associated with the industry dropped on the opening bell. Pfizer, which had been the strongest thus the one purchased, fell less than one might expect, but nonetheless fell.

Final tally: An option being sold later that morning at 3/4 meant a percentage loss of about 45 percent! We see how an "out of nowhere" or "wrong" comment will cause much $$$ options pain. But for an "instant," comment and reactive three to four percent drop in the price, that 45 percent of an options capital could be surrendered in a single day! Somehow the disparity of losing 45 percent when only 4 percent "guilty" seems a hint as to a gamish nature of short-term options. Ouch!! Bring on the roulette table? (To be fair, three weeks prior, a purchase of Novellus (NVLS) and their following day surprising inclusion into the S&P 500 was a "right" comment or good unanticipated news that sent their call option's purchase soaring...the author enjoyed the "game" that day.)

## Simple warning for short-term options involvement: Don't...or just don't do it too often.

It would certainly seem that the IRS is one entity which, if inclined, might be willing to release its internal figures as to how options investors fare. Do they lose money as commonly as we all believe? And is the IRS better if investors do better? If, as an unbiased source, the IRS makes known that say 80 percent of tax returns showing options buying lose money, that fact might discourage continuing options trading and the losses that follow. Short-term losses do not benefit the IRS, but gains benefit the IRS with an increase in due tax liability!

Yet, if investors handle purchase options risk correctly, results should be far better than suspicion might otherwise suggest. For example, investors who purchase call and put options that represent strike prices close to the current market price couldn't lose both at the same time. Subsequent stock price movement, up or down, must make one option strategy profitable.

Dominant short-term thinking is synonymous with instant gratification, instant answers. Buying on Monday morning expecting in minutes or hours or by Wednesday to be counting out profits is certainly more difficult than real "investing," where time is your ally.

Short-term winning this time, might mean surrender the next, or it will eventually. It's too difficult, almost mathematically impossible, if attempted often enough. The "odds" are with "the house," especially when trading thinly traded options, because specialists and floor traders can set pricing as they wish, which isn't from investor demand and supply. Their doing so is never designed to benefit the options investor. They are very bad consistent bets.

Obviously layering short-term after short-term strategy, one after another, means the investor never participates in the profitable trends that always develop in some markets and/or sectors, nor do they retain the edge that time and study permit.

*More Proof*

A simple study on United Technologies and Federal Express commencing on December 17 and October 8, 1998 and ending on April 19 and April 22, 1999 respectively, sought to determine how much more of the total intermediate-term trend points available could be had, if sold after each advance, go short (or purchase puts, enjoy the next short-term drop then buy back in prior to the next upward move, and continue to repeat the processes. In other words, with *perfect* timing, how much more money might have been pocketed? Granted, a two-trial stock study is only mildly telling but for this learning purpose, it is still useful. With the investor buying at the commencement and selling at the end, all the while sitting through the middle portion of the move to gain total points equaled to 51 and 72 respectively, for each 1,000 shares purchased realized a $51,000 and $72,000 gain respectively.

With perfect timing, and the capture of each advance and decline, the dollars reach equals $73,000 and $94,000. In each case about $20,000 more. If perfection isn't had—and wager it won't be—even being 75 to 80 percent correct, still results in an inferior return versus a simple intermediate term buy and hold. For all the short-term effort above and the resultant totals, commissions were NOT accounted for, nor the emotional stamina, or the stress to endure constant activity and monitoring.

## Moral:
### Remain passive throughout an evident, strong, intermediate move.
### Forget timing and trading the retracements.

*Still more short-term shenanigans? American Express 7/26–7/27; 2000:*

Investors have learned that financial stocks will fall if interest rates are rising or are expected to rise. If an economic report suggests more economic strength than expected—*at least this week*—an investment in call options or a stock of a financial services company will probably sink. There can be the then horrendous occurrence with options that "implied volatility" changes, or the options specialists opinion changes, and thus, the "delta" relationship changes. (The delta refers to how options move relative to their stock price.) What was only a .25 delta relationship advancing becomes a .50 relationship falling.

By definition, this means: for each 1 point rise in the stock, the call option advanced 1/4; but with the stock declining the following day, the option lost twice as much, or 1/2 for each 1 point decline. (This occurred because the specialist set up the bid pricing lower than normal—or being straight—to induce options selling, which could be quickly purchased, at very low prices, which can be done so very subtly.) Three days later, the stock advanced a stout 1 3/8, and the call option, the one from above...advanced 1/8! An advance of 1/8 on an 11 times greater percentage difference in the stock movement! Why? Most likely because the presumed "implied volatility" had *decreased* and/or the specialists are controlling the option's price.

## The Lesson This Time:
## Life in options isn't fair—except to the options specialist.
## In the short-term you are apt to be right, then wrong,
## many times during a trading day.

AMD, Advanced Micro Devices, the large semiconductor manufacturer fell, in sympathy with its industry in the fall of 2000 from a price level of about $30 to the low $20s. AMD was due to report earnings in a period when missing expectations meant a -20 percent to -50 percent decline immediately after a disappointing announcement. (One example at that time, Home Depot: a 50 point nosedive to about 34, so investors were correctly apprehensive.)

On 10/11, after the market closed, AMD reported earnings better than expected and the stock went up a point or so in after hours trading. The following morning, their always optimistic CEO, Jerry Sanders, made an appearance on CNBC and made a wonderful pitch for his company, adding how he felt, in no uncertain terms, that the stock was ridiculously undervalued. The stock remained up for that day—but not by much. The following morning in the midst of a Wall Street buying riot in technology stocks, AMD fell for most of the day, often down a single point and more.

How much money would you have bet that with a good earnings report, CEO acclaim on a national stage and a buying binge in their industry, the stock would have soared? At least advanced? All right, not fallen? A bundle. And we all would have lost—at least that day. But this is what short-term investing—or trading—is made of. You can never know for certain—especially with the purchase of an option where even less is certain.

One more "last" example...any list of short-term tragedies is never, never, ending. On November 8, 2000, Sun Microsystems, absent any negative, specific company reporting, along with a technology drubbing, and in the midst of the Florida voting debacle (remember?), fell 7 points during midday to about 90. Their December 105 call options could have then been had for about 4.25.

After a lower day on Monday 11/13 and a broad NASDAQ turnaround, the market and SUNW made a nice advance on 11/14. The stock was up 8 5/8 to a 94 close.

Yet the same 105 call option, with the stock a net 4 points higher, and in all of two days—hardly a rationale for options time decay—was then worth the <u>same</u> 4.25! *And computation from the respected Black Scholes Options Pricing Model suggested the option should have landed a theoretical value of 5.11!*

Here is an example of a delta of .20 with price rising turning into a .50 with the stock down 2 points to 92 the following morning. The professional explanation? The implied volatility from the stock had changed to become greater; hence, the lower option price. Sounds good at first listen? Nonsense!

Volatility is measured over a multiple period, usually 20 to 30, even 50 days. Was a price change from 94 to 92, over two hours, sufficiently unwinding to warrant the delta to drop in half? Of course not! Some proof that the options model, which is typically used to set pricing, is less than ongoing perfect. The real explanation has to do with nervous options holders refusing to believe SUNW would continue toward the 105 strike price, and consequently began an abnormal selling trend without normal buying to offset the exit surge.

Still one more time where the short-term options player is wallowing in a mine field. You'll win some and lose many while security in strategic expectations is never present. Nor should it be expected to be. There are forces too easily advanced and outside of your control which can turn ideas upside down overnight or even in minutes.

### Is Short-Term Trading Really Pointless?
This is not to infer that all short-term trading plays, especially when trading stock are really random, trend-less, pokes in the dark, not unlike "Wall Street roulette." There are real opportunities, theoretically ever-present, during any type of market period where stocks, or indices, or options, are either bid too high and "overbought," and thus, due to tumble, or are sold unmercifully low, and are then due to "bounce," or move upward. These short-term invites abound minute-by-minute to any of the approximately 6,000 stocks within the three central marketplaces, and the 80 to 100 indices, derivative instruments, and 4,700 stocks options with many sets of expiration months for both calls and puts, arbitrage, IPOs and so forth. The idea that all these investments are close to being in equal buyer/seller neutrality, also known as "neutral balance," where the price lies in ideal equilibrium between buyers and sellers, is absurd. Opportunities appear every minute—someplace.

But so too are many items, such as goods for sale, that are equally out of our reach. And there may well be a lesson here. Opportunities of all varieties are useless unless they can be taken advantage of the majority of the times they appear.

There has always existed the uncontrolled investor emotion of bidding too high and selling too quickly. While chances for "the most overbought and oversold investment" are constant, they are difficult to <u>consistently</u> advantage if the tact is in and out; strike and retreat; a buy 'em-in-the-a.m. and sell 'em-in-the-p.m. game. If you pick your spots when stocks get into "hyperbolic" price patterns (pricing that becomes stratospheric) and have a shade of patience, and if you are very selective, short-term investments will sometimes yield sparkling results.

It is also axiomatic that short-term trading requires about six non-break hours of immense and intense concentration throughout each trading day. Most people do not have that much self-discipline to truly concentrate that long on one or a handful of ideas, day-after-day-after-day, or for minute-by-minute-by-minute. Try it and you'll see, it is far easier said than repeatedly done. (In fact short-term efforts might produce results on an equivalent par with less attention paid. This is because price moves randomly over short periods, making the possibility of capturing the price that motivates a transaction, may occur while the investor is only occasionally present rather than fixed upon a day long, 390-minute, concentrated watch.)

It is also agreed that short-term investing is always intuitively tempting. Who doesn't revere in instant gratification? It is however very, very dangerous to wealth attainment, especially with purchasing our unfriendly options, where much perfection is mandatory and reality won't be cooperative. Yet who objects when a novice tries to invest in this manner? Novice investors start out at almost 50/50. If our neophyte wanted to repair cars and had zero insight, it isn't likely he'd complete any repair. If wanting to try his hand at construction and doesn't own a hammer, this might bring failure. However, with a few bucks, and a borrowed computer, our intrepid Andrew Carnegie might think he or she can initiate a path to "investment riches." Accept this tenet: Less options activity is better and short-term specialization is apt to be met with frequent failure and disappointment.

Another major hurdle with the short-term trade is an unwillingness to part with fast paper profits which investors have learned can disappear because of the unexpected on almost anything: news, analysts' comments, false rumors, etc. The oft temptation then is to sell <u>too quickly</u>, making the capture of a significant portion of any move an impossibility. This, by design, results in having small profits even when correct, and rarely—if ever—enjoying a "killing."

The obvious retort would be that when trading in and out several times per day, you needn't make $10,000 per trade to make any money. *(The author recalls very vividly a well-to-do client being reminded of this very fact. He was not interested in making a few hundred dollars, but rather making potentially thousands, even if it meant losing the small profits.)* And yet while small and frequent profits add up, so do small and frequent losses. The commissions that accrue, the added stress and demands of locating increasingly new strategies, and the constant necessity of hour-by-hour attention increase with the added burden of the psychological claim to remain constantly vigilant and reactive each and every day.

*Still More Short-Term Reasons to Pass at the Next Get-Rich-Quick Investment*

Take the want-to-be trader as a full-time investor or career "professional." It is so drastically unlike most common salaried vocations since no compensation is ever made for the "good try." The mere <u>attempt</u> at their craft/passion/vocation of making money invokes no automatic paycheck. And a dichotomy then exists between having to invest and wanting to be selective. Doing nothing equals an income of nothing. Being too active suggests random outcomes, or maybe a negative income. Compare this blunt realization with what constitutes having an earned income in all other professions whose earnings, more commonly, are payable by the attempt of a successful work effort. And, unlike other aspects of corporate life, there is no one to share decision-making with. The account is their province solely. Unless they alone resolve trading short-term strategies profitably, each goes home with less, even though there may have been a diehard attempt.

One more hindrance making the short-term so boorish to master, is the at-times inability of price to move outside of definable parameters. Countless times the markets and individual stocks lie between an overbought or oversold area, cannot advance or fall beyond expected prices, fail to follow through in rally attempts, and the like. What happens next is the cruel indecision of not wanting to stand idle but realizing there isn't a resolve as yet, and knowing that the longer it takes for resolution and eventual price movement outside of the range, the more probable it will occur. Intelligent investors can afford to "miss" these types of "opportunities" especially when not knowing what might be next—should invite the investor to the friendly sidelines. The full-time trader has no such luxury. Play or perish. In real world Wall Street, participate <u>too</u> much and you will indeed perish!

Bottom line: As a short-term trader, each cuts his or her own paycheck and the determinant between having and having not, is clear. All the human frailties we all possess becomes painfully evident, such as an inability to remain disciplined, learn from experiences etc, etc, etc. It is generally no walk in the Hawaiian sunshine.

### Then Can Nothing Be Counted on over Short Periods?
*Maybe. Well…maybe not.*

The most obvious impediment regarding the short-term view is that its movement in price isn't rational or controllable to any consistent degree and "winning" results are demanded quickly so at least the profit you witness, you can in fact keep. You may try, and undoubtedly you will, to intellectualize what will surely occur in the next two to three minutes, hours, or days, and then expect results to play out as scripted. Not only will it not—but it shouldn't. No more than predicting any type of short-term human behavior is ever an assurance. Anything that starts and completes so soon cannot have a major rationale recurring component to blueprint a correct forever profitable path. (Even when we might have been correct, it might be a case of simple mild luck, not a prognosticator facility.)

If you were intending to day trade at 10:00 a.m. with the hope that by 10:15 a.m. you'll exit richer, ask yourself honestly: how many times in only 15-minute intervals would there be repeat chances to make money? With the intention of holding a position for several weeks at least time surrenders to the possibility of multiple chances. But minutes? Investment proficiency isn't being deployed over minute-to-minute periods. Even if we have learned to dissect a price pattern, such as when to enter and exit recurring times with some grace—and profits—for how long might the edge remain?

Psychologist and Princeton Professor Daniel Kahneman, in a Dow Jones Asset Management interview asserted, "People see skill in performance where there is no skill." Kahneman would have us believe that the laws of probability might well explain investment performance and not a few years of thoughtful out-performance. His sense is that people want to see patterns of investment success where none exists. Investors often create illusions suggesting that their correct investment calls are the determinants of skill rather than chance. The interesting professor, no doubt, would buy into the theory of efficient markets.

Equities pricing can move in the short run almost anywhere, anytime, and for any reason. Trying to continually capitalize on what isn't intellectually predictable is an odds-based pointless exercise of time and is why most short-term investors have very limited consistent success. Accordingly, the education of traders, the short-term crowd and their stockbrokers, is very, very expensive. Expect to be wrong many times in the short-term especially if the turnaround—in and out—is minutes or hours, for wrong is then the norm, not the exception. The best short-term investors in the world wouldn't disagree. But that is also the landscape, and it isn't about to change.

Short-term trends are murderous and "low probabilistic investing" at best, with no time guarantees. With options purchasing, time isn't an ally, it is only a foe. Nonetheless, with time horizons beyond day-to-day or, worse, minute-to-minute, some fairly typical recurring price patterns and similar investor reactions, provide some hope beyond mere fate. This hope is predicated from recurring tendencies that form from many experiences turned into profitable transactions. Even the single time or two when the tendency doesn't work isn't cause for abandoning tried-and-true profitable strategies. Invest only in the most opportunistic appearing—and do so infrequently. If not, and you stay around long enough, the short-term can reduce even the best investors to mediocrity.

The key—if there can be a consistent one—is to base a short-term investment strategy on something where a probable edge can be repeatedly exploited since the penalty for mistakes is immediate and often painful and where time doesn't permit a bail-out. It is the toughest arena of investment and maybe the most difficult of professions, since being net correct is the only measure for continuance and all mistakes are 100 percent payable by the "party in error"—and guess who that might be?

Even with the release of the next artificial intelligence software—always unique and cutting edge—designed to guide us onto the daily land of wealth sans the human frailties, we should be properly and permanently suspicious. Prediction of inherently random events isn't itself foreseeable. No software—neutral networks included—will ever consistently predict the next four or 40 minutes of the human investment decision making process.

Let's end with a short but apparently true story from one of the interviewees from the book, *Electronic Day Traders Secrets*. Marc McCord, in response to a question regarding his largest investment advisor loss in a single day, *"Lost it all (1.7 million)...When you lose 1.7 million and you have to call up Mr. Jones and Mrs. Jones and say, 'Listen, you know you sent me $15,000 and I turned it into $40,000? Well now you owe me $10,000 to close your account."* One thought comes to mind for any advisor in a similar predicament: *"Mark, do the words, attorney at law, civil judgment, and subpoena, mean anything?"*

In reviewing this section I decided to note personal options transactions for the few times they were utilized in calendar year 2001. For 12 transactions (probably a bit too much in frequency, but the markets did not trend long enough in '01) a 75 percent success rate was enjoyed as 9 of the 12 options trades were net positive. This is good...and it's also abnormal, but this is also after having twenty-five years of professional experience, first-rate trading technology, and learning the ropes very, very thoroughly—and having some luck shine on your side. (A good bet would be 2002 won't be a repeat.)

There are three points. One, what has been and will be read regarding options material herein is good factual information and <u>will help you</u>. Two, despite the success, the short-term will remain a difficult arena and one you should not expect to try to become too proficient in. You make <u>real</u> money, and generally much more frequently, during trending intermediate and long-term periods. Three, kindly assume point One—please <u>adopt</u> point Two.)

## Why Trends in Place Have to Continue

All right, nothing has to continue, but there are many reasons why trends that acquire momentum will continue to continue in the same price direction.

First, the normal psychological state for most investors is similar to most people—to be part of the plurality. If most of a group is acting in a singular manner, they will automatically pick up those who won't think independently until the last holdout succumbs. If stock prices are directionally moving, most investors will get on board eventually, because deep down, they do not want to be "different." There is an anxiousness in not being excluded from the masses, or with "those in the presumed know," or in not knowing what everyone else seems to know. There is a psychological calmness to "group think" and resultant group action. If you were inclined to want to purchase something, wouldn't you, like most, look to find stocks already moving up—the same stocks that "seemingly go up all the time"...and those most likely to continue to climb?

In Robert Shiller's book, *Irrational Exuberance*, he labels group mindset an information cascade where "even rational people can participate in herd behavior when they take into account the judgment of others and even if they know that everyone else is behaving in a herd-like manner."

Second, the concept of technical analysis will create self-fulfilling trends. When past price formations have occurred or indicators have gone to telling levels, and investors have made money, and the same patterns and indicators appear to be reoccurring, those same market technicians—their students, friends, offspring and heirs!—will act again in the same manner since those now-new patterns will be presumed to provide the same ultimate results. An example(s): this occurs repeatedly when stocks stop their descent at the same prior price level. It occurs when investors know from the past when the Dow goes up 80 to 90 percent if their stock picks will also rise. Meaning as the train starts out of the station…their investment choice will gain in value.

As a corollary, with the price action within trends that are moderate, where their angle of ascent or descent is not too great, there is an almost "built-in" basis for continuance since their price action doesn't get too far away from normal moving averages, for one example, thereby causing extreme up and down movement, which would send investors to react very affirmatively one way or another with their mass possibly altering the trend. When price action appears regular, investors feel no need to take action. Contrast to a 20 and 30 point straight-up move with paper profit monies dancing in your head, in a mini-buying panic—it may be quite hard to remain tacit. This often appears on a day of great relative volume and a very large intraday range of high-to-low price.

Third, changing minds usually takes time. Investors who have researched and planned and then executed their strategies are loathe to give up too quickly; they'll stay the course. So too does the investment community, which cannot allow the public's perception to be that they flip-flop from bullish to bearish and back to bullish at every turn. It wouldn't inspire confidence—and investors might remember.

A small analogy takes place when a company acquires monopolistic economic market standing. An example may be Microsoft in computer operating systems. By their market position, they own their markets; they alone set standards for all others to comply. It is extremely difficult for new competition to alter the leader's perception of the entire market and get participants to make changes away from the standard. Thus, the monopoly proliferates. It's also the excellent reason to invest in companies controlling most of the markets they operate in. Competition from outside is going to be rough.

Fourth, with the information flow so great, investors today have been exposed to so many books, investment programs and financial advice that they have bought into the basic tenet that investment takes time. (In uptrends, patiently holding stocks over long periods is the way to go. It always works.) So investors view in and out decision-making less favorably. They too will side with the course in motion—especially if it is up.

Investment today, like our world today, runs upon instant access to information and quick decision-making. With brokerage firms, investors and most foreign democracies all connected or wired so to speak, the probability of mass action is with us. So when investor reaction gets started, it can have a rapid effect where everyone will have the capacity to know and almost simultaneously react. This is terrific when prices are going up and you are long, yet not so terrific when not, as the fall of 1987 so sadly demonstrated. And lest you forget, that market crash was during the infancy of instant trading and communications.

Since computerization is used extensively on Wall Street to move thousands of bits of information, it means anybody with the slightest ambition can take notice as to what is and isn't moving, reporting and happening. Two decades earlier, to chart a stock involved daily pen and pencil plotting. Today it's all computer-driven. Investors can now see from the comfort of their own living rooms which stocks are advancing and which are declining. Investment software means trends in place now give easy notice.

Fifth, trends in motion get noticed, by investors and the press and Wall Street's army of salesmen. Inaction—the sit and wait—can't be justified as readily as it can during an "east to west" price pattern (a lateral move). If you own stock and you see it falling dramatically every day, you are more apt to *"get off the train" or get off something*, and unwittingly add to the carnage. Alternatively, if each day the Dow is writing a new record, it doesn't take too long to get investors out of money markets, away from inaction, and into participation. And the pros will buy into anything so as to "not get left behind." Trying once again to keep up with the S&P 500. All of this becomes self-fulfilling. A trend feeding on itself.

Sixth, the human condition wants direction, and it wants trend. Investors do not want to buy 'em today and sell 'em tomorrow, then redo the process. If a trend appears to be "forming," most investors will follow in that direction hoping for its continuance. This, too, is almost a self-fulfilling prophecy. Not knowing is the precursor to inaction on Wall Street, leaving investors to desire trends as a justification to invest or remain; they often, to their detriment, see trends where none are present! Call it a certain mental requirement, true psychological rationalization to execute the investment strategy.

Seventh, most investors are not unlike most people in that they do not wish to spend too much time on things that do not capture their real interest. Most of us would rather leave things the way they are than fret about what might or could or should be done. Maybe call it being lazy, or label it a lack of ambition. Investors do not want the task of constantly monitoring their portfolios or make a passive act an active one. Thus…they'll remain in, and with, trending positions.

Eight, most investors lack conviction regarding the holding of their investments. If their stock starts to go down more than expected, they will turn to the sell bias wondering what, if anything, might be wrong, and vice versa (and therefore hold on) during an advance. This tendency leads to a "follower mindset"—like sheep being led astray. The result will be, again, a trend-following act; refusing to think independently.

Ninth, proprietary research has to date proven that even short-term trends do indeed remain intact despite logical reason they should not.

A study competed by the author in February 2001 on the Russell 1000 with the addition of a few hundred technology stocks, sought to determine how many consecutive trending days a stock might make before reversal. If upward for three straight days, what are the probabilities of a 4th, then a 5th, etc? Intuition might seemingly be as days pass continuance of a consecutive move would drop very proportionately, i.e., going from two to three straight-up or down days is far more probable then the sixth running into a seventh. This obvious presumption has been proven wrong.

It is a virtual 50/50 bet (actual results were 45 to 47 percent) that stocks trending beyond two days will get to the third, and if the third then the fourth, if a fourth then a fifth, etc.

This study destroys the supposition that most investors make: Assuming after some preset number of days, they should automatically liquidate their position since "it just can't keep going up or down." Apparently there is about a 50/50 probability it will, and about 50/50 it will again the next day!

## Net Bottom Line:
## Do not automatically terminate even short-term trending positions.

Tenth, with the confines of a trend, there exists natural "protection"—call it comfort. Upward trends generally remain upward and retracements tend to be short-lived and of little harm. Ditto regarding downside pricing. It can be said when investing in conformity with the dominant trend, the likelihood of continuance and thus profit is very great. And the fear of any immediate trend reversal, upon initial transaction entry, so against probabilities. Odds indeed do favor "the trend is your friend" proverb.

Eleventh, commission expense to execute strategies is of no consequence. A presumed opening opportunity in a trending position will get executed—"put on"—more often, since the added thought of "covering" the commission factor isn't as much a consideration as it once was. Investors consequently may stay with the flow of price trend and continue to "get in." Once upon a time, an investor would pay hundreds and hundreds of dollars to purchase stocks or options; when the position was sizeable enough, as in thousands. Today, commission costs are meaningless and have resulted in the extension of price trends. Where once a $300 commission may have been required to initiate a strategy and might have demanded some contemplation, it becomes a secondary issue today. A rapid bearish pattern of pricing might easily induce an investor to short stock/purchase put options, etc. without the commission burden. This "freedom" has clearly helped exacerbate price moves up and down. Ideas now get into place.

Twelfth, trends in place clearly protect against the effects of otherwise contrary to expected or invested, for news. When a company is in perhaps a bullish trend and issues a poor earnings expectation, or is downgraded, the stock can often continue forward because its internal momentum mutes any outside influence. Conversely, a stock falling rapidly will very often continue down, despite announced good internal news.

We can therefore say that a prevailing and strong trend can protect the investor against many outside influences which might otherwise affect price to their detriment.

Thirteenth, a study published in the Journal of Finance, February 2000 issue, summarized a 16 year period—1980 through 1996—showed stocks from the NYSE, American and OTC marketplaces returned a statistically significant .53 percent more each month from factors attributed to their continuing momentum. More—but obvious—proof that trends in place endure.

Fourteenth, and perhaps the most obvious reason why at least bullish trends proliferate, is that most investors when watching their profitable positions work higher, have already learned from those recent periods, that being patient (term it pragmatic) *"worked last month when the stock fell, and then recovered, so why wouldn't it now?"* The odds are, they reason, the stock will move higher still since it did the same thing in the prior months. *It always worked its way up so why sell?* They consequently won't have their finger on any "sell trigger." There is then less automatic selling pressure and when they witness minor price depreciation, it's accepted as normal price action and soon to be followed by another rise, yet again! Pop the corks!

"Buy side" investors who have been waiting for a decline *"so I can finally get in,"* know from the recent past that they had best *"not wait too long since the stocks price will only move higher."* There is from them continual buying pressure to "want in" as prices advance so *they* too don't get left out of a good thing. So, to no one's surprise, buying "the dips" helps perpetuate an upward trend. These two forces, acting together, push pricing still higher and higher and sometimes higher still, or in continual declines, lower and lower and..."will it ever stop?" It's follow-the-leader mentality in the extreme. But it works, as it has for decades.

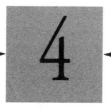

# Investment Basics
## for
## Trend Analysis

## The Price Trend—The Basics

A trend in securities pricing might be defined as "the evident continuing direction of a price series—either upward or downward sloping, over duration of time." The cause for this directional movement in all securities, at all times, is the dynamic of buying and selling pressures.

When share demand creates more buying strength than can be met with the same magnitude of selling, then prices rise. If sellers offer more supply than can be met by buyers, then share prices simply fall. Thus the ebb and flow of the incessant demand/supply equation:

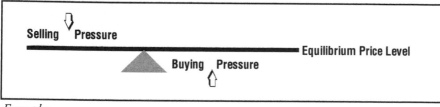

*Examples*:

If the selling share interest is 5,000 and the buying share interest is only 1,000, the pressure—weight if you wish—is to the selling side, (the down side) and the price probably falls. The buy/sell equilibrium tips for this instant over to the sell side.

If a 100,000 share block to purchase is then submitted and but a few 100 share lots are present to be sold, the dominate buying fervor forces the price upward. How much, depends upon the buyers want and the sellers greed—at that very moment.

The explanation for this buy/sell dynamic is based on many, many factors, whether rational or not. Part of the intended price movement is traced to the scientific—analytic and predictable; some of it is art—a feeling or a "gut reaction." At times, prices move not only because of the regular disparity between the buy and sell struggle, but often in the absence of liquidity. In other words, investors "pull their bids" (as occurred Oct 1987) and prices fall or, conversely, sellers "cancel their offers" and prices rise a bit more easily. So price movement isn't always just the torrid rush to initiate buying or selling. If but one person, one day, makes a bid to buy IBM at a buck, the stock theoretically, could open at $1. Don't hold your breath—but the demand supply equation is what moves price in actual practice. (The more realistic analogy to IBM is in aftermarket trading where a lack of liquidity can have prices travel through prominent gyrations because of the lack of the normal number of players.)

How might one side of the price dynamic—demand if you will—get started? Less genuinely than you would ever assume.

Assume a large investor, maybe a pension fund, desperately wants to buy a two million share block of stock and the sell side at that moment is thin. This buyer can push the stock price up on their one transaction. If others, unknowing of the mindset of all other buyers, simultaneously wish to also buy, or having witnessed their desired stock suddenly "getting hot", may be the cause for their immediate placement of bids. Casual buyers now view the stock as moving and they join in. If ordinary selling pressure abates slightly, the stock can rise further and still draw in others. Now, sellers sensing higher prices, stop offering their shares. By day's end, the business press will be asked to explain the "sudden strength," and presumptively lasting. The following day, investors might awaken to a larger-than-expected profits guidance and may start selling to get out on good news and not lose the quick bounty. Consequently, the stocks sprint comes to a quick halt.

Where once investment decisions took time to execute, never mind to analyze, now come about in a fractional second, on trading desks from all over the world, with just a few clicks of the mouse. It is even likely that trading decisions will become quicker still, and even more pronounced in magnitude, as trading execution technology evolves worldwide. In the strange paradox, the savvy market timer—who can rule profitably—will acquire long sought and overdue acclaim...assuming any can be found!

Intermediate price trends that play out as real, don't tip their start in hours or in one to two days and almost anything can cause movement for short periods and have nothing lasting behind them. This is regardless of whether the "smart money" (Wall Street's label for its own professionals) is involved or not. Because our two million share example is still a single buying decision. Of course, this isn't meant to be interpreted the same as if the stock were rising on <u>extremely light relative volume</u>, since its assent wouldn't be nearly as believable with a puny volume. The difference is small players and non-committal volume compared to a single, albeit large investment decision.

Yet, the number of shares involved from one party, in a single transaction, may have a very short-term profound meaning even though it must be counterbalanced by equal conviction on the other side for the trade to be completed. Why?

Let's say the number of shares that make up the average daily transaction in Ford stock is 400. Assume someone offers 100,000 shares for sale. We recognize that in order for that transaction to be consummated there will have to be found buyer(s) willing to purchase 100,000 shares and then it might casually appear that things are then in balance. What becomes significant however is the number of individual buyers that it might take to have the 100,000 share matching buy-side fulfillment. Based on our average trade of 400 shares that may mean 250 individual bullish convictions stepped forward to buy. In terms of probability their collective bullishness may no longer be a factor in the very near term as they have already collectively purchased. The point is that measuring trades on a tick by tick basis, of course via computerization, should have some predictive, very short-term inference in instances as above. And it has remnants of the now popular concept of Money Flow.

If the company whose stock you own reports a huge earnings surprise or other good news this does not mean the stock is going to go up—no more than it must. It might or might not, right now. It will depend upon the assumptions that buyers and sellers have already factored in their activity at the moment of the news release.

Simplistic as it all appears, this is the way pricing evolves. There is no other one-to-one causation factor other then the changing wants between buyers and sellers at the instant of transaction and which can be instantly altered, displacing either side's momentary dominance. With the fewest of exceptions, each next price change is independent of the preceding price transaction. That is why predicting short-term price movement is so challenging—if even close to consistently possible.

## The Psychology of Price Movement

It is admittedly presumptuous to believe it is possible to reason why security pricing moves when it does and the where smart money is headed. Were someone ever to really corner the "why" of price action, it would never appear in print. But let's explore some of the phenomena anyway.

If disproportionate buying and selling pressure is the root cause of price trend, then what drives the pressure in the first place? Apart from forced sales and required purchasing (e.g., 401k funding), investor perception of good and bad things ahead: good news events; an ongoing flourishing economic period (e.g. 1990s); soon-to-be-announced higher earnings; an industry about to be reported upon favorably; a new product or move to expand their business; a technical—a price trend—reason; company receipt of a very negative security analyst review; huge and unexpected layoffs taking place etc, etc. The reasons-to-buy list is long...as are the reasons-to-sell.

Investors, large and small will base investment decisions on certainly finite methods, but many nonetheless. And there is little gained in reciting all that might apply. But one thing can be counted on; all investors are affected by price movement. Their willingness to be motivated by what they see going on is a very powerful force. Desiring to buy, yet wanting to wait, but being seduced by a rapid upward advance, will cause most of us to join in.

Yet why? What suggests that right now is appropriate and the expectation, higher prices in the days and weeks ahead, is anything more then hope? The last three minutes of witnessed trading?

To many investors, hope is the only basis. In fact, it might be the only basis for prediction other than the market's effect or the degree of unannounced external effects, earnings announcements, significant company press releases, etc., all of which we are not supposed to know beforehand.

Suppose one day, presumably unbeknownst to almost everyone, a 250,000 share purchase order is to be submitted for a thinly traded stock on the NYSE. Perhaps coincidentally, two buyers simultaneous place unusually large purchase orders. The reason for these buys need not really matter; whether instigated from tips, thorough research or advisory opinion, they are all purchase decisions. And let's assume the sell side is a bit thin. The stock might spike upward, sending the message to other investors that the stock is then headed higher. Casual traders in the stock notice the upward trend and might participate. Want-to-be sellers, sensing the quick spurt, might pull their bids or shares, for sale. The average Joe, seeing his wanted stock running away, climbs aboard. For the moment, the stock might be well up.

Now let's suppose you had proprietary knowledge that there are three large sellers waiting to unload if the stock moves another half point into their target sell-price level. Maybe you utilized proprietary trading software to detect suspicious selling from large institutional blocks—orders of 10,000 or more shares. You might believe this is useful and influential information. Is it really? Let's dissect it.

What if one or all three of these sellers defer their intent or simply cannot sell at that point—something comes up, a required investment meeting can't be scheduled or, hardly surprising, and they merely change their mind. Now how helpful was your prior "exclusive" knowledge? Not much. And whether this occurs in five minutes or repeatedly throughout the day, it is very typical of price psychology. There isn't as much lasting conviction governing the buy/sell dynamic as we might have hoped. It is to follow the first mentality, with even shorter term focus, the most random and precarious.

How about the idea of future price prediction? It is the zenith of naiveté to think we can look into the future to know with assurance who will buy, with what intensity, and with how much continuing fervor. How might an upward trend take in other buyers—and never mind the sell side. Trying to crystal ball what the masses will simultaneously do in reaction to changing price movement can be a tortuous exercise.

And once having bought, how much determination will sellers have to resist unloading? The answers are always the same: no one knows today how investors will react and no one will know with hard conviction tomorrow. Human beings cannot accurately or consistently measure the collective future mindset of investors. We cannot very accurately predict the order flow of subsequent equity prices.

Judging prospective human-decision, making is not close to perfection by other human beings. And since these decisions often come about spontaneously, it can't be plausible to be close to correct regarding their future intentions.

It is also a sad fact that investors' perception of where future prices are headed is colored by their purchase price. Consider, for example, the investor had rejected prior selling and then watched their shares fall. In an overdue upward bounce, they would be first to sell in the assumption that since they have been subjected to only losses, any gain now is to be savored. New purchasers might conversely assume the upward "bounce" is the long-awaited start of something on the upside; maybe the stock had been down for so long that the time is truly now to begin an upward move. In reality, the older owners are more likely than not to be wrong if they automatically sold on the assumption that further weakness will follow any short-term reprieve. The fact that they have experienced near-term frequent weakness should not blind them to the potential that the stock just might have bottomed. Lessons: You should not assume what isn't in prices; your cost basis has no material effect on where the stock ultimately locates.

## Security Price Patterns—Charting Pictures of Investment Reality

If we can't predict where prices are headed from short-term human investment actions is there nothing which might guide us? Fortunately there is some relief...we just have to be willing to look for, and follow, the evidence before us.

All stocks have chart patterns—fluid drawings—of their price movements, up, down, and sideways. They can provide superlative insight into future movement and their recurring price formations can be excellent for the timing of eventual changes and investment enters and exit points. *Even children can ascertain upward and downward pictures of trending security price action, so investors should have a lock on to this directional aide!*

A classic upward trending bullish pattern is a series of price bars with the daily, high, low and closing price levels forming a pattern of visually higher trending prices, but not necessarily perfectly upward trending. When the security turns down, retracing some of the price movement, the lower prices are still higher than in the previous low series of prices. (Retracement means very short-term price action moving countertrend or opposite the direction of the then-dominant price trend.)

In Figure 4.10 the chart of United Technologies is a picture of a near classic upward trending intermediate advance. (The curved and wavy solid lines are moving averages, more about those later.)

## Figure 4.10

UNITED TECHNOLOGIES SEP 1998 - MAY 1999

12/27 8:58 am Printed using SuperCharts©Omega Research, Inc. 1997

A steady advance, not too fast (too extreme) nor too slow (lacking buyer conviction), may be a windfall for either the options or stock player who may have purchased near the start and allowed this picture to remain the sole criteria from which retention or an exit would have been considered.

The short-term retracement in price trend from Point A to Point B did not alter the basic upward trend in place, nor did the violation of the trend at Point C, because the decline was mild. An exit strategy would have been correct, using price as evidence, in very early May 1999 when the stock broke its upward trendline which it had not since its early October 1998 commencement. This was an intermediate advance of almost seven months, far outside the norm but as warned, without evidence of an in-process price decline. Why assume one will occur and sell out of the position and maybe out of further profits?

Downward-trending bearish price patterns work in reverse. Price has a downward slope with continuing lower highs and still lower lows. The OTC market (Figure 4.11) during the steep March through mid-May 2000 sell-off period displays these phenomena.

Figure 4.11

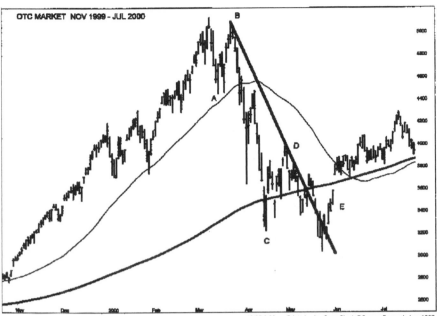

12/27 9:06 am Printed using SuperCharts©Omega Research, Inc. 1997

With each upward and then later downward price action, the overall price trend continues a weak and downward sloping. Retracement is in evidence: with the main trend downward, very short-term retracement pricing is upward, Points A to B and C to D. The plotted downward trendline having been drawn from the high reached in early March through the lower high points trending downward into mid-May, would have then been broken by an upward price movement which began in very late May. This would have been the signal to then place an exit strategy, for any short strategies, at about Point E, the "trend breakout" point, in the assumption a rally would begin.

One further point: the intensity of price movement, the degree of rising or falling slope, is strong evidence of investor conviction. A price slope of 50 or 60 degrees or greater, as opposed to 25 and 30 degrees, is meaningful proof of investor confidence in the existing trend.

It stands to reason a stock leaping forward in larger amounts week-by-week with a higher degree of slope is suggestive of higher levels of confidence. This will bring investors larger profits than one moving barely above neutral or with a slight degree of slope over a similar time frame.

**Provided the slope isn't too extreme, thus unsustainable,
choose equities with strong trending price slopes—
upward when bullish, downward when bearish.**

Neutral, or sideway trends, are shown in Figure 4.12 of Advanced Fiber. Throughout the period displayed, the stock remained range bound within the 15 to 20 1/2 price areas.

Figure 4.12

12/27 9:16 am Printed using SuperCharts©Omega Research, Inc. 1997

Sideways, also known as east to west periods, are killers for particularly short-term options players since money can be lost at both ends. Call buyers lose in the want for any sustained advance while Put players feel similarly disposed desirous of a fast continuous decline. In these types of price patterns, an advantage would be to the option seller, also termed the option writer. They pocket money when the stock doesn't move outside the strike prices (price levels). They may have chosen to sell puts and calls at. Intermediate term stock investors wouldn't be toasting anything either because the stock remained range-bound for the entire six month period.

## Multiple Chart Pattern Evidence

If one concept or stock pattern can provide clues as to direction, it would be obvious that two—or better still—several, all coincidentally pointing toward the same conclusion might make our intended strategies even more plausible than likely random occurrences. When in occurrence, is there more proof of prospective direction? These situations tend to be the exception, but do happen and are quite worth observing.

Consider a long-term price support area also coincides with an RSI of 35, even as our intended stock purchase target continues to plummet. With these two indicators pointing toward a near-term bullish probability, the likelihood is that there will be a dramatic rise. To sweeten the example, imagine the 200 day, daily moving average is in the same price support price area! Now making the right decision should be like shooting fish in a barrel.

In early December 2000, noted with the downward arrow on the Powerwave Technology chart (Figure 4.13), the price pattern gets into upside overdrive and becomes too far above its 200 day moving average as it takes on the look of a hyperbolic advance. As noted at the bottom of the chart just beneath the downward arrow, the Percent of Close indicator has additionally turned to overbought. These three pieces of evidence paint a very compelling probability of downside price action which occurs very rapidly over the ensuing ten days.

Figure 4.13

12/27 9:28 am Printed using Superchart©Omega Research, Inc. 1997

Multiple technical price pattern occurrences all supporting the same conclusion at the same time isn't common but does happen. This is an excellent reason why programming your computer to seek out these opportunities through pattern recognition, or from stark numbers crunching, would be a worthwhile effort.

In summary, all these price observations are made by viewing securities within their respective price charts, either plotted on paper (the old way) or screened automatically within various computer software programs. Stock patterns, even those with the most conviction, are never straight lines in either direction; rather they have a "stair-step" movement. When bullish, they rise for a few days then fall for a day or so, then perhaps display an upward thrust. Falling trends often act similarly, but in reverse.

## The Trend Continuance & Retracement Issue

A key issue, amongst many, in forecasting future price levels from "reading" price patterns, is how investors handle inevitable contingent price retracements, often termed corrections. These will inevitably occur for as short as a few days to as long as a week or two and sometimes even longer. It is when price moves against the dominant price trend currently in place.

The Critical Questions: Does the investor do nothing, trusting that the primary trend in place will continue (and their profits, if any as yet, will still be there)? Or, does the investor attempt to advantage the recent presumed "overbought or oversold" short-term movement of prices that is causing the retracement and initiate a counter dominate trend trade—thus assuming a new change in trend direction has begun?

And what constitutes a normal retracement of the primary trend? A quick answer: The degree—and almost literally—to which pricing has moved away from the "normal" day-to-day "bounce," the "noise," within any intra-trend price action. If it is not major in price magnitude and not much longer than a week, then assume the retracing price action for the few days is normal "price noise," and is regular and random buy-and-sell retracement jockeying.

The long answer: Trends will ultimately die, as certain as they always begin. Knowing when, before they succumb, is luck, art, but is also sometimes learned from hard experience. Prices will almost always tip their hand to direction and usually fairly quickly. Be sensitive to price changes but be completely unassuming as to developing price patterns, until actually proven. You should allow what you witness in price action to guide you. Do not assume what isn't in evident pricing.

Here are a few hints as to the probability of a price trend continuing:

- The age—calendar time—of the total move.

- Its total magnitude from commencement.

- The slope of price—that is, how fast or slow its movement.

- After brief, short-term "relief" countertrends, does the security quickly resume its path?

- Are long-term technical barriers about to enter, RSI, or support/resistance, etc?

- The price action of the broad market the stock is a part of.

Important variables for the amount of retracement you should provide latitude for, assuming the price change is only a retracement, are the computed volatility of the stock and the amount of the price movement against the primary trend, considering its total price moves to date, and time.

Stocks within, and maybe destined to remain in, continuing trends promote themselves by their continuous directionally action. They simply trend progressively. If they cannot summon investor interest after many days of retracement and even a day or two of very significant counter price retracement movement—the combination of both—and if the dominate market trend reasserts as it had, this might be a warning that a primary trend change is taking place. Normal retracement price activity, if that's all it is destined to be, should be relatively tame in time and magnitude.

An intermediate term upward thrust having advanced maybe 50 percent over a few months and having become extended (overbought) should be granted some downside relief for perhaps a week or so, and maybe a third of the prior price advance. The allowance for the amount of time to alleviate an overbought/oversold condition is somewhat proportionate to the duration and magnitude of the previous move. The stock's volatility and its investor's urge to buy or sell, would also logically determine an extent of price retracement. But a reasserting strong broad market or individual issue price action that refuses to retrace much in price should be taken at face as a probable desire for continued upward momentum. These are the two forces you wish to act in concert with: use the market as the main timing source for trend continuance; and use the stock when it's exemplifying strong relative price action. Retracement is expected to be only temporary price action.

To summarize: As the extent of overbought or oversold becomes more and more pronounced, the wise investor becomes increasingly more price sensitive and is quicker to act on price movement adverse to their position—price action—yet having first allowed the trend to play through as long as price evidence is in your favor. When expected retracement isn't mild, get concerned and sensitive to the next few days of price action. Your investment might be changing its primary direction.

The wish to get in at a trend's beginning, with the emotional and intellectual comfort of pricing evidence, is not possible. This is because only the passage of time can prove if our expectations worked and pricing proof is not known until after the fact.

Blind guessing as to change, that is selling or buying too soon, often leaves too much money in other people's pockets. This is being too assumptive. Try not doing it; instead learn how trends really play out.

The "perfect" advancing trend is not so strong as to invite sellers to grab quick "overbought" profits, therefore causing too significant of a downward retracement, but it is firm enough to repeatedly entice buyers. It's almost a sense that trends just endure but don't create notice, prompting a declaration that would order investor reaction: to sell if price had gotten overbought; to buy when price has gotten far too punished. Rather they are mild continuance, upwards or downwards being the preferred route. "Perfection" in a declining trend is the reverse; the upward, retracement moves, small and unseen; the downward, continually weak, but not crashing. Ideal continuance for a trend is that it mildly play out, and not get affected (shortened) by too much extreme sudden movement which would likely alter the root direction as shown in Figures 4.14 and 4.15 (page 59).

## Figure 4.14

JOHNSON & JOHNSON DEC 2001 - SEP 2002

12/27 9:42 am Printed using SuperCharts©Omega Research, Inc. 1997

In both instances, the obvious downward price pattern begins to quickly accelerate and bottoms in mid-July 2002. This type of price action tends not to have "legs" because a price falling too rapidly elicits the "bargain tag" and too many eyes are witness to these infrequent patterns. Thus, you get very recurrent immediate countertrend movement, as was the case here. We would liken these to investment "jewels" waiting to be stolen. An ideal balance of trend movement rarely lasts for lengthy periods, generally not for many continuous weeks and almost never for months. Price extremes will always seem to pop up. These are opportunities—pay attention!

You have to allow for regular, daily price ups and downs and depending upon the stock's volatility level, maybe more than you would prefer. Simply agree that stocks have a right to close up or down, any day, even several days running, that contradicts their primary trend and the market's broad moves, without it having any effect on its dominate price trend. After a reasonable period of time—unless your intent is very short-term, when action would be necessary—if there isn't a resumption of the pri-

Figure 4.15

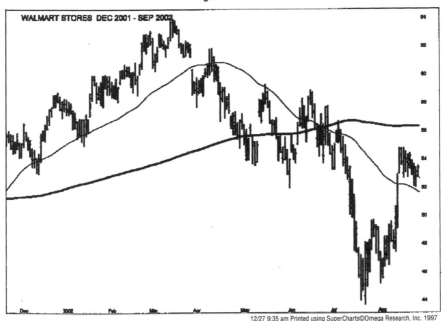

12/27 9:35 am Printed using SuperCharts©Omega Research, Inc. 1997

mary trend and certainly if the market reasserts itself then the retracement you have been witness to may have become a trend reversal—a new dominant market direction—which would invite exit consideration from the prior bias. Case in point, Veritas Figure 4.16 (page 60):

Note the beginning of the advance in late October 1999 and the subsequent upward bullish trendline completing at Point B. Unfortunately the stocks top (price) was at Point A—nearly 68 points higher—and that's the good part. If an investor waited a bit longer—all of two weeks—in the assumption that the bullish trendline would support the falling price he or she would have been saddled with an existing price at maybe Point C, 90, some 88 points beneath the high of 178.

### An Obvious Lesson:
### Never use a trendline as your sole determinant as to the timing of a sell or purchase decision.

## Maybe Pass on the Illusory "Opportunity" Afforded during Price Retracements

Market retracements away from the dominant price trend will tend to be short-lived in calendar time and generally mild in percentage and or point movement, with few exceptions. If we attempt to narrowly define what constitutes a price retracement, it

## Figure 4.16

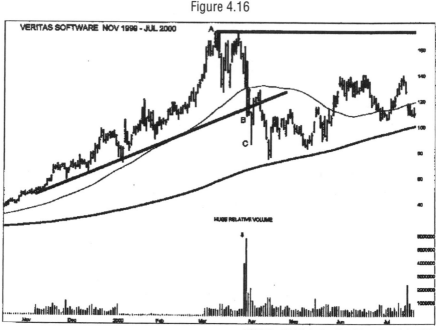

12/27 8:59 am Printed using SuperCharts©Omega Research, Inc. 1997

might be a contra price pattern lasting at least three days and less just market "noise." The normal, maximum, duration of a retracement appears to be a duration of 8 to 12 days, or 1 1/2 to 2 1/2 weeks. Retracements lasting longer are far and away the exception but do occur. The market's Sept 2001 through mid-Nov 2001 period being a good lesson for the anomaly.

Unless retracements are to last well beyond their average maximum duration, they might offer only opportunity and not the probabilistic event that we should always insist upon. Opportunity and probability are not the same. Opportunity in our markets is always present; whether it can become our reward is all together different.

Retracements that might last are generally those that arrive after significant price direction—that of almost hyperbolic variety of extreme upward or downward price action. An excellent recent example was the period in late September 2001 after the World Trade Center bombing and after the markets had reopened. The following days were swift and very deep to the downside. This pricing pattern invokes notice which will have unsure hands selling first. As might be expected, the resulting retracement, then bullish, lasted well beyond average and would have been highly profitable to have participated in.

It might be reasonable that remaining idle, that is, not trying to initiate a new strategy to catch "the illusive bottom or top—through these accepted, normal, contra movements—is superior to impatiently and generally unprofitably waiting to find their next expected occurrence. We have all too frequently been wrong. Too many investors during the late 1990s advance were determined to short the market in its upward price trend when they reasoned an overbought state was at hand. Similarly, during the mid-2002 technology fall, it wasn't uncommon to continually search for a near-term bottom when too oversold was an assumed price condition when a lasting rally just had to be in the offing.

Remaining silent until these reversing price patterns run their course means we can simply align with the dominant trend whenever that pattern develops again. (With positions already in place, we might allow any mild price damage to complete itself, with the later probability that the prime price pattern will again become on track.)

*Let's try and derive a mathematical example:*

The average number of trading days in any month tends to be about 21 and in the course of a calendar year about 250 total. If we accept our definition of retracement, then in terms of actual number of days these contra price trends can be found will be very small in comparison to our total of 250. Conceding that one appears about each six-week period and lasts perhaps an average of six to eight days means that maybe eight price patterns develop per annum. If they last an average of six days we can assume a total of about 50 days. Within a dominant price pattern totaling 250, a 50-day figure, or about 20 percent, is the maximum time when investing contra to a dominate trend might cede opportunity.

If we next approach the question of how often we might be capable of entering and exiting on the actual days these periods begin and end, we can subtract from eight periods, at least a single day, for each beginning and end, since we rarely can expect to be in on the day of any bottom and out at the precise day of any top. The days of real opportunity are fewer still—maybe 35. Next, let's try and guess what happens if we miss perfection by more than a single day, we are then down to 25 days, giving us a 10 percent probability.

Now let's dissect a single retracement period that might last perhaps three to four days. If we delay entrance and exit by just one day—we miss the ideal entrance and exit price meaning we have lost two days out of a four day potential period. If we miss by more than a single day, there isn't any reward. If an expected rally—remember trying throughout the bear market—lasts only two days, you have assured yourself yet another loss in trying once more to catch the bottom.

The point to the preceding paragraphs is not to spar with the mathematics but to accept the obvious inference: trying to entertain entrance positions in retracement pricing patterns, on balance, won't provide a sufficient odds-based successful results. The dominate price trend will still retain far too much of its influence most of the time.

*The experienced conclusions:*

- Sit through retracements unless they appear to fall outside the ten to 12 day maximums or they are extreme in price movement and thereby typically non-continuous.

- When the probabilities for success when investing against the primary price trend hovers around 10 to maybe 15 percent, it pays both emotionally and financially to do nothing. Let the existence of these non-probabilistic opportunities go by; there will be several thousand alternatives yet to appear in your investment future.

## Tactics at Prospective Turning Points

Let's place some numbers on a hypothetical move. Assume a stock has advanced handsomely to a current price of 72. At this level the technical indicators start to warn that a price top may form. A 17-day RSI of 77, maybe a market RSI of 70, and a very high broad market percentage level above its 200 DMA, are all warning levels consistent with prior tops. Yet, despite the potential of a downside move, if our stock holding hasn't started down, we would not exit our position; rather we would allow for price to get even more extended if it is to become a reality

Maybe our price ultimately hits 75 and then starts to drop to 72. This is about 4 percent beneath its intraday 75 high and normal day-to-day price erosion. (In almost every case —excepting hyperbolic price pattern—nothing can be done to consistently retain very small random movements.)

Let's next assume it drops to 69 we now have experienced a 10 percent correction from the 77 top and in most cases only a mild hint as to anything <u>abnormal</u>. We don't know yet if it's just a regular expected retracement from an overbought and current primary bullish trend or the start of a bearish trend reversal. If we had previously decided even a 10 percent correction, although paltry to some, is sufficient for us, we might begin to exit our position. And we would place a sell order for 50 to 70 percent of our holdings. But let's say this time we had not.

We allow for a few days of back and forth price action and then find our stock fell deeper into the 62 area or about 15 percent beneath the recent 75 high. (And again if we had a 15 percent valuation stop we would institute a 50 to 70 percent exit strategy. Had we utilized a prior 10 percent stop level, would have already removed the remainder of our position.) But let's believe we had neither in place. We are down 15 percent and wondering if we are in a trend-reversal portending bearish pricing or are we still in a retracement and if so, do we add to out current position. should we buy into the assumed retracement? We can't know yet, since even 15 percent is still not significant enough. Yet, if the broad market has also fallen 5 percent it, by definition, isn't enough. Maybe we should buy more stock and presume the price action is only a retracement. However, we always demand some upward price action before we buy "go long" anything.

Now assume our stock starts upward to 67. Is the advance to 67 a retracement in a <u>new primary bear</u> market trend or simply the continuation of the old bull market? When will you know for certain? Only with the passage of time. It's more than an issue of label, for if the move to 67 is a bullish trend within a new bear primary trend, buying these "price dips" is wrong if you do not immediately exit since a furtherance of bear activity will drive prices ultimately much lower than 67 or 62. We don't need to be buying more stock as prices gyrate lower and lower and lower. If we had a final valuation stop at -20 percent, we would completely exit at about 60. This would have meant we always retained 80 percent from the buy price. We would not have suffered through long and tortuous -30 or -50 percent price carnage. We would have controlled exit pricing by <u>our</u> level of expectation and emotional comfort.

In summary, as a broad guide, if the market or sector you're in as a whole hasn't corrected in excess of 20 percent of the primary price trend, price movement is probably retracement. Unless your position is acting worse than 20 percent or you have pre-designated valuation stop levels at -10 to -15 percent, in which case you would have already employed exit strategies then remaining in retracing positions with the primary trend should be sound advice in most periods. This is based on the market having the dominant effect on where prices move in almost all periods.

Market price variation of less than 20 percent can be anything, retracement or reversal. You cannot know at that point, unless you are prepared to develop split exit strategies or have very slight valuation stop levels. If you wait for a full 20 percent hit before exit realization you are going to part with a fair amount of wealth and there isn't too much that can be done about it. Using smaller valuation stops, at 10 percent, means you give back less from the top, but you also will exit out of even mild retracements and then may have to reenter if the primary trend reasserts.

If you can exit, pay appropriate tax, then reenter, and do it less than having remained dormant through retracements up to -10 to -15 percent "windows," you are a financial wonder and should be drafting your own book! Yet it might be possible in qualified accounts, since current tax isn't at issue. However, in personal accounts when staring at a short-term gain with the attendant tax liability—dream on.

# *Price Trend Pattern Evidence*

## Basic Technical Chart Pattern Analysis

There are but two prime price trend charts to look for and a handful of the best of time-tested technical indicators. Price trends are basically: bullish, bearish, or neutral (noncommittal) with neutral being placed in the camp of basing or topping. Neutral is a non-trend pattern since its movement is sideways or directionless.

*Caveat: the next several pages represent chart patterns and after you study a few, they tend to blur together. These are necessary, illustrative chart representations of bullish and bear-ishness. If reviewing just these few becomes laborious, think of the task of manually review-ing several hundred or more each day. It is an ideal task for very sophisticated pattern recog-nition software.*

### Bullish Chart Formations

These are the most utilized patterns from which the vast majority of investment decisions are made and investment wealth created. This is because, in theory, a stock has NO top on price into the future. To wit: a 50 stock can't drop 51 points. However, it can rise several hundreds of points over many years and still continue to climb much higher over a period of decades.

## Upward Trending Price Action:
## Continuing upward trending price action not too extreme nor too slow.

Figure 5.10

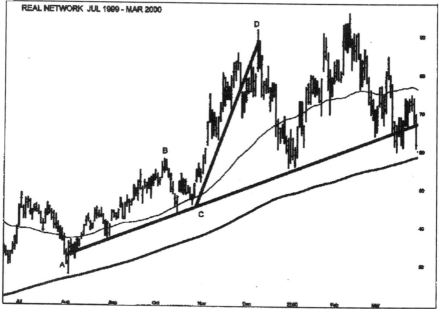

12/27 9:54 am Printed using SuperCharts©Omega Research, Inc. 1997

The chart of Real Networks (Figure 5.10) during the period from July 1999 through very late November 1999 is illustrative of an upward trending price action from the Points A through B and then onto Point C. A fairly serene upward slope despite the retracement pattern from Point B to Point C. Note the rapid rise from Point C, in late October, through Point D about mid-November. That ascent is at an approximate 67 degree slope—in plain English, it is far too rapid, thus unsustainable. It rose approximately 85 percent in 21 trading days or about 4 percent per day. Annualized for the next 12 months, it would enjoy about a 1,011 percent rise. We will learn shortly it is termed a "hyperbolic rise" and soon destined to fail, miserably, as it should have—and abruptly did—in early December 1999.

The chart of Advanced Micro Devices (Figure 5.11) is similar to the previous one with the mild upward bullish trend from Point A through Point B. An almost 4_ month advance which returned nearly 100 percent to investors who weren't thrown off from the obvious upward bias and deferred by today's so-normal "want to be right—right now" or the "me first" quest for instant gratification.

Ultimately, the stock started to run too far, too fast, from Point B to Point C to once again doubling and more a short 60 days later. Now the rise from Point B

Figure 5.11

ADVANCED MICRO DEVICES OCT 1999 - JUN 2000

12/27 10:06 am Printed using SuperCharts©Omega Research, Inc. 1997

through Point C was at about a 54 degree slope—not nearly as fast or steep as with Real Networks. Yet, while not of a hyperbolic look, it isn't too far from frothy, and thus the stock in early May 2000 breaks the upward trendline with some significance and falls into the mid 30s or about a 30 percent slide in three short weeks. A scant $13,000 "bye-bye" if having held a 1,000 share block throughout the total dip...drop...carnage!

## Double Bottoms:
### "W" type of chart formation, two recent and similar level "low" prices (separated by calendar time in weeks or months), with an upward price spike in-between.

The Cadence chart pattern in Figure 5.12 (page 68) is almost a classic example of a double bottom, a "W" looking picture. In mid-April 2000, at the upward arrow, the stock makes a low then rises to Point A in early May. A retreat back to approximately the same low of early April, now in late May at the other upward arrow, and then an advance to Point B around June 1st. A mild breakout occurs, but the stock moves laterally for several days before moving well beyond the breakout point, the price level represented by Point A to Point B.

The Merrill Lynch technical chart (Figure 5.13, page 68) provides a number of excellent technical analysis examples even during a very brief period of time.

Figure 5.12

CADENCE DESIGN SYSTEMS  FEB 2000 - OCT 2000

12/27 10:13 am Printed using SuperCharts©Omega Research, Inc. 1997

Figure 5.13

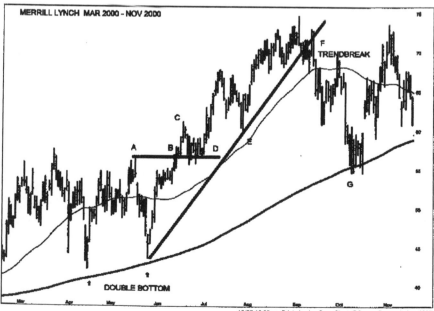

MERRILL LYNCH  MAR 2000 - NOV 2000

12/27 10:25 am Printed using SuperCharts©Omega Research, Inc. 1997

The initial low, the upward arrow in mid-April 2000, is followed by a strong advance to Point A. A drop to the prior low of mid-April, in late May, is somewhat supported by the upward trending curved line—Merrill's 200 day moving average; it's bullish upward trending slope almost always offers the price support that occurred here. The stocks run to Point B in early June, then immediately "breakouts" through Point A to Point B "testing" or resistance price area, then on to Point C, and becomes "proof" of the breakout and the expected higher pricing, as occurs to Point C.

The stock then declines to the Point D price area (once a resistance area but now considered support since it has been broken) before rallying to the mid 60s. A correction or retracement of the main intermediate bullish trend in early July is stopped, and supported, at the bullish upward sloping trendline, at Point E. The later rally to Point F is then followed by a trend break and later fall to Point G, where once again, while the construction of the 200 day moving average is upward trending and bullish, the stock stops its nasty descent at the 200 day line, even if falling slightly beneath. Virtually everything within this chart is very close to text-book technically perfect— or exactly as a technician expects pricing to play out. One should be so fortunate that it might occur every time in a similar manner.

### Bullish Breakouts:
### Price action moving above former price resistance areas or above lateral trendlines or moving averages.

At the risk of being too fussy over precise definitions, continued movement above a former resistance line or resistance area or moving average can be classified as a standard (normal) breakout.

In Figure 5.14 (page 70), The Entergy Corp chart displays a 200 day moving average line (the thick heavy line) being penetrated to the upside about late April 2000. In mid-April the stock price has risen to the line and briefly gone above. This price pattern frequently comes back to "test" the apparent intent to breakout. For Entergy, this happened almost immediately then the price moved laterally, noted by the area (the two upward arrows). The stock then broke out again to test the 200 day moving average area in early May, before moving well beyond and upward into the fall of 2000.

A more classic example of a breakout above trendline resistance occurs with the chart of Baxter International, Figure 5.15 (page 70).

The long horizontal trendline from mid-Nov 1999 through mid-June 2000 was one of resistance near the $35 price level. Yet Baxter sailed through the apparent long-term resistance point in mid-June (shown near the upward arrow). This shows a classic breakout above a prior longer term resistance trendline. As illustrated, this has bullish implications, although there can be an immediate testing of the apparent breakout as we see in early July or, the testing as seen with the Entergy Corp chart.

Figure 5.14

ENTERGY CORP FEB 2000 - OCT 2000

BREAKOUT

12/27 10:30 am Printed using SuperCharts©Omega Research, Inc. 1997

Figure 5.15

BAXTER INTRL DEC 1999 - JUL 2000

BREAKOUT

12/27 10:40 am Printed using SuperCharts©Omega Research, Inc. 1997

Just as in the case of the Dow Jones Industrials, which between 1966 and August of 1982, were incapable of breaking out above the 1,000 level, when long-held resistance finally gave way, there were then very powerful bullish forces at woik. The Dow moved nearly 15 times higher in the next 18 years! And a great number of "paper" millionaires were created.

## Bullish Trendline Breakouts:
## Price penetration above a downward sloping (bearish) resistant trendline, or above the top trending bullish trending line within bullish trend "channels."

The price pattern of Introgen Inc. (Figure 5.16, page 72) displays an obvious breakout from the severe downward (bearish) trendline drawn from early March 2000 into mid-May. As often happens, the breakout in mid-April is almost immediately followed by a fast retest and further lower price action which resolves itself near the middle arrow, where it then begins an approximate 50 percent rise into late April.

The two arrows outside of the one in early May denote the look of a "double bottom" and, as previously mentioned, a normally bullish sign. Here, from the stock's low point in mid-May to the 80-ish high around July 1, the rise is almost 100 percent—decidedly bullish.

Our next chart of Advanced Micro Devices (Figure 5.17, page 72) shows a breakout in very late October 2000 and an almost immediate reversion back toward lows. This is termed a "breakout failure." One probable reason for the failure is that the breakout attempt occurred during a severe, decidedly bearish declining pattern that applied within the overall market as well, instead of a sideways "base building" price pattern when, a more-likely resolve would have been an advance which held. (The chart also displays strong resistance—almost a four-time attempt at penetrating the 46 area top—from May through mid-July.)

## Prior Support Price Level:
## Price decline to, or at, where no further price decline was seen.

The Amazon chart (Figure 5.18, page 73) indicates a support area at the $60 price level that survived multiple attempts at downside penetration. After a few of these unsuccessful attempts, shrewd investors got wise to the pattern and initiated buying after each drop to the $60 price level that could not be penetrated. This minor strategy worked until the significant technology collapse in early April 2000.

The pattern for the Dow Jones Industrials (Figure 5.19, page 73) illustrates a second time how the mid-March 2000 through late June 2000 support area—the horizontal line immediately below 10,200—supported each decline. The Dow's failure to fall below this support area led to a series of successive advances each time the area was tested.

## Figure 5.16

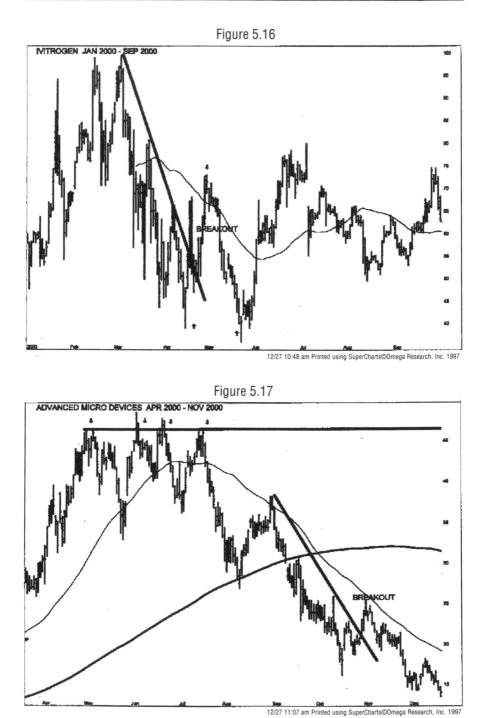

IVITROGEN JAN 2000 - SEP 2000

BREAKOUT

12/27 10:48 am Printed using SuperCharts©Omega Research, Inc. 1997

## Figure 5.17

ADVANCED MICRO DEVICES APR 2000 - NOV 2000

BREAKOUT

12/27 11:07 am Printed using SuperCharts©Omega Research, Inc. 1997

Figure 5.18

12/27 11:12 am Printed using SuperCharts©Omega Research, Inc. 1997

Figure 5.19

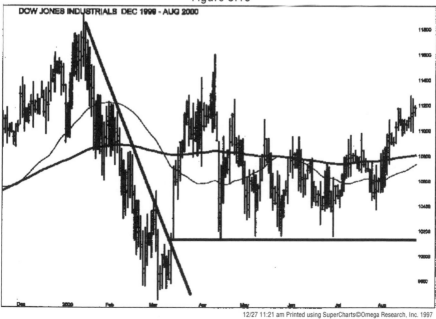

12/27 11:21 am Printed using SuperCharts©Omega Research, Inc. 1997

## Percent Below Moving Averages:
## At extremes, prices go only so far below moving averages, 50 and 200, thus becoming too "oversold."

Please note: the following are intra-week figures (percentage levels computed on a daily basis). They are based on market indices where inherent capitalization, as already noted in Chapter One, will always skew results. Without an un-weighted study of all stocks in these markets, you cannot get a pure percent measure of where the over-bought level is or as, we will see below, where the oversold level is. Yet the following experienced figures will offer a fairly apt approximation, since most investors will follow these broad market indices anyway for guidance, no matter how constructed.

It can be reasoned that an un-weighted average of where stocks bottom-out would give us a useful percentage number where we might be tempted to start buying. The conclusive usefulness for any one individual stock would remain subordinate to a close inspection of that individual stock's price movement for clues. In other words, if the actual figure from an inclusive un-weighted study was at a -22 percent level below the 200 day moving average, it would not necessarily mean that it was the right time to make a purchase of this stock. Hence, all the mathematical computations to secure the un-weighted exact figure might not offer the ideal we would think it would. *Because we are using individual security chart patterns that have no limit on maximum and virtually none on minimum values, we are left with zero insight as to what constitutes extremes, per individual issues.* Without an indication of what is construed as a stock's maximum/minimum percent over or under a specific moving average, how could an investor be guided? Contrast this with the 17 day RSI technical indicator, which is not just stock specific and includes upside and downside maximum levels inherent within its construction.

Finally, since most stocks (our formal options study indicated greater than 80 percent) will begin and end significant moves with a trend parallel to the broad markets they are a part of, it would seem a fair statement that when the market's percent, below its 200 DMA becomes too great, most stocks will have coincidentally bottomed out as well, and consequently might begin to advance in lock step. It may be wise to cast some reliance upon the figures below.

First, in measuring the broad markets alone, meaning both the Dow Jones Industrials and the NASDAQ, some of the maximum intra week percent levels below the 50 DMA have been:

| DOW | 10/1997; 8/1998; 10/2000 | AVG - 14 percent |
| NASDAQ | 10/1998; 4/2000; 10/2000; 3/2001 | AVG - 24 percent |

The maximum intra week percent levels below the 200 DMA during the same test period:

| DOW | 3/2000; 10/2000 | AVG - 11 percent |
| NASDAQ | 10/1998; 10/2000; 3/2000; 7/2002 | AVG - 30 percent |

## Bearish Chart Formations

Bearish price patterns are always limited since prices can't go down more than 100 percent and fundamental changes (company, industry, economic, monetary) are always potentially designed to improve, not retard, matters—meaning, by definition, that bearish directional magnitude is always limited. This suggests never staying married to the downside when short or bearish unless price retains a falling bias, which it cannot indefinitely without a bankruptcy.

The CMGI chart (Figure 5.20) shows graphically what longer term bearish price movement looks like—consistently trending lower highs and lower lows—*repeatedly*. This seven-month event gave away over 120 stock points, but a tragic -85 percent of shareholder value was disbursed from this Internet incubator company in the huge Internet sell-off and coincident NASDAQ bearish trend that began in mid-March 2000. And this chart is lucid proof that *stocks do not have to stop their plunge...until they are ready to.* There isn't one hint of support for the stock over the duration of this downtrend save a little bottoming process in August. Yet even with a chart this bearish, you would be a winner betting there were plenty of shareholders who rode the stock all the way down, and likely moaning, "I can't sell now, it's too late," or "It just

Figure 5.20

CMGI INFORMATION SERVICES MAR 2000 - OCT 2000

12/27 11:33 am Printed using SuperCharts©Omega Research, Inc. 1997

can't get too much worse." Guess what? Oh, yes it can.

What this chart does not show was the bullish run just prior to the bearish nose-dive. In that bullish move, there existed a double top, the concept of which hints as to problems ahead and will be discussed next. The point being, that as the stock dropped, there wasn't a support area(s) which, when being violated, would have told us to consider selling: instead, there had been strong bearish evidence only months before.

### Double Tops:
### The opposite bullish "W" pattern, or "M" type of bearish chart formation.
### A double top "M" is a bearish price pattern.
### It is the opposite of a double bottom price pattern.

The price chart of Micron (Figure 5.21) displays a convincing double top formation first begun in early July 2000 and noted with the down arrow and again in mid-August with a second downward arrow. The resulting drop of almost 70 points and 70 percent of shareholder value into November suggested the pattern as being a precursor to the actual subsequent falling price action.

## Figure 5.21

MICRON TECHNOLOGY MAR 2000 - NOV 2000

12/27 11:45 am Printed using SuperCharts©Omega Research, Inc. 1997

## Bearish Breakouts:
### Price action moving below former price support areas; lateral trendlines or moving averages. *(Once again, the word "breakouts" is really a misnomer, it is correctly a "breakdown.")*

Oracle's chart (Figure 5.22) had a triple top in the 45 price area commencing in April and running through late August, with the three downward arrows noting the highs. The break of both the 200 day moving average in late September and trendline break in late October, at the 30 price area at Point A, gave way to further downside as standard technical analysis would suggest. Top to bottom, this is nearly a 50 percent tumble. When significant support areas give way in a weak broad market or industry sector there can be nasty downside disasters.

### Figure 5.22

12/27 12:01 pm Printed using SuperCharts©Omega Research, Inc. 1997

## Bearish Trend Breakouts (again, actually breakdown):
### Price penetration below a downward sloping support trendline or below the lower trending bearish trending line with bearish trend "channels." *These pattern types are very rare.*

The Altera Corp (Figure 5.23, page 78) displays a bearish trend channel from late August continuing downward into late November. The lower portion of that chart in the early part of October 2000, shown with the downward arrow, is where the bearish trend breakdown occurred. The result was a further approximating 25 percent. You can detect the breaking of the 200 day moving average at about the same time. Both technical breakdowns are symbolic of a price pattern very likely to recede much, much, further.

Figure 5.23

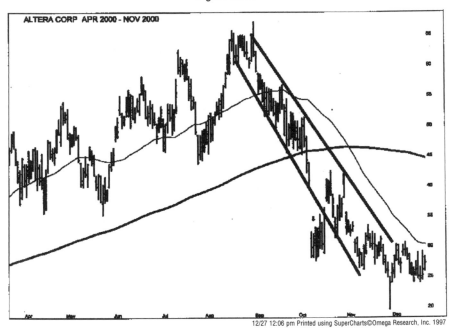

ALTERA CORP  APR 2000 - NOV 2000

12/27 12:06 pm Printed using SuperCharts©Omega Research, Inc. 1997

### Prior Resistance Price Level:
### Price advance to, or price at, where no further rise was seen.

America On Line (AOL), (Figure 5.24, page 79) graphically displays a triple top and obvious price resistance at Points A, B and C. Each attempt at moving upward past this 62 area of price resistance was impeded by selling. Given what transpired, their shareholders would have been thrilled had they immediately exited at any of the three attempts, or 20 points lower, since the stock hit an intraday price of 14 11/16 on 11/30/2000. To put it mildly: a tortuous price drop on a good company, having done the expected in earnings and sales, is not always enough. We can speculate what AOL might have fallen to, had they missed their EPS numbers.

Figure 5.24

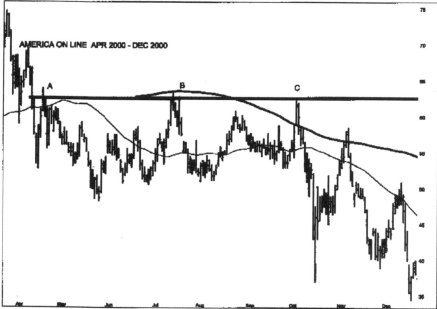

12/27 12:12 pm Printed using SuperCharts©Omega Research, Inc. 1997

**Percentage above Moving Averages:**
**Upward price action reaching an extreme percent above moving averages,**
**thus becoming too "overbought."**

The maximum percent above its 200 day moving average, that an individual stock may get before becoming too overbought and then destined to falter, is very different than that for the major indexes. There is ample evidence that indexes rarely get more than about 25 percent above their respective 200 day moving average. For stocks, the story is quite unique unto itself or is "stock specific."

The last several Dow Jones and NASDAQ percentages above respective 50 and 200 day moving averages follow, and can, provide some help as to when an intermediate overbought condition may be surfacing. Use these with the same "warnings" as expressed when looking for percentages below 50 and 200 day moving averages in the preceding Bullish Chart Formations section.

As already mentioned, the <u>maximum</u> percent level above 50 and 200 day moving averages for any individual stock to signify an overbought status will vary considerably, and there is, as yet, no concrete number where any individual stock topping action will consistently occur. Unfortunately, this means only hard inspection, paying attention to price, or a very broad and un-weighted based study, will give us any useful answers. The broad market percentages that follow offer great insight.

| Period | Dow Jones NASDAQ Percentage above 50 DMA | | Period | Dow Jones NASDAQ Percentage above 200 DMA | |
|--------|---------|--------|--------|---------|--------|
| 3/18/98 | + 8 % | | 4/22/98 | + 15 % | |
| 7/21/98 | | + 9 % | 7/21/98 | | + 18 % |
| 4/12/00 | + 9 % | | 2/01/99 | | + 33 % |
| 7/16/99 | + 11 % | | 5/10/99 | + 23 % | |
| | | | 3/10/00 | | + 57 % * |

*\* This may prove to be a multiyear top at the 5000 level and it coincided almost perfectly with stock mutual funds record intake of 39.1 billion in February 2000—one month prior to the NASDAQ top.*

## Hyperbolic Price Advance:
## An extreme upward price spike, almost vertical and impossible to maintain.

One of the most persuasive chart types to follow onto profitability, it also follows most investors' normal—and wrong—mindset. To wit: selling quickly after advances so as not to give profits back; holding onto losing positions and not feeling that losses have, in fact, occurred. The "if you don't sell, you can't have a loss" thinking is "flawed thinking." All too typical, there are short-term and longer-term hyperbolic advances, the later characterized by very extended 17 day RSI figures and a much longer, by calendar time, upward lift to price.

Each one of the following charts will look almost identical…yet they are all different companies. Each will show pricing moving upward at an extreme degree of slope and at the price top—ideally a very large intraday range with abnormally high relative volume. Lastly, the falling price pattern is almost identical in the time and magnitude from the commencement of the upward unsustainable move to its peak price. *If it took eight months to rise 75 points to its ultimate top, it likely will bottom…eight months later, and 75 points lower, almost completing the right side of a standard bell curve.*

Investor thinking at these tops isn't hard to reason. The majority of bullish investors still desirous to purchase would probably defer after watching the stock soar nonstop, so their help in pushing bullish sentiment higher still, is limited. Current owners have made a great deal of money—at least in percentage terms—very fast. As that quickening, upward pace accelerates and causes more anxiety and more attention, when the bubble is about to go, almost everyone has been made nervously aware. The price pattern itself causes this. Everyone hits the exits simultaneously and with an almost "sell me out at any price cause I've made a lot of money anyway" plea. The result is *price carnage*. And these stocks collapse without the aide of a falling overall market environment. Yet in one—NASDAQ March 2000—their descent would become murderous.

Further observation has shown this price pattern is best when price had been making new recent highs as opposed to coming off a fast downward move where stocks habitually become overbought, sometimes easily and, at times, even hyperbolic. A price pattern making constant new highs feeds the "protect the wealth" mentality so that at the first major sign of a cessation of the advance, investors head for the door all at once to protect all they have earned. However, if price is coming off a bottom and then becomes extended, akin to an "oversold upward bounce," it gives most investors only a bit back of lost value. That type of upward price momentum has far less urgency attached and, similarly, if price becomes hyperbolic after a very favorably viewed news announcement. (In this situation, investors might have a tendency to allow price to remain hyperbolic a shade longer, assuming higher highs might yet occur, although no lengthy evidence of upward price movement had taken place, with perhaps the news prompting the hyperbolic price has yet to be fully appreciated.)

"Financial physics" would make us believe no stock can run straight upward for very long. If the angle of ascent is closing in on 90 degrees—that is virtually straight upward—they must, and ultimately always do begin a rapid descent.

The Safeguard Scientific chart (Figure 5.25, page 82) has volume bars at the bottom (as will all the others which will follow). These are straight upward lines which indicate the daily amount of activity in the stock. In this chart, the arrival of the top from the hyperbolic rise beginning in mid-February 2000, is shown at the two upper arrows. Directly beneath is the usual heavy relative volume accompanying the rapid price drop. Also, inspect the very large intraday range at the day of the top. (This usually means investors were very uncertain and nervous.)

You will also note, the time it takes to lose what had been gained from the start, is about the same as the advance took. Each hyperbolic takeoff yields a picture usually as a mirror—opposite in decline compared to its advance. If hyperbolic, its decline indeed arrives…painfully!

The next hyperbolic pattern is of Protein Design Labs (Figure 5.26, page 82) and shows the mirror-opposite picture of advance, in time and declining magnitude, once the selling starts.

Our final chart of Rambus Inc. (Figure 5.27, page 83) has two hyperbolic stages, with a double bottom in the mid-April through mid-May time-frame between each, and each acts as expected. Pity the poor soul who may have been induced to buy in early March, then unknowingly with his "advisor's" blessing, took another "chance" in early June buying more shares—(also known as averaging down) "to get on board before it takes off." (An investor should almost never average down.)

Hyperbolic patterns are ominous patterns when being long stock. When they begin the look of developing, pay extremely close attention and exit immediately after

Figure 5.25

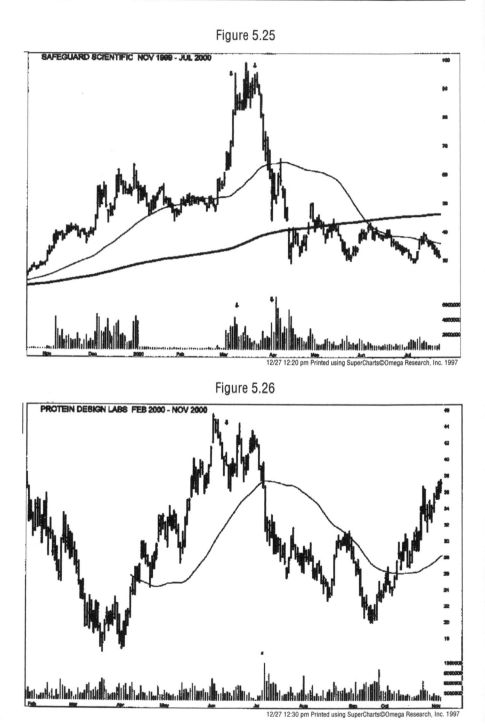

12/27 12:20 pm Printed using SuperCharts©Omega Research, Inc. 1997

Figure 5.26

12/27 12:30 pm Printed using SuperCharts©Omega Research, Inc. 1997

Figure 5.27

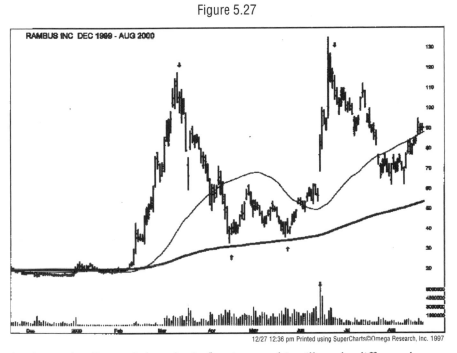

the signs we've discussed above begin forming…and it will not be different the next time.

### Neutral Chart Formations

**Neutral Price Action:**
**Prices range bound between a continuing series of highs,**
**without breakthrough, and lows without a breakdown.**
**A continuous east to west "in between" bound, high and low price pattern.**

Medtronic (Figure 5.28, page 84) is one stock that offers a neutral price pattern over a fairly long period—in this example, about eight months. The stock was range bound from the 57 to the 46 area. Strategies such as buying calls or outright stock as the price nears the 46 support area, and shorting stock, buying puts, or liquidating long positions as the stock approaches the 58 neighborhood are appropriate until the stock penetrates beyond the 58 (resistance) and 46 (support) price parameters.

Even when viewing a "longer term" neutral price pattern, as with Medtronic, if the investor was looking at the very short-term, the early September 2000 through late October period was quite directional. (Price patterns are dependent upon the period you are looking at and always have some directional movement if the investment period is short enough.)

There are even times when prices run up to resistance or down to support levels and trend there for extended periods, invoking a back and forth bullish to bearish to bullish opinion as to the next price direction. One example, when an expected drop from a resistance price area doesn't materialize and assumptions kick that perhaps the stock will push through…since it can't fall etc., etc! Weeks later, if it hasn't fallen, the investor might then assume a overdue drop would occur. As time is passing, directional expectations often flip-flop.

Figure 5.28

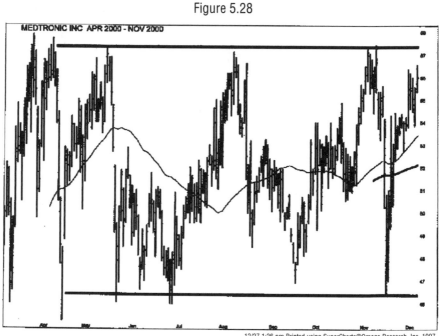

12/27 1:26 pm Printed using SuperCharts©Omega Research, Inc. 1997

# The Technician's Group & Methodology

## The Technician's Time

The individuals who view equity price patterns amidst all kinds of trends are called "technicians" and their attempt at future price behavior is usually termed (price) pattern recognition. There was a time, and not very long ago, when technician's work was considered on a par with fortune tellers and weathermen. Today there is much to recommend in their efforts, their art and methodology.

Their craft is termed "technical analysis." They believe that all that is known about a stock is always reflective within its current pricing. That price is all that investors really care about since they can't "spend" or live from their earnings of the company they invest in, or the terrific news announcement, or the latest technologic doodads they produce. Unless they outright attempt to buy the business they benefit only from price, appreciation and depreciation (if selling short) but not from product usage, or glossy annual reports, or witty analysts' comments. Does it matter if the stock has a great financial balance sheet, beats the Street's earnings estimates, but still sells at a P/E of 2! If investors won't advance such a presumed bargain, why be in it for any lasting period?

There is no doubt of an opportunity cost when an equity portfolio or large stock position remains stagnant for any extended time. To wit: one receives no interest while awaiting redemption. (I once came across a public paper company that was actually earning <u>more</u> per share than it sold for! Talk about a reason to go <u>private</u> but not the best to include in a 401K portfolio.)

Technicians equally espouse learning the technical "habits" of the companies you wish to invest in. This can be termed how "technically responsive" the stock might be. Some stocks are very technically responsive while others are not. Some stocks consistently react to certain indicators and not as much to others. Unfortunately you don't get uniform or perfect reactions every time.

How do you find out? Carefully witness the price action. Does the stock make its high in the morning and then tail off? What is its usual daily maximum move? How does it react when the broad markets unexpectedly react? Does it react opposite to the expectation of news? Can it outpace its industry's movement? At what magnitude of intraday price levels might it be supported or resisted? Is the stock flat-out trendy—once it starts up or down it continues in that direction for days or maybe a week to two—regardless of what else is going on around this? Is it fast to sink? Are huge intraday swings quite normal most days? (It's nice to know all the above rather than panic during fancy price gyrations.)

## Measuring the Technician's Craft for "Correctness"

The flexibility one grants to defining whether a technical indicator or chart pattern worked successfully as a prophetic tool, will usually determine how accurate the indicator or chart pattern is. For example, if a stock declined toward its 200 day moving average and if that average was upward sloping or bullish, you should expect the stock price to be supported by the 200 day moving average line. Yet what determines whether, after the fact, that it has occurred as anticipated?

What if the stock falls beneath, then rallies? Or falls beneath and remains slightly below for many, many sessions, then drives upward? Or maybe the stock price falls to and touches the 200 day line, then advances for several days, then falls back to the 200 day line or maybe beneath? We could create a multitude of "rules" for determining what makes any indicator work. Certainly a high percentage of the time, the static criteria we demand to help us must work correctly. Yet that might be 70 percent, 80 percent or only 55 percent. Dependent upon our definition of "correct" criteria, all our examples may have worked or all failed!

If we were trying to decide on a percentage basis which of the above three occurrences merits a "correct" label, (i.e., that the 200 day upward sloping moving average did indeed support a stock's falling price) then absent defining parameters for how much of any advance would qualify, and how quickly it should occur, and how long the advance should be sustained—be it in days or by percent increase—then the correctness, albeit usefulness, of any indicator would be in doubt. The answer of course depends upon how liberal or conservative the defining parameters are set.

If the 200 day line must support a price decline without being penetrated intraday, and must immediately advance without pause, and must rally at least 20 percent within ten trading sessions, we are setting criteria quite differently than merely asking that the stock price not immediately fall substantially beneath the 200 day average as our definition for a "correct call." Criteria too liberal will prove nothing and any subsequent testing of price movement can only be explained by chance alone.

Strict parameters are generally more useful as forecasting aides because they are far less prone to sending "false signals" which can be expensive and, at minimum, increase unnecessary trading activity and commissions cost.

## The Fallacy behind Automated Price Targets

For intentions other than short-term trades or curtailing losses, nothing is more presumptuous and senseless than assuming price targets—yours or anyone else's—and executing transactions at arbitrary price levels. It is also very likely to be expensive.

Automatic exiting violates a basic investment maxim: to allow profitable positions to expand to their ultimate level.

Robotic-type purchasing simulates random price bottom prediction. In falling times, buying runs counter to trend—another expression of violating basic investment principle.

When you own a stock, or have call options, a price target means selling at a higher than current price. If you are short, or have purchased put options, it is a price lower than current. For instance, assuming a $60 price as an automatic sale level for your long stock investment, this means at any price movement above $60, an investor can only wave at lost profits.

Broker research is rampant in removing stocks that have met their—the operative word being "their"—price target: *"The stock has met our price target and we are removing it from our recommended list."* Following this line of reasoning, these firms are suggesting that they are the marketplace, that they can dictate accurate price levels. It's not quite this way. Theirs, or any other fundamentalist opinion at its core, makes assumptions that stock market prices and corporate values need to equate almost equally at all times, similar to each having a Beta of 1.0, and must move in tandem! This is far removed from what is consistently true. The markets always tell us what a share price is worth in a future period, not equations, and clearly not automatic price targets.

If a sale is to be contemplated at some price level for fundamental, technical or other reasons the first priority as price nears is to *witness* the price action. Don't just simply liquidate at some planned price point. There is no reprieve in automatic exiting. If the price tries to move further, it's wiser—and richer—being in and not watching from the sidelines.

Factually, we never know how far investor sentiment can move price. So why prejudge the ultimate bias of the marketplace? What if momentum builds? Maybe the broad market will provide effect? Even irrational investor momentum might race price to unimagined levels. Why would we want to lose the potential advantage of these affecting variables by a mechanized act? "I'm selling, no matter if it gets to $60 or I'm going in to buy if it falls to $25."

**The masses set price levels, not ourselves and not the press; we should observe first and react second. The lesson being: become more observant and less assuming.**

# Significant Technical Analysis Concepts/Patterns

In this section, we'll discuss some of the more common, yet more important indicators and price patterns that technical analysts and successful investors utilize. It is more than probable that studying and learning the following very well, would be far more than adequate. There are maybe 30–40 technical pattern types and 75+ indicators. Few play out meaningfully enough or often enough to justify their learning.

### *The Concept of Support & Resistance*

As prices, time and time again, fall to a price level but have difficulty falling beneath, the price area at which they terminate the fall is termed as its "support." The area supports or deflects the price from falling lower. Conversely, prices repeatedly failing to rise above certain price levels are being impeded by its "resistance." Technicians usually draw east to west (horizontal) trendlines at these price points to make easy visual recognition of these support and resistance price levels. Sloping trendlines, upward or downward (termed diagonal), use the support and resistance concept in the same manner.

The longer in calendar time (months and longer are much more meaningful than weeks or days) and the number of attempts prices try to violate these areas usually signifies the probability they will retain their significance. And this is pretty much as one would expect: buyers knowing that prices will stop falling at this support level will begin buying as the stock descends to it. Sellers will start their selling strategies as the stock draws nearer to the resistance area.

There is nothing sacred about the precise price level. Slight penetration, certainly for a single day, or a small percent decline/advance or beneath/above these areas (trendlines, in general does not mean they are not still at work. This might be because there are some stocks, where activity tends to be largely institutional, that require more time to implement strategies. At support and resistance areas, by the time they might be willing to act, the price levels get broken, albeit slightly, by perhaps only a few points. However, if there is greater penetration—above (for resistance) and below (for support)—and it remains for several days, this would invite a hard look at a possible price trend change occurrence. Yet we never wait to make a deserving sale on a stock until it falls back to its support line. Waiting for these occurrences before exiting could cost us many, many multiple points.

A curious phenomenon occurs when a stock gets *above* its prior resistance. This price action is termed "breakout." This new area, in theory, now flush with buyers sensing the old resistance which impounded price for so long, but now being broken, will beget buying and an anticipated long advance. Their collective actions and new cost basis—the price where they all now purchased—form a new support area at the prior resistance level. Why should this be?

In theory, it took quite a bit of effort from buyers to break through the old price ceiling. That price level is perceived as the new area to begin buying at, since that price area took in, theoretically, so much buying strength to surpass the old resistance. We say, if the prior resistance level is broken, its price area now becomes a new support price level.

Conversely, prior support levels when broken become resistance areas since a large amount of selling had to take place to get the price beneath the long-held price area of support. The next time the stock tries to rally above this price area, it is apt to have difficulty, since new buyers will know at which level where large selling had taken place.

It is noteworthy to understand that although a stock breaking its support might well eventually fall to a lower level, it will rarely do so in a straight line. In other words, in the very short-term it can turn around (i.e., still advance) if it becomes too oversold, showing that even in a largely bearish pattern there is short-term upward opportunity.

The market's short-term trend will have a very important impact upon most stocks' support and resistance areas. A market rapidly falling will take most stocks with it. Any support a stock may have had, can be short-lived if the overall investment climate is rapidly weakening in intensity.

### Overbought/Oversold Price Conditions

During extreme market periods, investor sentiment is one-dimensional. When euphoric, any news is reasoned as positive and investors continue to buy with higher expectations—"just to get in" or "to be part of the party." During pessimism, nothing is slanted "positive." Prices fall—often continually. The degree to which these times cause notice, or make the "front page," is what exacerbates sentiment and leads to the classic "overbought/oversold" tag, whereafter, investors have learned a contra trend move—a retracement—of less duration and usually intensity, takes place.

During shorter periods of a few days, stocks get overbought and oversold very easily and are usually best judged by their stock chart formations or keen price inspection. When buying gets too rabid, even intraday, price can get too pronounced, or overbought. This is usually above or below their on-average 3 percent change from the prior close.

Beyond a few days, it can be on a chart basis through visual inspection. In other words, prices advanced or declined nearing 90 degrees. Or it can either be after many consecutive days (five or more) or, most likely, after two to three rather dramatic days of point's magnitude.

Eventually, the expectation is that overbought means a fall will shortly take place and as with an oversold condition, a near-term advance is on the horizon. Whether these expectations—the retracements—are to be lasting is crucial for participation. If they are not, then the dominant trend will re-continue and a fast liquidation is necessary if a countertrend position has been placed. If a "new" trend is in the offing, then being patient is the optimal preference. The answer to the question, according to the late financial journalist Edward Hart, is earned in "the fullness of time." We shall know for certain later, not with prescience.

### Double Bottoms & Double Tops

When stocks have a price low, followed by a second price low of usually not more than a few points higher or lower than the first low price, usually separated by more than a month, this usually signifies the stock has hit a "double bottom" and will begin a rise of some consequence. The theory for this is that if the stock price has been unable to decline below a prior long held price low for a period of time, then the "holding" of this second low price offers some proof that the stock won't likely fall lower again. Therefore, a sustainable advance can begin. The successful test of this is when the price starts upward from the second bottom price low, it will rise above the prior high after the first price low.

These types of rationalizations may be self-fulfilling investor wishes, but they do work. It is a very bullish chart pattern and most times, probably in the 70 percent area, a rally of some consequence will shortly occur.

The opposite pattern includes an example of where two close high prices have been detected. In this pattern, the stock is unable to move higher and is said to be "toppish" with a decline expected soon. It is a considered a bearish price formation.

### Hyperbolic Advances

Of all technical price patterns, this one might be said to give way to an almost *guarantee* as to useful predictions. The success rate has to approach 90–100 percent in the absence of a takeover. It does so because prices going almost straight up cannot last forever—or very long. They must stop or the underlying company's shareholders would own everything. Nothing runs lofty...for infinity.

Price patterns get to this extreme level often during an emotional buying binge when buyers simply want shares and dismiss any contrary reason for acquiring them; they are willing to pay almost anything. They use "market orders" to "get me in." They dismiss the "greater fool theory," theorizing they'll be the smarter one, selling higher later. Depending upon where they purchase, they can be very correct...for a while. Nonetheless the day of reckoning will occur—not if—but *will*.

These fortunate investors have watched their investment run almost straight up, but more times than not, they're doing so under anxiety. They may be happy—but they're also anxious. Like most of us, they didn't expect that much success so soon. It's abnormal. Consequently, not unlike others, when they realize the upward thrust is over, they all want to exit to save nervous profits. Selling takes place in droves—often at any price. It is close to panic-driven, yet gifted opportunity for savvy short side or options put buyers. It is classic fear at work.

When the price tends to approach almost straight vertical on price charts, or near 90 degrees, the RSI is approaching or is above 75, volume is relatively huge. Intraday price range is quite significant and the end is within a day or two. The retreat—the bearish, downward move—tends to mirror the advance in time and magnitude.

If a stock started its run at 30 and peaked at 75 in three months, a safe bet is at the 75 top and extending out three more calendar months, the stock will again arrive at about 30. If a significant support area can be found, the 200 day moving average in a firm upward trend pattern will perhaps be at the higher of the two levels. But drop in price it shall—it always does.

### Diagonal, Angled Trendlines

In a bullish trendline, technicians draw a straight and continuous line between an intraday low and a subsequent reacting higher intraday low. When they connect points from an intraday high and a subsequent lower intraday high, they are designing a bearish diagonal trendline.

Slight penetration of these lines (maybe less than 3 to 5 percent) generally means nothing and prices tend to remain directionally as before. However, after a trendline breakout, if the subsequent price movement does not move outside where the price violation occurred, it is said to be suggestive of a trend continuation failure and the prior price direction is likely. Example: a prior bearish trendline being broken or penetrated to the upside will have bullish suggestions to it; yet then breaking below would suggest a reassertion of downward price action.

### Price Breakouts & "Breakdowns"

Breakouts are chart patterns that signify that a stock's price has gone above a prior resistance area or diagonal trendline and is then assumed to be headed higher. Considered bullish, there are enough instances to support a bullish view. However there are many times when breakouts are quickly followed by a retreat to the breakout level to "test" investor's true intentions. Do they really intend to march the stock higher or was the move above a "false breakout?"

The longer the resistance area held, the more likely a breakout will have duration and keeps moving upward. And if the breakout is on heavy relative volume it should have even more meaning.

A "breakdown" occurs when a prior support line or price area has been violated and price action moves lower and remains so. The price then would be expected to continue downward.

## Technical Indicators & Definitions

Technical indicators offer investors mathematical help in identifying overbought and oversold conditions. And since they are generally a single value or so, they are far less trying than having to visually review price charts constantly. They are a perfect match for data processing. Formulas can crank out end-of day numbers which then can be screened to find buy and sell candidates. Usually technical indicators are not open to much interpretation; their result can be acted upon without much bias. It makes a technician's life much easier.

There are almost too many common technical indicators (several of the popular investment software products include well over fifty) most of which work only occasionally in estimating price direction. It makes the most sense to develop or utilize those indicators that are proven accurate with peaks and troughs in price action. Put another way, at the extremes of price—signals that suggest a new bullish or bearish impending move. (Indicators that merely follow the existing price action can hint as to a change but mere chart inspection offers the same insight.)

To test an indicator or utilize one of the many available, find a stock that is badly oversold and see if the indicator can be fine-tuned to initiate a "buying signal" as the stock starts upward. This will show that the newly designed methodology will show it will work, at least at bottoms…and at least once. Many, many stocks with this bullish indicator signal would have to be back tested to have predictive merit.

Irrespective of whether a designed or current indicator makes intellectual sense, as long as it works in predicting movement, it should be utilized. Students of technical analysis would agree that some of the better indicators, RSI and Money Flow, are conceptually elementary mathematical models that are really very, very unsophisticated. It's been questioned how could something so simple in design work. Yet they work very well. But, they still cannot cause a stock to move for an extended time period outside the required buy/sell equation. So we should agree they have an ultimate inherent limitation as to predicting the future. Since some do work despite our wish that they were more far more esoteric, we shouldn't dismiss the better use that the best of them offer. If they work—trust them, since it's from the levels they suggest that investors have learned to act.

## Designing an Indicator

It is common practice to design technical indicators that attempt to measure stock movement without regard to other affecting variables—the market as a whole or a stock's industry. Since we know that the market's effect upon an individual stock is very strong over short to intermediate time frames, why not do so? If we don't, are we suggesting a stock is an island unto itself? Do we want to eliminate the most affecting consistent variable? Doing so will occasionally work, since any stock can move counter to the market for a period, but those times will be few.

Measuring a stock's upward response as the market rises and maybe even surpassing it, and when the market is down, perhaps not falling that day or falling less than the market, would be very telling for a stock's bullish strength, were the markets ultimate direction to be bullish. Naturally, the reverse would be true looking for bearish potential trend.

The revered Money Flow Indicator is designed to be isolated unto the stock alone. Yet, might there be a better approach? Because it is an easy argument to make that when a stock starts downward (or, in Money Flow parlance, "it is experiencing liquidation,") to say the stock is reacting to the probable market's impact anyway, why design an indicator that has the direct market's effect in it? It's a catch 22 issue. *Why be in a falling stock, regardless of what a bullish __market__ signal might be telling us? Why choose equity from an indicator type when its principal –near and intermediate term impetus—will be from something not being measured by the indicator?*

Even this author's idea of a weighted price computation might be superior to Money Flow (each intraday actual transactional price, multiplied by its trade volume for that transaction, added together for a daily total, then divided by the sum of the final daily volume; this ultimately equates to a true daily weighted price; weighted by volume that is—assumed conviction). However, both may be inferior to designing indicators that trace the stock relationship to its dominate short to intermediate most affecting voice, the market's movement—the more propelling force. It seems conceptually inferior to side-step the markets effect no matter how automatic it may appear within equity's price performance, anyway. Whether it is in practical application will only be realized through lengthy back testing.

## The Frequency of Measuring

The measuring frequency of how often we test technical conditions is crucial—daily is generally preferable before weekly. In this application, we may capture intraweek movement that would otherwise escape our detection. If we measure the percentage above or below a 50-day moving average of the Dow Jones Industrials, on a weekly only basis, then any extreme intra week overbought or oversold condition that might help us, would be missed. If the Dow were to turn up or down intra week and signal a move having gone too far, we would be clueless. Waiting until Friday's close to measure weekly changes implies that intra week movement isn't important to monitor. *(Once upon a time, it might have been true. In today's investment world, a stock moving 10 or even 15 percent intraday is not uncommon and large percentage swings take place over the course of only a few days.)* End-of-week-only measurement might prove to be very, very costly, since one can lose mightily in-between Fridays. Activity between Fridays is hardly irrelevant noise and clearly for one predisposed to short-term or purchasing highly volatile issues. In an era with instant reaction, being prepared more frequently than less is highly suggested.

One caveat: weekly measurement does avoid the pitfall of becoming too reactive.

It can be shown that for a long-term investment philosophy, to buy and repurchase on a consistent basis (the age-old "Dollar Cost Averaging" method) during upward trending weekly periods, thus remaining fully invested until the stocks weekly picture turns down, can reward the investor even more than monitoring on an intra week frequency. In other words, utilizing weekly closing figures means that weekly closing price becomes the determining factor for overbought/oversold, the breaking of support and resistance areas, and other technical measures for timing decisions.

A weekly review also eliminates the "noise" made by price gyration. The downside is that price movement can often be severe intra week if a stock is volatile and its sector and/or the market itself are beginning substantive moves. It wouldn't be "known" until "Friday night" where substantial damage or opportunity might have been sustained or lost.

Example: Cisco Systems, CSCO, perhaps the lead technology company in the world, still suffered devastating market capitalization losses from its March 2000 high of almost 82 through the Fall of 2001. Tracking the stock on a <u>daily</u> basis meant the stock first broke its 50 DMA at about 65 in early September 2000 and its 200 DMA at about 63 in mid-September 2000. Using <u>weekly</u> charts to determine an exit point meant an exit after a break of the 50 week moving average in late September at about 58. Not too bad, yet an exit using the weekly 200 week moving average would have been at 30 in mid-February 2001, which isn't just bad, it is out and out awful!

Weekly reviews of <u>moving averages</u> will not usually coincide anywhere close to a top or a bottom, whether it's a single stock example, or any number. Weekly computation of moving averages as an example of a technical indicator is simply too slow. A better approach might be to judge an exit or enter position on a weekly basis but with faster response indicators, possibly the RSI which will certainly show support and resistance areas. While weekly reviews of these indicators means more of an after-the-fact review than if a review is daily, if the trend in place isn't reversing very quickly, if the equity instrument you own isn't too volatile, and if support and resistance levels aren't being taken out, weekly reviews can still be sufficient for most technical indications. Just remember to apply consistent criteria to guide you.

For example: if you utilize some RSI level, you should always use daily or weekly computations to enter or exit transactions based on respective levels where the indicator has proven useful.

## Multiple Technical Proofs?

The many-is-better belief is founded upon the suspicion that if several indicators computed using different formulas all point to a bullish outlook, then there exists more likelihood that a bullish price result will occur. Any single indicator can provide a false signal, but several in-like predictive modes won't. It presumes that the best indicator might not be worth following unless others agree with its bias. It thus reasons why positions shouldn't be initiated with a few indicators in harmony.

It is common to have most indicators reach the same conclusion, at the same time, as most utilize similar computational elements, and almost always at significant trend changes—that is to say, at the end of a protracted downward or upward period, such as markets well oversold or very overbought. Therefore, the predictive value of waiting for many indicators pointing toward the same conclusion before going forward with a researched idea at important turning points, is very suspect. Any one of the better indicators will be just as telling unless each is measuring something very different, and that too, is not very likely. "Many" indicators having to fall in line aren't likely to improve the strategy's potential.

However, when *certain* indicators along with price chart patterns *and* excessive relative volume all appear to be signaling the same direction concurrently, the odds greatly favor following the signal they portend, and even more so when the broad market is also in directional agreement. While it is not often many will fall precisely into place at the same time, designing software to target those infrequent anomalies is exceedingly wise and, not unexpectedly, wealth creating!

One example: a falling price that stops at a long-held support level, is coincident with a very low RSI, has huge relative volume, is also at the stock's 200 day moving average, and has been down perhaps four to five prior days with a market and or sector deeply oversold and turning upward etc, etc., all signals a prescription for a striking and rapid advance.

## Conflicting Evidence: Charts & Indicators

There are times when indicators may be signaling perhaps a bullish movement, but the chart pattern is decided bearish or vice versa. Classic evidence of these occurrences is during bear market spiraling-downward periods when everything, according to historical indications and indicators, is reading oversold. The cardinal rules are:

**The security chart pattern construction should be viewed as dominate with technical indicators secondary for all periods beyond a few days.**
**For periods outside of a few short-term days, if the chart is bullish—**
**be long (out of equities). If the chart is bearish—**
**be short (in put options and residing in cash).**

We all would be far richer were we to allow the markets to tell us when the bottom is at hand and not try and test the bottom with a non-conforming chart pattern—as in the above example, with one continuing to make new lows.

If a trend is continuing down, it will more likely than not to continue down. Forget catching the bottom and the assumed bargain, since it may arrive—in reality, many points lower. One example: NASDAQ October to late November 2000, when many apparent "bargains" became far more so throughout that devastatingly bearish tech period.

Terribly bearish stock price patterns portend…more terribly bearish chart patterns.

## Specific Technical Indicators

### *200 Day Moving Average*

A stock's 200 day moving average is a plotted continuous trending line gathered from the last 200 days of closing prices and indicates long-term trend. *In actuality, 200 days is about 10 months of price data.*

Repeating this process will net a slow moving line trending upward or downward. Dividing closing prices by 200 figures means the line will be unable to alter its own trend quickly. It will be slow to change its trending bias. It's questionable as to why investors use 200, and not 250 or 150, as the standard long term proxy for a stock's bullish/bearish positioning. But no matter, they do, although a minority use 30 weeks, 150 days, interchangeably.

If a stock's current price is above the moving average, it is considered long-term bullish; below, long-term bearish, at least at that point in time. It also does not mean that event, though it's located beneath its line that does not provide an opportunity for occasional spirited short run advances.

The trend or slope (angle) of the 200 DMA trend line is important. It is most important to visually note the approximate angle of ascent—if it is upward towards 25 to maybe 45 degrees and is clearly portending a strong upward continuing price bias. But most importantly, it will stop almost any decline along its continuing trendline. This is called "providing support." The probabilities of this type of support phenomena are about 85–90 percent! A day slope that is too flat has less ability to halt a decline. However, one exception to its ability to provide support will occur in severe market downturns, themselves abnormal periods when normal expectations and occurrences won't apply.

Stocks moving from beneath the line tend to be repelled as they approach it. This is called "meeting resistance." However if they get through and rise above the line by more than 10 percent, this will often start an advance of some duration is being considered long-term bullish even if, as they frequently do, they come back down to the "breakout point" (the 200 DMA price level) and retest the price level. A subsequent advance would be accepted as a successful test and the price level would be viewed as a support area. A minor break of the line usually isn't significant and usually will be resolved to the upside. If a break occurs and more than several days pass with the price still beneath the line, it might mean more downside will occur. Several days of observation gives investors sufficient time to make a determination.

Technicians use the 200 DMA trend as a core technical tool.

*Mathematical Construction: The 200 DMA, is determined by summing the last 200 days of closing prices, dividing by 200, and plotting the resulting price figure. For the next day's computation, the last day (the 201st day) is dropped and the latest day (today) is added. We sum the 200 days as before and divide by 200.*

### Closing Percent of the Daily High—Quasi Proprietary

The astute investor frequently negotiates their strategy toward the close and they, and this indicator, assume the price momentum is to be expected to continue based upon a percentage of the close. Rational or not, it has been learned that the closer to the stock's high its closing price becomes, the more likely that bullish momentum continuation will be the impending result. Conversely, closing nearer to the intraday low is more an invitation of price weakness. A 50-day period is used for the indicator. Note: bearish extremes are at greater than 60 percent; Bullish at less than 40 percent. At these extremes, a countertrend move is very, very likely—and very shortly.

*Mathematical Construction: Take the oldest 50th day closing price and subtract from it the 50th day low price. Next, take the 50th day high price and subtract from it the 50th day low price (this is the stock's intraday range) Next, divide the result from the first portion by the second portion and multiply by 100 to determine that day's percent that the close was of the high. We then move to the 49th oldest day and repeat the process until we arrive at the latest day. When complete, we have a sum total of 50 days of percents, which then divided by 50, yields that day's Closing Percent of the High Indicator.(This and others are short math examples, but a simple computer program will make the computation(s) instantaneous.)*

One day example: High Price 100; Low Price 90; Closing Price 98;(98-90/(100-90) x 100 or 8/10 times 100 or 80 percent for that days result. This figure means that the intraday close was 80 percent of the intraday high.

### RSI, Relative Strength Index

RSI stands for Relative Strength Index, introduced by technical analyst Welles Wilder in 1978 and is a mildly involved mathematical formula of closing prices and the average points magnitude of up versus down days over some user pre-selected period, with results ranging from zero to 100. This indicator tries to determine when a stock is too overbought or too oversold, based on computed extremes. The assumption then, is that the equity will next move in a counter direction.

## It is the best pure technical measure of extreme buyer/seller enthusiasm over an intermediate period.

The data period of 17 days has been found by this author to provide excellent intermediate predictable usage. Just an exceptional indicator!

What it essentially measures is the number of advancing points divided by the number of declining points and computing a ratio of each. Rather simplistic in concept, but it works very well! And it probably works just because investors have been shown to react to its extremes—almost like any self-fulfilling prophecy.

(In early August 2000 the SOX, the Philadelphia Semiconductor Index hit a low point of 36, just about coincident with the index's price low. The subsequent rally which soon followed made for a lot of money. The SOX 17-day RSI was an unheard-of 78 in early March 2000 right at that index's price high! The NASDAQ, in March of 2000, while at 5000, had an RSI of 72.

The RSI is a common technical indicator easily found in almost all investment software programs. It signals top price action when it is above 75, better still above 80 and after a consistent period of time. It suggests a bottom being in place when less than 35.

Caveat emptor: the first occurrence of a high or low RSI must be viewed in conjunction with what has preceded that level. If a bullish trend is just <u>starting</u> or, after a very protracted decline, or after even a full fledged bear market, a fast RSI of 80 plus (normally indicative of an overbought condition and a severe warning of a soon-to-follow decline) should not be immediately followed by a sell order. It is more likely the stock will find its way higher. However, if the advance was lengthy in duration (calendar time) or magnitude (huge percent movement) then the 80+ figure should be viewed as much more important. One more point is the slope of the RSI: if it arrives at overbought/sold very quickly, it is more probable to have an effect than if it slowly arrived at an extreme reading.

Like all indicators, an extreme RSI figure is a "warning." It is not signal, an automatic exit out, or an entrance into any position since only, and *I really mean only*, adverse price movement should be the final decision maker.

*Mathematical Construction: Total the daily net advances for the UP days over the past 17 most recent days (for our 17 day measuring period), then divide the result by 17. This yields the average UP close. Next, add the daily net declines for the DOWN days over the latest 17 days. The result is the average DOWN close. Then divide the UP close by the DOWN close and add +1 to the result. Divide this result into 100. Lastly, subtract the result from 100, and you have calculated the RSI figure for the most recent day. For continuance, we drop the oldest day, then the 18th day, and add the latest day, which is today.*

Considering the remarkable predictive worth of the RSI, it should be explored in an attempt to modify it to become even more useful. That modification might have to do with intraday figures, since the standard RSI is measured only on closing price and/or may be some relationship to broad market performance.

| | PRICE TOP AREAS | | 17-DAY RSI VALUE AT:<br>PRICE BOTTOM AREAS | |
|---|---|---|---|---|
| Dow Jones 30 Industrials | 1/2000 | 66–67 | 3/22/2001 | 17; |
| | | | 9/21/2001 | 15; |
| | | | 7/24/2002 | 20; |
| | | | 3/12/2003 | 31 |
| NASDAQ | 3/2000 | 72 | 4/2001 | 29; |
| | | | 9/2001 | 18; |
| | | | 7/23/2002 | 28; |
| | | | 10/10/2002 | 38 |

There are too many examples of individual stocks to list when their RSI levels were 65+ at tops and 20–30 at bottoms. To list but a few:

| | | | | |
|---|---|---|---|---|
| Cisco Systems (CSCO) | 3/2000 | 72 | 9/2000 | 26 |
| East Bay (EBAY) | 3/2000 | 67 | 12/2000 | 36 |
| Johnson & Johnson (JNJ) | 12/2000 | 68 | 3/2000 | 26 |
| Juniper Networks (JNPR) | 9/2000 | 75 | 10/2001 | 25 |

### OI, Options Indicator for Market Intermediate Forecasting—Proprietary

The OI is an extremely simplistic proprietary indicator developed to measure investor options sentiment, but not very different from general near-term investor options whether a bullish or bearish sentiment. It is a mild alteration of other options models, but it has worked exceptionally well—more conclusively when indicating market <u>bottoms</u>.

Going back to 1980 for long-term proof, whenever the five week moving average is beneath 1.00, this is essentially telling us that over the past five weeks more put options have advanced than call options. The markets are too oversold and due to advance within a few months. In any event, at any <u>under</u> 1.00 reading, there is very little market risk over the next three to four weeks.

Overbought is a bit less valuable, but readings above 2.00 are a hint toward too much optimism.

Through the Fall of 2001, during seven calendar periods, this indicator registered above 2.0 suggesting an overbought condition. During the same time-frame, on approximately 15 occasions, it registered under 1.0 for quite a bullish outlook.

*Mathematical Construction: Its construction is simple math. Take data from Barron's options information section, the CBOE weekly advancing call options figure, and divide it by the CBOE weekly advancing put options figure. Add the number for five consecutive weeks, totaling them and dividing by 5, then initiate a continuing five week moving average. It couldn't be simpler and... it's worked for nearly a quarter of a century.*

### Gauging Relative Price Strength Comparisons

The importance of this "concept" is to monitor if an equity investment is moving greater than the market as a whole—this means a percentage advance more than the S&P 500 on positive market days, or down more on a percentage comparison during declining days. It is desirous to be in the positions that outpace the market's upward strength and, if "shorting" stock or buying puts, to associate in stocks that are weaker than the broad market. Greater relative strength, or weakness, means faster investment profit.

Example: During a terrible declining market period, the investor who is short a stock or who has purchased put options would want to see their stock rise less when the market might advance, and fall much faster and deeper when the market sinks.

One significant warning: the idea of superior relative strength is meaningful, and sought only when the market and individual stock is moving in the same direction. There is a fool's luxury being in a stock that "holds up" better than others in down periods. Since while these investors enjoy greater relative strength and lose less than others, they lose money regardless! Losing less than average is not what investment is designed for.

*Mathematical Construction: Measure the stocks daily percentage move and divide the result by the S&P 500 daily percentage move. Next, design the criteria for the stock to prove superior relative strength—e.g., demand the stock have 50 percent superior daily greater relative strength than the S&P 500 and of course you could simply measure one against the other and obtain the stock's simple percent comparison ratio. Insistence that the stock show greater upward strength on positive days and less weakness on down days is more demanding and further proof of a stock's relative strength.*

> Example: Stock is +1.6 percent for the day.
> S & P 500 is +1.0 percent for the day.
> The stock is 60 percent greater in relative strength (1.60-1.00)/1.00*100
> The pre set criteria is a 50 percent superior relative strength level for the stock.
> The stock having a 60 percent daily number is for this day exhibiting superior relative strength.
> The stock receives a +1 for a one day positive comparison (if the stock fails the criteria test, it receives a zero).

*Lastly run a ten day moving average of the daily comparisons and multiply the result by 10 to arrive at the stock's relative strength ratio. Maximum would be 100 percent with a minimum at zero percent.*

*And you might expand the study period beyond ten days, design your own criteria or choose relative strength indicators found in almost any investment software product.*

## *Note: Avoidance of Volume*

One of the most overworked phrases is that without increasing volume a trend can't be continuous, or real, and that only with heavy volume is directional continuance assured. This is pure folklore. Volume is activity, and prompts investor interest. Simple magnitude of volume isn't indicative of a futuristic buying or selling interest bias.

Trends flourish with or without the same <u>relative</u> volume—it need not increase to prove anything. Only under extremes of relative volume, which denote very unusual interest and generally for good reason, should volume ever play any part of a buy/sell opinion. A far too mentioned measure.

# Beating Wall Street...
# Some of the Time

## Direct Your Investment Focus toward Industry First

According to an article entitled "The Cat's Meow" printed in the November 2000 issue in Bloomberg's magazine, "Wealth Manager," by senior markets editor, James Picerno, and from a study completed by Wisenberger a division of Thomson Financial, it was noted that investment in the broad market as a whole (almost a play on the S&P 500 through the period 1983–1999) gave rise to a spectacular 14-fold gain. This is $1,000 playing out to about $15,000 over those many years as the generational shift of baby boomers to save and invest—coupled with new 401k regulations—produced dizzying returns. Yet before you start clapping, note what the balance of the study said: were one to emphasize sector (industry) performance, some label it as simple momentum investing. That return, under perfect timing, would have brought about a 250-fold rise in investment worth 24,000 percent. No, it is not a math typo, it is 24,000 percent. Every $4,000 investment chunk turned into $1,000,000. Now you can surely stand and applaud and sip the finest champagne you can find since the inference is profound!

Before the old school rallies to the buy and hold defense, we all know that perfection isn't in the cards over extended periods and perfect industry timing is an honor only for textbooks. Yet if timing were only half correct, would a 12,000 percent return be enough of a lure?

Academics argue that no one can time markets and sectors or individual stock selections with any consistency, to which, one probably would have little quarrel depending upon the definition of accurate timing. However, if sector/industry timing, when very, very correct, brings about returns that are astronomical vis-à-vis buy and hold, can any more of a stronger investment case be made for their focus and attempt at replication?

These means are an ardent focus on evident industry price momentum. They are not any lazy "sit back and let's watch fate dictate our investing future; we'll just ride out -40 percent sector/market baths on the assumption the calendar will bail us out."

Why not at least try an industry momentum focus!! Are 24,000 percent or 12,000 percent returns sufficient incentive? Let's hope so.

## Beginning the Hunt for Wall Street's Riches— Begin from Pricing Proof!

When the bargain stocks (or individual industry sectors) "stocks look cheap" and come into vogue in the Wall Street press and actually begin their assent with some enduring upward moving price action, this is the time when we should start to take a serious investment look. "Dead money"—e.g., small cap stocks 1983–1987; 1996–1999—is a preeminent example of earning relatively nothing on invested monies over multiple years. Needless to point out, not where investment dollars should have been allowed to stagnate. Now patience is a great virtue to have but it can be a very expensive one.

A $50,000 equity portfolio remaining dormant for several years costs any investor plenty. $50,000 at a 5 percent interest return in bonds or money markets over 36 months still yields about $2,500 each year. If compounding, it suggests "portfolio waiting" has an "opportunity cost" of perhaps $8,000 plus. (It is not dissimilar to having collector cars or expensive art which equally returns no immediate value. There is a holding cost with collectibles—even with some securities "collectibles." Yet while the price for waiting can be hefty, at a market turn, equities will always still be the place to be.)

Depending upon the definition of time, price trends that lead to gains are always in evidence. There can be a trend for a few minutes or an hour. If one reverts to six months ago, there will likely be a very discernible trend from that date to the present. There are clear long-term trends as well as our favored intermediate-term trends. There can almost never be a trendless security with a sufficiently liberal definition of time. That is, securities do not function in a straight line or stay unchanged for very long. And depending upon luck and some skill, some money can be made in any type of trend past the very shortest of intervals.

Trends move along until the investor buying and selling pendulum reverses, and therefore should:

**Never, let it be assumed to be changing direction, until there is actual continual price evidence supporting that directional change!**

Even with available technical hints as to what may occur, the trend in place should be plainly viewed as unto its own.

According to Jake Bernstein, a well-known trader and author of over 25 investment publications, *"I swear that if I had even one dollar for every time I took a profit too soon for no valid reason whatsoever, I'd be one hell of a lot richer."* A frank admission by maybe the learned best: that assuming trend changes is not wise, and far too often very, very costly.

**You cannot know how far up or down or to what extremes investors will push pricing. Wait for the evidence to appear! Do not just guess tops & bottoms! No one really knows...since only mass investor sentiment shift will cause a lasting change.**

One of the most curious of Wall Street phenomena is when everyone appears so bullish and all the external events so positive that the market or a stock then declines. It is quite easy to understand, and, for a change, it is quite logical.

During grand bullish periods, investor sentiment gets very extreme and it seems everybody who dispenses advice is universally positive and so, too, is news and, better still, prices have that upward tilt. When this trend becomes so bullishly pervasive, it will only have arrived after a period of continuous price rise when almost anybody who might have been predisposed to buy and had any effect on pricing, would have. The last portions of bullish money—the last buying "stamina" available to lift equities—becomes quickly absorbed by normal selling and some profit-taking, and the balance of buying/selling pressure then tips to the sell side and prices shortly decline.

As postulated, of the three trends an investor could seek to specialize in—long, short, and intermediate—the latter, by way of experience and some study proof, can have the most monetarily profound average effects when correctly leveraging a successful investment.

Through experience and research, the duration of an average intermediate trend move is generally about ten to 12 weeks. According to Victor Sperandeo, also known as "Trader Vic," the definition of the duration of the intermediate term trend is "lasting a minimum of three weeks to as long as six months." According to his research, dating back to 1896, the average market return during an advancing trend was 20 percent. He also determined the average days of intermediate advance to be 107—a shade more than three calendar months. *(The reader will note these figures are all consistent with our November 1998 study lasting over five trend periods.)*

The intermediate trend starts as a short upward or downward movement from a prior countertrend which has presumably ended or, from a lateral, sideways movement. One determines the certainty of that new trend only after it has begun, well after the fact—by simple observation and never prior to. Generally, intermediate term trends do not just start and fire significantly in one direction. There is usually a "testing" of the presumed "new" trend before we begin to think of it as the advent of an intermediate launch of perhaps several months or years.

It's always amusing to hear an investor make the statement "they would only invest at the start of a trend and never invest in a trend until it was clear on the charts." The natural fallacy being—you cannot see evidence of a trend on a securities chart until after it has begun. Thus, you cannot—were you to adopt that tact—enter a trend from it's onset. There is mutual exclusivity in wanting to be in at the start but waiting to be sure from chart pattern formation before the transaction is entered is wise. There is a fine line of feeling comfort, yet waiting too long and giving up potential is the cornerstone of an investment purchase. It is a way of saying, you don't own the last "10 percent" of any equities price. You can't have it except by luck. And, it's a big "and," the top you think you are getting might only be for weeks or days or...even a few hours. So revel in the glory for a moment. Equities are perpetual and higher prices almost always occur sometime.

The Dow Jones chart (Figure 7.10) below is from the November 1997 to April/May 1988 period (the middle period trend of the five that our 1998 study

Figure 7.10

12/27 12:47 pm Printed using SuperCharts©Omega Research, Inc. 1997

looked at) and indicates many trends and a host of examples of price pattern recognition within its confines.

The far left side of the chart at Point A would have certainly been a downwardly biased trend ending at Point A. Commencing at Point A through Point B is termed a short-term advance, approximately four weeks in duration with a 10 percent Dow upward move. The trend from Point B to Point C (also in duration of 5 weeks or so) is downwardly biased and short-term by definition. Point C ends at a price level, 7,350 Dow, where the prior low was made at Point A. (This "double bottom" gives the savvy investor the presumed edge, since most times a recent low point in pricing, followed by a second attempt at lower pricing—but not meaningfully exceeding it— is construed as a "successful test" of the Point A bottom, and is sometimes referred to as "the reaction low." Assuming there had been even a prior attempt to fall below Point A would mean at that Dow level, termed it's "support," is even more formidable.)

The next test is to see if the next trend can exceed the prior high at Point B. As is evident from the upward trend from Point C through Point D (the upward arrow) the Dow 8,200 level—the prior stopping point—is where we see prices trend even higher and exceed the prior Point D level. When this occurs, the advance is presumed to have tested the prior high, Point B, and broken through its level, known as its "resistance." It has thus broken out—not surprisingly termed a "breakout." Therefore, by definition, we have a short-term trend now turning into a probable intermediate trend, continuing to move to approximately Point E, where the trend ends at about Dow 9,200. Pricing that starts at Point C and continues upward is a series of higher high prices and higher low prices—when small price declines occur—on to Point E. Point E to Point F is a retracement of the advance and subsequent final failure to move above Point E at Point G which is indicative of the start of a trend reversal. This is a classic real-world advancing, intermediate term trend illustration.

(An important caveat: after the second bottom at Point C, which did not fall below the prior low or Point A, we might have assumed a bottoming process was in place because there was some evidence and then went long (bought securities). But were we to wait for the upward move to get past Point D—the confirmation of the move and "breakout point"—and to have felt more certain, some 800 Dow points would have been missed! Ooooouch, once more!)

## Using Leverage to Multiply Profitable Opportunities

To capitalize when correctly assessing the intermediate direction, the use of leveraging money, as in the instance when one is investing in options, provides in many cases either the only ability to obtain the "effect" from a presumed advance/decline in a stock or the market, or when used properly, the most efficient usage of capital to attain profit. (The word "only" means that an option purchase at-the-money—where stock and exercise price are about equal—will cost about 7 to 10 percent of the cost of an outright stock purchase. Not having enough money to outright buy stock would otherwise mean not capitalizing on an idea especially if the stock is high in price. At least in these cases, options offer some ability to participate.)

Options can be seen as an inexpensive way to earn "the play" on a stock without tying up significant portions of an account. *Buying 500 shares of a $50 stock versus a 5 calls purchase. In dollar terms, that means $25,000 compared to perhaps $1,500 (5 options at maybe $3 each). And if the call options were "at, or better still, in-the-money," each point movement of the stock would equate to about an equal profit amount in the stock purchase.*

Options are in some degree the way "margin buying" used to be on Wall Street. In the 1920's, margin requirements were only about 10 percent ($1,000 worth of stock required a $100 "deposit")—not too much different in required money in percentage terms than at-the-money options pricing today.

### Options utilized intelligently can offer extremes virtually unheard of because so little money is required to secure extraordinary percentage returns.

As our study noted, the options returns dwarfed those of the underlying stock during one period at a striking 18-to-1 ratio! It should be obvious that using leverage properly can yield spectacular results.

In some situations, however, such as purchasing stock on margin, it can mean losing perhaps twice as much when wrong. The only options risk is the original purchase cost. So option upside can be vast and the downside purchase expenditure, limited to just the capital outlay at the onset, and even that can be limited dramatically.

Merrill Lynch (MER), the largest full-service brokerage firm in the country and the author's first security's industry employer, late in the summer of 1998 experienced a gradual decline along with most equities, then began re-accelerating downward—call it plummeting—into a nasty correction. It ended on October 8th, when the stock's price bottomed at an intraday low of 35 3/4. If an investor witnessed a 20 percent rise in the stock prior to agreeing, an intermediate advance might have begun—*and it actually took all of a single day of hesitation*—and then summoned the courage and purchased, here are the actual stock and option results at various dates:

| $10,000 Purchase Decisions: Stock, Margin or Options | | | | | |
|---|---|---|---|---|---|
| MER | Dates | Price | In Cash | On Margin | Options |
| Bottom | 10/8/98 | 35 3/4 | | | |
| PURCHASE | | | | | |
| After 20 % | 10/9/98 | 45 5/8 | 219 Shares | 438 Shares | 12/50 Call Options @ 3 3/8 30 option contracts |
| SALE | | | | | |
| Study End | 12/9/98 | 71 1/2 | | | |
| RESULTS | | | $15,659 +56 % | $31,317 +112 % | $72,000 +520 % |

Once again, the use of options leverage proves the superior investment by a land-slide! The options returned $56,000 more dollars than a cash investment in the stock of Merrill -46 versus 520 in percent return. And this is no isolated one-time event, since in most instances 80 and 90 percent of equities will trend in the same direction as the broad market during an intermediate move and a profitable leveraged option investment will always dwarf a cash or margin return. The mathematics of leverage is that compelling!

While the observant pessimist can assert, "Of course the leveraged investment is superior when it works but how often does it?" All right, certainly not often enough to warrant displacing your life's savings. But being very correct a few times from start to end of any normal intermediate advance is eye-popping! Obviously, if you were right with a stock purchase, you almost have to be more right with an options invest-ment, assuming you learn the rules well.

Perhaps it is better to ask how much is given away when not participating in a successful leveraged investment. How many does one need to have been net better off? The leveraged numbers, when correct, are just too lucrative to not invite a deserved look.

## Selecting the Right Investment Vehicle—
## Hint: Not from Fundamentals...Its Relative Price Action

The simplest and best approach in choosing amongst investment alternatives is to research for the one that is evidencing superior relative price direction—either up or down. This should be obvious. Pick the "cherry" of choices.

Choose the strongest relative pricing strength in advancing trends, in short, the "worst" meaning the security with the <u>weakest</u> price action in declining trends.

Most obviously, choose an investment that is moving in the same direction as the market and is following the same trend of the market as well as its industry. It is preferable that both be directionally the same. Don't try and predict which stock will act contra to the historical 80 to 90 percent of stocks that trend coincident with the market. It rarely pays, or often pays very little even when it does.

Resist the temptation to snap up the laggards, especially when investment is short-term or even intermediate-term, or where time is everything. This means if the market is trending downward, the investment that you should choose in either options or stock is falling faster. In rally attempts, it continues to look weak (i.e., it rises less than the market or its sector companies). If the trend continues down, an investment exhibiting superior relative downward price behavior will fall faster and return greater profit to you. In investing with an expected advance in mind, you should avoid selection of investment choices that are not the leaders to the upside. Choose stocks that would be rising at the fastest percentage and are participating in the advance, and not in stocks that are not responding.

The method for determining exact relative strength needs to be one of formula and not mere observation. Yet what appears as obvious direction from chart pattern observation certainly still works. Most software programs have relative strength variations built in, but in their absence, simply divide the closing price of a potential stock by the Dow or the S&P 500 to cede the percentage change and keep the running results. Greater numbers mean the stock is outperforming—displaying better relative strength and vice versa.

| The "Sample Company" | | | |
|---|---|---|---|
| Dates | Price<br>% Change | Dow Jones<br>% Change | Relative Strength<br>Computation |
| 4/1 | 100 | 9,000 | 100/(9000) or .0111 percent |
| 4/2 | 102  2.0 | 9,090  1.0 | 102/(9090) or .0112 percent |
| 4/3 | 99  -2.9 | 8,800  -3.1 | 99/(8800) or .0113 percent |

The <u>stock</u> is showing better greater relative strength than the market in a falling period, and in an uptrend, a one to perhaps own.

One last point in deciding which investment to pick from, is the "industry effect." Most stocks within most industries will tend to have strong co-movement in their market price and, almost universally, short-term. They tend to move up and down directionally together, and at roughly the same degree. For example, when banks are strong, it pays to get into that sector rather than spending too much of your evenings trying to dissect which of its component companies will run the fastest.

Conversely, if the drug industry is weak, for almost all short-term periods, all of the drugs will weaken and even the strongest-acting—those with fine relative upward strength—will also succumb to the downside. Exceptions do occur, but this aspect of proper selection shouldn't be forgotten. Align your immediate investment choices with the current price trend.

If we were to prioritize the importance of an individual company, its industry sector, and the market as a whole, it might be in those respective orders. A very strong stock will be more important than its limp industry and neutral market environment. Yet a suddenly downside shift in its industry would likely curtail the stock's potential upward movement. It might not derail it, but could affect it. So these three elements can all be independent and, under some circumstances, dependent. Under ideal investment conditions, all three are trending alike, and none are trending in opposite direction to one another.

## Find the Probable Cause for Movement: Is It Specific or General

It is so important to catch the distinction if a stocks greater than normal daily movement is being caused by general comments that move everything as if "painted with a broad brush." Some comments may be fair and some not—or news that is individually directed or when more attention might be necessary. The companies that grab the business headlines are presumed to typify the majority—this isn't often factual.

> **Internal Effects:** Business press mention
> Company generated news
> Security's internal daily buy/sell dynamic,
> including volatility
>
> **External Effects:** Market price movement
> Industry price movement
> Economic events
> Business & Finance News, etc.

If we review each of the above for the suspected cause of price movement we might have been able to control, had we known, only the security's day-to-day trading—and that to a very limited degree—stands out. Only if that day's price movement is truly outside the range of normal, or meets technical factors, we might be forced to take action. Otherwise, it might be seen as just another day's consensus tally around buying and selling. "How could I have known today it would move up/down 2 points?" You couldn't, no more than on most days, absent some technical indicators or publicly made comments.

All these other elements that affect price come to us "out of the blue" and their resulting effect—good or bad—is just part of the monitoring process on the day of announcement. An equities daily magnitude of price movement will be largely governed by its own volatility. It is thus important to know how much "bounce" there is in what you are buying since that alone can explain price behavior. Large volatility levels mean a wide high to low price range can occur in response to any type of event. Be prepared.

For example, if an oil analyst announces the price of oil will drop dramatically, and shortly after—usually instantly and most certainly instantly if we had just purchased Exxon—shares plummet. This isn't probable cause for a sale based on anything fundamentally, inherently wrong with Exxon, maybe only the industry in general, and that opinion might not last long. It might quickly be proven to mean there is something inherently wrong with the analyst! So a quick raid on the oils might allow for a fast turnaround if either the news is soon refuted, or after all the stocks have moved, in this case, down too much. (And to be fair, the analyst might be, in time, proven right by the price action.)

Remember: Wall Street has very little memory. Using yesterday's news to rationalize a buy or a sell can bring on brief emotional relief, but is forgotten by investors almost as quickly. Were you hurt if you had intended a sale in the oils that day? Sure. Could you convincingly rationalize what protective action you might have done to prevent the drop? No. There was no way of knowing. And different news might have given you 2 points!

If the business press one day touts our holdings as having a new exciting technology and we add a few points—so be it. It's nothing we could have planned for.

If the Federal Reserve decides to "punish economic growth" and raise interest rates and stocks sell off including ours, what can we do? Did we know beforehand of their decision? Did we formulate how the investment community would react? Even if our security holding announces they are having financing troubles, it doesn't mean we are to be blamed. How might have we known? They appeared okay yesterday.

If you cannot know beforehand the events which could affect pricing, why worry and beat yourself up over things you could not have controlled the day the information was made publicly available.

We certainly can use judgment after these effects are made known, and should if they alter price direction in major ways, or if our investment has internal problems now being made known, or if the buy/sell internal dynamic is about to change in a more pronounced manner which we'll discern fairly quickly if we remain price observant. Otherwise, it's just the day-to-day forces of supply and demand. They cannot be known prior, absent any learned technical response as price moves toward these levels.

As we can see from above, most times, particular daily price movement won't be something that our investment was the cause of or should make us liquidate the position. It is terribly unfortunate to be on the wrong side of elements affecting money when you can't see it coming. If our specific investment isn't to "blame," then hardly are we.

However painful, if you are holding positions being "hit," these temporary periods can make for easy "pickings" if you are careful to judge the real importance of comments and news. Temporary movement, when overdone, provides immense short-term potential—but be sensible first.

When no specific individual company news can account for movement after broad-brush news or events, assume that the reactive quick price trend is temporary and the prior trend likely to reassert.

Granted, there are times when companies with problems refuse to be forthcoming but one, maybe two, days out of the ordinary price action without specific news might portend significant problems. Once more, allow price action to be your guide. Does it matter if the company refrains or even tries to support its price, yet it still continues lower? It shouldn't.

## Is the Stock Market's Six- to Nine-Months Forecasting Ability Meaningful?

Is the stock market sacred six to nine months or two to three quarters ahead and are forward looking prognostications really useful information?

It would seem that the answer is based upon whether we are interested in a possible market top or a market bottom. At bottoms, the economic future based upon collective business opinions would suggest as they turn from cautious to more optimistic. Investors might be prone to assume that while things aren't good at the moment perhaps in a few quarters they might be and justify buying. Yet at market peaks, there is almost universal enthusiasm where investors rarely assume a selling posture. Things are simply too good, and the beliefs are that things will remain splendid. If the markets foretell where stocks might be headed after long upward movement, but can't speak in the present—for warning—then their "voice" reliance is seriously in question.

To find a downward picture only from "a rear view mirror view" long after it's happened isn't investment relief. So what if the NASDAQ topped in March 2000 and the "market" knew in nine months that technology earnings and revenues would slow. If we discovered in November/December 2000 with prices off 50 percent, what the market "knew" nine months prior but wouldn't talk, then what good is the market's prophetic talent? *"Geez, the tech sector is announcing less then anticipated revenues, earnings, reporting warnings every day, layoffs… oh so now, with the NASDAQ being underwater can we rationalize as to why that March 2000 price top coincided with peak earnings?"* Wonderful and so useful knowing three quarters of a year later—after the fallout!

This is like suggesting to the heirs of the Titanic on Christmas Eve 1912… "Tell 'em to have passed on that trip." Thank you for the timeliness. But a straight dose of Wall Street reality—company and market fundamentals do not always lead price; the market tips us on the basis of rather apparent price action.

# Was It Fundamental, Technical, or Repeated Coincidence?

## *The Ancient Fundamental vs. Technical Analysis Debate*

For as long as there have been securities markets, investors have debated the merits of fundamental versus technical research. Fundamentalists would postulate that a company's consistent capacity to earn far greater than expected profits, year after year, is about the lone driver pushing higher and higher prices. A technician would agree that throughout market history, certain fundamental characteristics have proven to be precursors to later higher prices.

The difference is that earnings or very high pre-tax profit margins and so forth are not independent variables singularly affecting price. A company can have great earnings this year, yet see a lower stock price than last. Why? It is rather elementary.

Buying and investing in a stock and buying the business are very different mind-sets. Price is what investment is all about. As a shareholder, what we really own is the price of the common shares issued by our company—we are "price holders." It is what constitutes <u>our</u> practical ownership. It is only what we relate to in monetary terms and what distinguishes worthy investments. Buying cheap and selling dear. *Price is subordinate only to the inherent buy/sell dynamic and nothing else.* On the contrary, all fundamentals are dependent upon many, many factors and it's a good reason why security analysts have so much trouble accurately forecasting the level of earnings, as one fundamental example. If earnings were an independent variable, then an investor would select only companies with the most prolific, then later sell at an EPS peak, thereby creating investment gains through earnings changes? Right? Of course, wrong!

We don't ultimately earn an investment dollar on elements other than price disparity. Price is an independent variable. It, of and by itself, is the loss/gain determinant. If we own 500 shares of a company whose fundamentals are worse this year than last and where its once earnings are now losses, but now the price is somehow higher, we have a profit on those shares. Its fundamental problems weren't what we used for counting out our money. No more than you would ease into a comfortable retirement with a 14 percent rise in fourth quarter earnings.

Common stock ownership and respective share pricing are the evidence of investment worth. Not what sales were or earnings might be and so forth. For while fundamentals, if exceptional, probably will in fact coincide with higher share price as years pass because investors have learned that they are ingredients for successful investments, they do not necessarily have to. Sharp as it might sound: great earnings and enviable fundamentals can mean nothing without a reflective higher price! Share price is always the basis for value, for investment worth, during ample earnings periods or not.

When an investor rejects XYZ in a "hot" momentum sector play and rather invests in a Kmart because they are expected to become more profitable 24 months out, he is betting that his investment future is in Kmart and not in the transitory hot retail area because the momentary phenomena might not be around in two years. The investor may be right about the eventual place Kmart occupies in American retailing, but he is dead wrong regarding the timeliness of the merit of the two alternatives. Losing real profit today because of what might become a disaster in years to come is suggesting that money can only be made along our timetable. How wrong can thinking get! Investment is for the present. Opportunities presented now are to be captured now and not ignored because of some future blow up.

We only value securities holdings on the expectation of future price, yet the attempted level is conventionally estimated from many dependent variables and then witnessed and ultimately valued, by subsequent price action to either "confirm or reject." Yet strict adherence to price action is the factual approach where investors should direct their attention.

Great fundamentals are usually consistent with higher stock prices during bullish periods with stock prices trending upward. During bearish periods, or "abnormal" times, fundamentals are quite secondary for preventing investor loss. Exceptional earnings may lessen downward moves but they don't—they can't—prevent them.

In mid-October 2000, the semiconductor industry, as well as most of NASDAQ, and lastly the Dow, had fallen significantly. Mattson Technology (MTSN), a semiconductor fabrication company, had fallen from 50 in March 2000 to 8 by October 18, 2000—no small loss. This was despite a good second quarter earnings report and a P/E of about 7, at the then price of 8. The stock had been as high as 32 in August 2000 after a good earnings release.

With market pessimism very high and with companies during that period reporting less than expected earnings (and dearly paying for it), being careful before investing with an expected EPS about to break was clearly prudent. Yet, technical indicators were also signaling a deeply oversold market perhaps ready to turn. MTSN was to report earnings after the close on 10/19 and with the stock so far down, far off its recent $32 price, it made sense to believe that the company might miss its expected EPS figure since sellers had been brutal in taking down the stock (anybody else who missed expectations).

On 10/19, the market rebounded mightily—the NASDAQ went up more than 7 percent. Investors wanting to buy MTSN, but waiting for the earnings release to confirm their decision and suspicion, found the company surpassed its earnings expectation by 20 percent. The stock quickly rose in the aftermarket to 14, an 80 percent move from the prior day-and-a-half low of 8. Being suspiciously concerned about a potential company earnings disappointment as the cause for the prior drastic falling price was misplaced. In other words, there was nothing wrong with the company and nothing based on fundamentals to explain why the stock so drastically sank. They were doing fine! Being a pure fundamentalist and wisely logically cautious cost the investor plenty. (Investors simply had changed their collective thinking shunning bearish and placed a new premium on the newly bullish market momentum. The ultimate excellent EPS report didn't explain the -75 percent bath the stock took from August through 10/18...yet negative market and sector momentum did! Proof again that fundamentals are subordinate to the investment price trend and are almost always for short- to mid-term trends and always when sentiment and momentum become the dominant factor.)

There is something very attention-grabbing between rigid fundamental beliefs and declining price reality staring you down day after declining day.

Over the long-term, stellar earnings are generally rewarded through greater-than-average and higher price. This is also because long-term investor perception is distinctly upward, raising all stocks by those with excellent fundamentals, as well as those without. But this assumes one is not in a bear market. In those dire conditions, good earnings often wouldn't help much. Doubt it?

Take the small cap universe of stocks, the Russell 2000, from 1996–1999, a bear sector period lasting for several years! Companies with fine earnings, offering great—almost historic—relative value as compared to larger companies, continued lower and lower and lower still.

A few summary conclusions:

A company presumed to continue growing rapidly, having a dominant position in their respective growing economic market, can be projected through its earnings to sell at some higher future price assuming:

- An overall bear market, or bear market in the holding's specific sector, is not currently in place.
- Wall Street/investors treat that industry as one where they place a high valuation on earnings.
- You do not have to make an untimely sale during a sour period.

This is when fundamental analysis provides real individual investment value for long-term investment and, as already mentioned, if one can build a position based on future expectation...and be correct.

For fundamentalists: sort your equity selections from price action first and lofty earnings/fundamentals second. Having both cannot hurt. If you hold a stock long-term, great earnings and favorable company perception by investors insulate a bit in downside price trends. In good market periods, companies with flourishing businesses do rise—and usually quite rapidly. The point is to not marry fundamentals and believe they alone protect value, because they don't.

Most securities industry research focuses on an EPS (earnings per share) figure times some P/E ratio. Price divided by earnings over the next 12 months to arrive at an estimated future price. If we next were to divide our estimated price by the current market price, we would find the expected appreciation or, in rare cases, depreciation.

The results are then sorted and the "best" declared to the public.

Estimated EPS 2.00 x Estimated P/E Multiple 25 = $50 Estimated Price divide by the $20 Current Price = 150 percent Estimated Appreciation. Also...

---

- IF the company earns $2.00 per share.

- IF the expected P/E multiple in 12 months out is 25.

- IF the company's industry is doing as well as would justify 2.00 in earnings and the 25 multiple.

- IF the broad market isn't in a price recession, bear market or severe correction.

- IF no significant negative news might impact the company at approximately 12 months.

---

...then our company might sell at the estimated $50 price target ($2.00 times a P/E multiple of 25). However, in a nasty market, we all pay the piper.

### The Fundamentalist's Tool Bag

A pure fundamentalist buys and holds their positions through almost all market periods. In this age of immediate response it takes no time for investors to react. If a bear market or sector is at hand, maintaining your positions throughout is a recipe for diminished value. And the best companies will take a bath!

Don't believe it? On 2/22/2001, Wall Street analysts, Morgan Stanley & Bank America Montgomery, downgraded the entire computer storage area sector, EMC and Brocade, as two examples, after 75 percent price declines? Why even bother?

Wall Street was highly recommending Enron well into late 2001, apparently unaware of the eventual deception, or maybe being blinded by their lucrative investment banking fees—some $320 million! Some proof as to how valueless fundamental analysts can be.

While Wall Street research can tell us how companies really function internally, they don't know how investors will react with any precision toward price movement—no more than anyone else. Why then, listen intently to their fundamental message? Good fundamentals will hold the stock up in nasty periods? Sure, bet on that!

A pure fundamentalist can only estimate price based on their assumed EPS figures and not on a P/E ratio, since it is market driven. Any analyst's later EPS revision is of little use since that part of the equation, they should get closer to, is correct. And if they fail within their own province, they indeed offer the investor nothing of value.

Even worse, in 1999, Wall Street was paying two of its fundamental analysts over 15 million for their opinions. Their ideas were frequently subordinate to change and heavily biased toward retaining investment management ties with client companies. Were investors really receiving first-rate research? Doubtful at best. It's the pro's evidencing the height of stupidity! 15 million, per annum, to tell us where a stock is going based on their (the analysts) notoriety. The Street surely can spend money more productively. The recent law suits might wake up management...their shareholders can only hope.

Fundamentals are relatively static observations until downward price momentum makes them liquid, that is rapidly being lowered to justify falling prices—sheer scribble.

Wall Street pays its research analysts very handsomely for opinionating on earnings expectations which are always subordinate to revisions based on computation of many and varied numbers of affecting variables, which psychologists know human beings cannot accurately assess. This ultimate EPS figure is then pegged to an expected P/E ratio, which, by the Street's insinuation, should not change?

In other words, if a company might earn $3 per share and sell at its industry P/E average at $20, then a $60 price target would seem reasonable. Then again, if the industry P/E multiple were to change, then our 60 target should as well...if earnings can be modified, repeatedly. Why then, not expected industry P/E multiples, even whose levels are historically less to be subject to change? Naturally if one were to revise both the EPS and P/E figures the Street's research would be even less valuable than it already is.

If the variables in assessing prospective price are premised on fundamentals so open to revision, it challenges the least even objective to find continuous worth.

Wall Street is enamored with any number of asset-pricing models, esoteric formulas and asset-allocation methods. Yet all of these expectations are premised upon the strange belief that the ultimate pricing of assets can be near scientifically calculable...label the inputs, press compute and a final price answer emerges—one we are expected to invest toward? Please!

This is not real world events. Price is driven by the emotion and actions of investors at various moments dependent upon certain known and unknown stimuli. Price, therefore, is hardly ever ultimately predictably exact, as Wall Street's scientific rigid fundamentalist opinion has us believing. Their design is a static group of assumptions, whereas price is dynamic and evidence producing...if you pay attention.

Getting it fundamentally right isn't an end game since the ultimate expectation that price, may or may not, follow from an accurate fundamental call. Knowing how the investments might react to events is far more important and lucrative than accurately assessing the event itself. Why? We don't make money on any fundamentalist's observation becoming correct. We make money when we reason correctly how investors will react to news, events, changes and so forth.

In defense, trying to peddle stock on the basis of a stock's technical price trend might be assumed as too unfamiliar to explain clearly or for investors to accept. It's easier to say…"the company makes satellites, they're doing well…buy some stock, it's a good investment." But investors should know better.

Fundamentals research may uncover a stock's "floor" price that may provide some reason for added use of fundamental analysis. This is the price at which the company may not fall beneath, since the hard evidence uncovered through diligent company investigation suggests that an unbiased value precludes continued investor selling. This could be at a significant discount beneath the company's book price or at available cash per share. In these two examples, if the discount is steep enough, the stock probably does have a "fundamentals floor," or a price which will not be violated if the company remains solvent.

Example: a company with provable $30 in cash per outstanding common share should have difficulty in selling too much below that level if the company isn't going bankrupt. Technical analysis cannot cause a stock to fall to zero. Nor can a group of technicians force a $44 stock down 45 points—only fundamental problems ultimately do that.

In his eye-opening book, *Robbing You Blind*, author Mark Dempsey, himself once a Merrill Lynch broker, cites a 1998 Zacks Investment Research study where of the 6,000+ securities analysts' recommendations in 1998, a scant and rather obviously biased 1.4 percent was suggestive of a sell recommendation to investors—a slight hint that Wall Street values its ongoing company relationships far more than fairly reporting an honest fundamental research opinion.

And to further paint Wall Street's strange fundamental ways—on January 2, 2001, in the midst of further NASDAQ technology carnage, a member reduced earnings expectations on the semiconductor sector. On January 4, 2001, after an historic NASDAQ rally sparked by a significant Federal cut in interest rates, a Wall Street firm then reasons why the semis should now do well—in just 48 hours they made a 180 degree turn! Let's hope that the one day enormous rise in stock price didn't influence the fundamental research—since it shouldn't…ever.

What a company, or in this instance, an industry might earn should be judged or researched, independent of the market performance of its stock(s). Although it seldom works this way.

### Wall Street's Most Highly Overpaid Club?

It had become commonplace for Wall Street's fundamental security analysts to downgrade a stock or remove it from a recommended list well after it has lost tremendous market valuation. A stock once touted at 70, and later drops to 22, is now not so highly revered, and maybe…even a sell is issued. The investment public cries, why have you waited so long? Issue the sell before the price gore. If you can't, how are you being helpful? What good are opinions when they arrive so far after the fact? The quick tendency is to agree—yet with some difficulty.

Stockholders are right in that prices can precede economic changes, but if an analyst is practicing pure fundamentals, they shouldn't know before the near future what economics might do to their companies. If, business sector conditions weaken (not evident until later in months and quarters), but their stock prices drop immediately, the analyst can't automatically assume the fundamentals are deteriorating without some provable evidence, despite the price fall-off. When prices are near bottomed and perhaps the industry is evidently in recession, the fundamentalist analyst is able to announce the downgrade (usually fundamental-based) well after the pricing effect.

Fundamental analysts should have their role defined and limited to "reporting upon the individual business health of a company and its affecting industry and relationship to the overall economy." They should stand clear of opinionating upon the technical expectancy of the price of the stock unless they clearly define their differing role. One should have nothing to do with the other in the pure discipline of practicing each role.

What this means is that if Intel is going to earn $2 per share from its business operations, its later stock price should not affect the analysts opinion of that $2 estimate. If the stock doubles, or halves, the company might still earn $2 and the analyst shouldn't be moved to change the fundamental outlook based on price. They should change the investment outlook, but not their fundamental opinion. Unfortunately, they often permit price to color their fundamentalist view. It is wrong in that manner. How often, as a company reports better than expected results, will an analyst coincidentally raise earnings as might be reasoned, and naturally price targets. This would seem consistent with valuation modeling, but at that point what are they bringing to investors that investors couldn't do for themselves?

When technology stocks were falling throughout the Fall of 2000 and Spring of 2001, analysts would drop earnings expectations as stock prices fell in the same frequency as they raised them as stocks soared in prior months. Yet their following of price raises the concern as to their independent analyzing of the true inherent business conditions within each company.

If they are going to alter their fundamentalist opinions with price change, they are more technically affected by price than practicing independent research. Might it be asked, what role and what value do they play?

From early June 2001 through 6/21/2001, JDS Uniphase (JDSU), fell ten straight days and brought about a few analysts' downgrades after the company later announced it expected to report poorer quarter(s) ahead. Yet the day after the stock's first advance, on 6/22, one firm cites "business as improving" and recommends the stock—amazingly coincident with the end of the price decline. Isn't it uncanny that as the stock price starts up and that within all of 24 hours, the overall company's business expectation is now expected to improve? *You need a wild imagination to buy the "coincidence."*

Ariba, Inc. (ARBA), hit a high price of $175 in the September 2000 time period and gradually fell along with technology and internet-related securities, continuing to cascade downward to the $2 area in mid-September 2001. During this World Trade Center disaster time frame, CS First Boston comes out and issues a downgrade...at $2. Thanks guys.

We would all hope analysts' expertise in understanding the companies they follow is independent of price and of their employers' desire to maintain business relationships with companies under fallen expectations. Further, that everyone would know that their investment projection is likely, and should be based upon, some part of technical analysis which they should disclose (yet an area of which they may have little training). It is an open issue as to whether investors gain much in listening when they talk, which is usually well after the obvious has occurred, and for which they can't be totally at blame—one of the inherent limitations of fundamental analysis.

And a word to those with two attendant ears: they are part of the total sales and marketing portion function and are almost never completely unbiased. They rarely have their own income directly based upon the accuracy of their forecasts. Perhaps the extent of the client relationships they engender and retain affects their bank accounts—no doubt it must since their accuracy of forecasts wouldn't very often justify a compensation review. This facet of Wall Street must change as well as disclosure in their personal holdings in companies that they cover, and the sooner the better.

## Vote Technical!

The conclusive factor as to why stocks move to specific price levels then repeatedly react as expected, may be a cerebral issue for those so inclined to pass away the obvious effect of technical analysis at play. In the absence of a disseminated specific stock news item, which we know cannot be assumed to be forthcoming, what else might explain why stocks so frequently stop their rise/fall at known technical levels, (such as 200 DMA), prior to support/resistance levels, trendlines, etc? If it's not technical buying and selling at these known price points, do we just assume it's coincident price action? That is very unlikely; the better guess is...impossible.

On August 9th, 2000, the drug giant Eli Lilly, had an appeals court rule to remove the company's patent for Prozac. On that single news item, the stock opened down more than 32 points. Yet where exactly, at the stock's 200 day moving average price—a usually supportive price level—was the 32 point drop ending at precisely its 200 day moving average level? A pricing coincidence? Sure it was!

August 24th, 2000, Next Level One Communications (NXTV) was downgraded by a Lehman Brothers analyst. The stock had closed the prior evening at $91.25 having approached $102 during the day.

The price ultimately opened down 51 points at approximately $41...right at the former long-term trendline support. It's not too likely it is another coincidence that a

55 percent pricing nosedive stops right about at the prior support area. (It was later revealed the price had been manipulated through a phony press release, but investors not privy to that information at the time stopped the carnage at the 41 point support level.)

Too many occurrences point to technical buying and selling at known prior price levels, than to be placid coincident price behavior when those price points are approached, and met, or however slightly exceeded. And it would be virtually impossible to measure whether the buying or selling was technical or fundamental in its origin, since the source for the act (anonymous investors) is usually purposeful and unknown.

Watch technical price levels—they certainly offer excellent tips as to future shorter-term price direction and are proof that technical analysis is always at play.

For long-term fundamentally inclined investors: if a substantially higher share price reflects itself after years of holding than the security has done, what the market's consensus via price said was correct. If not, then the enviable fundamentals and all the inherent value, irrespective of how grand, in practical investment return meant very little—didn't they?

## Does Practicing Technical Analysis Cause Price Movement?

Investors who rush to buy a stock from a company that has just announced good news to the marketplace are acting from fundamental factors. There can be little other reason that price movement so frequently begins or ends at commonly known technical support and resistance areas, such as 200 DMA, prior support levels, etc., without it being symptomatic of investors practicing the art of technical analysis. Yet what might be relevant and important is how much of price movement is "technically" dependent. Do certain stocks have more investors who act at technical conditions than others? To this question there would seem to be a qualified "yes," but it would appear to be company specific.

It appears some stocks are hitting walls of resistance and crash while others won't. Some stocks are repeatedly highly reactive to the common technical indicators, while others aren't. Other than shrewd observation and knowing what you are buying, what else would help explain a consistent price reaction based on technical conditions?

There is a concern as to how long any "once reliable" tendency might continue to maintain itself? To this hypothetical concern, the safe and certain answer is that blind reliance upon the past without captive present observation may lead to faulty information or little prospective worth. Investment priorities change. Risk and judgment, and time horizon and profit expectation shift and prioritize eventually.

**Lesson:**
**Learn very well, the <u>current</u> technical tendencies of your positions!**

# Catching Market Bottoms—Long- & Intermediate-Term

It would take the most brazen investor to believe there is a knowing way to capture exact bottoms in specific equities or broad markets during severe selling periods when fear exacerbates the normal buy/sell dynamic into frantic emotional decision-making. No one can, or does, blow an "all clear whistle" at developing bottoms, or at panic sell-offs.

During these final bearish, even sacred, support technical factors can be taken out and "new" assumed support levels put in place with often similar transitory bullish assurances. In panic selling or periods close to it, there is virtually nothing that should be viewed as gospel. The worst can happen. Rationale isn't pervasive.

The strategy to be employed, to participate at market bottoms, encompasses a few ideas:

> - The distinction as to whether a bottom is a long-term bottom at the climatic end of a bear market, or an intermediate bottom in an ongoing bull or bear market, takes on significance. The timing of entrance into long-term bottoms is less important, because there should be years of gradual advance in front of the investor.
>
> - In the instances of an intermediate bottom, or as we shall learn later in this book, in a short-term bottom, we don't generally have time as an ally. The points then:
>
>   - If you are looking at the start of a long-term bull market, precise entrance is far less important since calendar passage should bail out premature, or late purchase.
>
>   - For periods other than commencement of a new bull market, timing becomes vital for success, and critical if the bottom is presumed to be only a very short rush.

The rule of history is that unless the Federal Reserve is in a tightening mode—forcing interest rates upward—and the market's weekly long-term trend has fallen decidedly beneath its 200 day moving average, you are likely experiencing only correction(s) in on-going, long-term bull environments. Sure, overly simple, but generally true.

Even with an agreeable Federal Reserve, after prices have been down, "with blood on the street," any rallies off the real bottom should have staying power. If they don't (that is if the "bargains" aren't sustained inducement for a lasting upward move based on calendar time, enduring months, and not a quick 15 percent upward rush) then perhaps a bear market is, or remains in place and where equities have little purpose.

Another reason why we want to know what kind of bottom we might be in, is because if the "bears'" party is not over, you do not want to be buying the "dips" (in prices), since in the weeks and months ahead there is apt to be more selling and more, albeit cheaper, "equity bargains."

However, if the bull market is really to remain, the former price carnage can make for lofty profitable choices. Remember, those lower and lower prices, still representing multibillion dollar businesses, will go down only so far. Yet some caution and technique should be performed first. Let's explore:

There is double fear at ongoing bull market presumed bottoms. One is being in, or getting in, and suffering further losses. The other, is being out and losing fabulous profit potential. It almost seems like a lose, lose, emotional decision for sure.

If the equity you wish to purchase at the assumed start of a long-term bull market has been price decimated and sells at very low point price valuation (10 to 15 per share), there can't be a great numerical fall in front of you. Stocks don't trade yet at negative numbers. In these cases, assuming the company isn't in great financial harm and is likely to remain an ongoing concern, it often pays to "guess" with perhaps a third of the ultimate intended holding, but only after some advancing price evidence.

Consider all these factors: if the markets retreat has been lengthy, beyond 12 months; and if the broad markets retreat has been very painful, -15 to -20 percent or worse; and if the decline appears to be slowing in intensity (down days are less point significant and are fewer in number in frequency); and if the calendar time between the low point (assumed real bottom); and if the time you intend to invest has been many, many months (quarters are better) with no lower price low; and if the <u>majori-</u><u>ty</u> of the following ideas are in place—then probabilities suggest taking some position. *(The U.S. market has a 210-year upward bias and it's not likely long-term multiple year sets of bear markets are as probable as are three-to-four-year cycle bull market repeats.)*

### First

Until the broad market averages start and remain upward for days, remain dormant. Allow the markets to lead you—not your stock choice. Why should the broad market be the barometer? Because it works and it is easily visible to all investors! (Investors tend not to be front runners—rather, they are followers. If the broad indices are running, it creates notice.)

Is it even a surprise that most stocks almost peak and trough coincident with the broad market they are part of? The lessons of the past tell us that 80 to 90 percent of stocks will follow the general wave of the broad market. Why initiate an individual stock purchase in this type of falling environment until some market turn is in evidence? *(An individual stock <u>cannot</u> cause the entire broad market to begin a new bullish phase. Markets move only from a change in mass investor sentiment.)*

During an avalanche of selling, what will save most investors' position is the overall markets turning up or stabilizing and then consequential investor sentiment improving! Until the broad markets either stabilize or begin an upward move, the investment sentiment of most investors will remain guarded and so too will almost all equities.

Watch the broad markets—the Dow, S&P 500, and NASDAQ—for hints of a turn. However, try not to measure whether a bottom is in place other than from its low point. In other words, don't try and answer the question as to a real bottom being put in, from one day to the next, since that results in a 50/50 type test. You should measure from the apparent low price, low level to the present day. A move of at least 15 percent might qualify as an in-place bottom. This is acceptable if you are playing for keeps, for the long-term; remaining sidelined throughout the first 15 percent of an advance will be tough. However, being certain of an assumed advanced becoming the real thing often exacts a price. (Intermediate investors should initiate any prospective bullish action even sooner, despite the attendant risk, since there won't be a long-term time-frame to make up for delaying.)

If a good rally is to develop and last, there will be huge profits to be had, even if missing the bottom. Ten to 15 percent is needed to be more certain. When haven't we all missed the bottom or the top 10 to 15 percent? Relax and take a slightly conservative stance. Stocks substantially down 60 and 70 percent from their high aren't recovering all of that loss even in a few months!

### Second

Forget how oversold your intended investment is; it can get worse and it will if more emotional sellers take hand and the overall investment climate continues bleak. Until upward broad price action is in evidence, temporarily forget the "bargain" you think you are witnessing. The reason: massive investor buying will be delayed until a sustained upward bias is viewed. Remember falling equity prices are not in a bottoming process—they are in a falling process. If you are bullish then you are wiser to watch—not participate.

### Third

A conservative strategy to participate might entail buying call options about 5 to 10 points out-of-the-money equivalent to the same number of intended outright shares of your equity choice. This may be preferable on the S&P 500 Spiders or maybe the QQQ's, or the NASDAQ 100 largest by market capitalization since you almost must make money if the respective market index you own moves upward. You may not if your single equity choice remains behind!

Why options and why out-of-the-money for the conservative posture? Since these options react a bit slower than at, or in-the-money options, even with a quick upward stock price movement, little would be lost if you were to buy late, and being less expensive than at-the-money options means less dollars are at risk, if you are wrong. Their upside, if a significant upward move is at hand, is still very good. Their downside is limited to their acquisition price and no bemoaning "Will it ever end," "Is there no bottom," as with relentless downside stock ownership.

If stock is bought first and there is more negative news, 20 to 50 percent dives occur. Holding 200 shares or 2,000, as all hell breaks out, is nerve racking! In our informational world, instant panic selling can get out of hand. A 10 point emotional slide with 500 shares is minus $5,000. To have purchased five out-of-the-money options at say $2, might mean 'so long' to $500-600 profit. There is some emotional peace in knowing you cannot lose <u>too</u> much. (Your loss with held stock, in concept at least, is the long difference between price and zero. If that's 78, then it's 78 conceptual points of pain.)

For an aggressive options participation, purchase options in-the-money on the indices. Even if the rally is very short-lived, upward movement should immediately reflect a profit.

### Fourth

Ease into the large positions you might ultimately desire. There is no issue if 100 percent of your available monies were put in near the bottom and the subsequent long-term rally were to last. But it reminds of the nutty idea, "Don't ever buy a stock that doesn't go up." When convinced a bottom is at hand, utilize maybe a third to one-half of your investment dollars. If it appears a true bottom has formed from price action over several weeks, the balance can be employed. Placing 100 percent into a unsteady market can become a near-term disaster and invite an emotional exit. Waiting to be certain will cost you potential, but it is sound protection.

### Fifth

Term it "dancing with the small numbers," but it is far more likely, at a market bottom, that low price stocks will rise a greater percentage than high price stocks. If you envision a fast 10 percent market run, a $10 stock will probably see $11 sooner than the $70 stock will head into $77. This is more than "so what," because percentage return is what investment is all about. If your $20 stock gets "all the way" to $23 in a rapid market rise, that 15 percent return isn't likely to be duplicated with the $100 stock. All of this refers to the very short-term move off a bottom, not for a lasting disparity between small price and large price, which is far more involved. (Unfortunately, the downside is equally punishing in percentage terms with small priced equities, but you do not want to be long equities during bear markets of any duration anyway.)

### Sixth

On a daily basis, try not to decide whether the bottom is in place. One day it appears as such and another day it doesn't. With rare exceptions, bottoms occur over time—a few weeks to perhaps several months. Watch the trend of the bottoming process. Do most stocks appear headed lower? Are there more times than not, that small rallies appear than small declines? Is the market capable of putting back-to-back advancing days, even several consecutive positive days? Do most stocks react well to good news and fall only a little on bad? In general, what has been the overall trending bias? Most of these questions take time to answer and trying to access the answers every day isn't useful or necessary. Watch the trending movement for the clues, but don't measure for the answer daily!

### Seventh

Forget the hero mentality: "here's my golden opportunity to get rich; I'll buy now, it can't get worse." You'll catch the bottom and be out at the top. Right, like before? Buying at precise bottoms and exiting at exact tops only happens on talk shows, at reunions, and in periods times of luck...and the next time won't likely be any different. Review the above before jumping in!

### Eighth

As simple as it appears, stocks that have a chart pattern that mimics a bell curve (wherein they drive upward, peak, then fall almost in mirror image to the advance, landing upon the right side of their chart completion) tend to have hit price bottom. At least, risk is then usually minimal. And when chart patterns have the look of having stopped their descent and then start to move laterally, it would suggest the extent of bearish sentiment might be over and thus, a rally could ensue—not must, or should, only could. Real bottoming processes look lateral on charts not still declining.

### Ninth

Lose your mind's rationale component—temporarily during dreaded falling periods. Stop over-thinking. Get offensive, especially near intermediate panic style bottoms. At lows, the logic we want to choose to guide us can be thrown out the door, since price movement during panicky times isn't sound. It is all emotional. It always happens this way at market extremes. When it's right to buy, place a market order or be prepared to move on a limit order—then get patient. You're likely to be happy shortly.

### Tenth

The entire prior not withstanding, it is better being <u>slightly late</u> in initiating a position—intended security target is moving upward—than being early. If the price trend is at least temporarily upward, it may well continue, especially if it's a new bull market commencement. Being premature means loss of capital. Psychologically, mindsets change when losing; positions can get axed too fast. Be slightly late—but not much!

### Eleventh

The market's 17-day RSI will tend to be at the low 20s area indicative of severe pessimism.

Caveat: the above commentary does not offer the potential of catching an intraday bottom in either a stock or the market as a whole, since entrance timing is based on longer time. As such, some portion of the bottom will have been given away. For an investor who wishes to ignore this and chance a very aggressive posture, wait for at least a market(s) intraday, 2 to 3 percent climb for the Dow and 5 to 6 percent plus for the NASDAQ—proof as to huge market strength—and extreme advance decline numbers, maybe at 8 or 9:1 or better, then invest. Remain in the position(s) until, or if, the broad market starts back down, then sell almost immediately. It might be the rally doesn't yet have the necessary conviction to last. True intermediate trend bottoms and rallies from their deeply oversold levels, should have many daily periods of upward activity.

It is necessary to understand that entry timing is entirely dependent upon what type of transaction term you are anticipating:

> • If long-term, make the market prove it has endurance and wait many weeks since prices, even 10 percent off the bottom, might not prove a 36 to 48 month bull market has arrived.
>
> • If intermediate-term, you might wait a week before taking a position.
>
> • If very short-term, you need to assume with evidence when the bottom is in place, since when it is, upward moves from very oversold conditions get very pronounced and can remain that way for many, many trading days. In other words an overbought status—when you normally would expect to sell—takes far longer to become a reality. You should allow upward pricing to run upward much longer than you might after a normal advance.

Panic selling, as on 10/18/2000, 10/19/1987, and 4/4/2001 are times when investors want out—anywhere! "Get me out." Lucrative, low risk, words to the studied investor. During these scary, anxiety-ridden times, pragmatic selling is not in occurrence. The sister concept is that prudent buying…should be!

When prices get to the level where they are of no importance, irrationality is at its zenith, the worst of fears, the lowest—lowest of risk…the perhaps short-term bottom…and the usual subsequent recovery bounce upward, is almost always very fast! And probably in the toughest period you will ever experience to be making a purchase.

As difficult as it is emotionally for players, buying must begin—*and "must" means "must."* There is very short-term potential and probably, and just maybe, the onset of an intermediate advance.

While it is normal human psyche to avoid involvement in a rapid falling price spiral as prices fall lower and lower and lower still, and while the exercise of a purchase order is very strenuous and counter intuitive, placement near that eventual intraday low is also apt to be with near zero short-term risk. In very abnormal frenzied investor selling, taking the opposite direction often leads to an irrational buying binge once started, from those wishing to capture perceived bargains and having the tendency to act first and think second. Mass investor impulse buying can have grand upward price consequences within minutes and hours.

When risk is greatest and you are most scared, reward is also at its highest. With risk at minimum and your mental state more relaxed, you are less apt to have reward in front of you since you have gotten to this calming state, prices would have had to have risen quite a bit and regularly. Buying at bottom is emotional buying, but it is an emotional period and logic comes out second.

Reward exists only for the investor who has purchased near that true bottom. Not those who thought that a $30 intraday price was a steal, and who now watch a rally ensue from 10 points lower. "Bargains" are never known prospectively—only from the distant view of time.

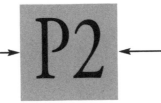

# Part Two:
# Taking Investment Action

# Mental
# Preparedness

## Preview

Were you right if for the stock sale you made today you captured the day's daily high and then watched the following day as it rallied four points, well above your sale price? Feeling vindicated, if you sold just before a huge sell off avoiding the price carnage, only to find the same stock one month later had risen 40 percent!

It depends upon your time perspective and how those sales proceeds may have been utilized toward the entirety of your portfolio. Was it worth being "correct" by grabbing a profit for a single day? Just how do we measure being right? These are tough questions and they come with ambiguous, difficult answers that almost never work out because there are no accepted standards after transaction exits.

Do you feel less anxiety being out of a position but impatiently watching profits you would have made, or more stress after initiating the strategy? Sometimes it is emotionally worse doing nothing. Often there isn't the calm in being idle that we imagined there would be. Similarly, since the market is fluid all the time, then upsetting over day-to-day expectations, is it a fool's routine and a clear way to ulcers? Logic supports the markets never do exactly as you planned, thus why frustrate? *And of course, it's always easier written than practiced.*

How about your focus prior to a security transaction, specifically, a shorter-term strategy? If we allow for any possibility of loss, or setup tilted profit-to-loss "odds" to dominate the likelihood of a thoroughly planned strategy working out, the investor may never act, earn, or feel the joy, both emotionally and financially, in having been very correct from their investment efforts.

It's easy to want investing to be on a rational par with physics or neurological surgery, so the intelligent and hardest working amongst us can "win"...well it's not quite a parallel. When you invest, only two things ultimately happen, there are not nine outcomes. The security position goes up; the security position goes down. And it could be said if you define success as selling higher than buying, knowing nothing might still cede nearly a 50/50 result. If we define "win" as departing with more than what we start out with and we take a long-term view coupled with our markets long-term upward bias, then just about everybody "wins." Granted, an oversimplification, but making some money ought not to be the standard. That's really too easy.

## Earning the Proper Mindset

The very beginning of this book made mention of a few critical reasons why nearly 20 years ago this author might have enjoyed the success with the Superior Oil transaction: the $1,200 that had been invested, represented an insignificant portion of net worth. So the size of one's bank account can dictate willingness to "risk" and ultimately to invest and quite often the amount of investment success enjoyed. Wall Street repeats the phrase that "scared money" never wins. If the dollars invested are too important, the emotion that ordinarily runs with tracking your effort will be allowed, more likely than not, to push a rational plan of attack outside of reason and possibly invite a premature sale. The prudent financial planning maxim therefore becomes:

### Do not invest monies in short-term movement that represents a significant part of your financial worth.

A 10 to 15 percent maximum allotted toward shorter-term focused investment is a reasoned starting point and a shade more attributed to any intermediate term non-options type strategy. Human nature being what it is means many investors will disregard the above, and chance more dollars anyway, but that decision is a precursor to needless upset and worry. Granted, neither the market nor the specific company you invest in knows the importance of what you've done—but you will. Carrying the added pressure of having to be right, in investment strategies you cannot control, is not necessary or smart.

It is a grand feeling to have money in the bank with bills paid and a secure profession and then be able to enjoy witnessing your well-planned investment efforts pay off to the ultimate!

Any type of investment theory that is very unforgiving demands a very disciplined and proven approach. Since the ideal investment trends we expect to advantage have an average duration of many months, and if the investor initiates a strategy late and exits too soon, the probabilities of being correct in large magnitude diminish. So it is quite important to devise techniques that will work fairly quickly if followed, because the luxury of time to bail us out isn't as likely were the time horizon very long-term.

All any investor can do—for that matter, all anybody can endeavor to do—is the best they have with their available resources. This means taking the time to prepare and checklist all the relevant items that might affect the intended investment prior to action. If this approach is not followed, the investor begins his or her investment with less of an edge, and the probabilities for success retreat, and just a chance "bet" has been placed.

When all—not some—all the relevant information that might affect a transaction has been considered, place the transaction with your head up. You have provided yourself the best opportunity to reap the awesome monetary rewards of being correct. This is the best you can ever do and what you owe to yourself, because hard work is supposed to be rewarding. It cannot be rewarding if you refuse to take action or become careless.

One of the most satisfying traits for an investor is being so sufficiently prepared from having witnessed challenging experiences, or from sufficient preparation, that you know exactly what action to take in unexpected situations or when rapid decisions are demanded. A feeling of calm and direction is felt, quite opposite to the stress and immobilization—and sometimes, outright fear—that is seen time and time again. Having enough confidence to know the probable outcome of your actions is very gratifying. This is where you want the state of your investment mind to rally from, so you can command confidence in the decisions you do make.

In the following chapters, there will be very specific strategies allowing an investor ample choices to succeed, but the fact that these ideas were culled from decades of experience does NOT mean that they work every time. Remember, investment is not science. And if events pan out 19 out of 20 times, it doesn't mean that one time in 20 it fails or is justification for abandoning the learned material. Investments never always work. But exceptions to long-held investment rules are atypical anomalies which regularly won't repeat. Simply accept they will sometime occur and learn from those experiences. Thus...

### Discipline yourself to really follow the lessons of your experiences and your knowledge.

There is no good reason to learn unless you are prepared to place that amount of expertise in front of a future whim where you decide to do as you wish and against the knowledge you have begun to master. A minority of times the "rules" will not work...but "80 percent" of the time they will. You want to train and discipline yourself to follow the successful experiences you have been taught and/or have already experienced. Why throw away your edge for a "feeling" that this time might be different? Your investment experiences are an invaluable asset—a priceless blueprint for what works most times. Follow them!

## Agree to Become a "Hostage"...Unless Pricing Proof Is Apparent

As we have already seen, investing under the tenet of short to intermediate term means that the expectations we have must be played out somewhat quickly for us to benefit, and by factors that nobody controls since we are all trying to predict the buy and sell psychology of thousands of investors, in a dynamic environment, subject to minute-to-minute changes. In many ways, it is contra to normal thinking. We are taught from birth to act in a manner that is consistent with logic, to "use our head." When expected results differ from that precept, we become frustrated. Yet the shorter-term the investment focus, the greater that feeling, is the logic. It's a tough acceptance to base the importance of money on so many factors we cannot control, but that is real world Wall Street in the short-term. Either accept it, or invest with a longer term horizon.

The human condition is programmed to act rationally and to plan along a logical continuum. This rational thinking won't change and shouldn't have to. Yet expecting the mass of investors to think equally "cerebral" with us for the next two minutes, or two hours, to be consistent with our timetable, isn't how Wall Street plays its game and it is what we can probably term being unrealistically egomaniacal.

To no rational surprise, factors do not have to work in the manner we wish, or at the speed we hope. When we presume the market trend will continue upward and our stock will follow, we are making that assumption premised upon our experiences, then giving rise to <u>probabilities</u>—not assurances. Therefore, to feel <u>anxiety</u> is a normal psychological investor reaction. But it is not supposed to cause inaction if you have given yourself the best preparation sequence possible. This is a learned art. This is the way it has always worked for consistent investment success when measured year after year. You will need to accept the fact you are dealing with the unknown and you control nothing after trade entry, yet everything relevant and prior to where your edge may be.

Studies have shown us that most people are more willing to stand pat and pass on the chance for great opportunities, rather than risk whatever they already have. A certain something is superior to a chance unknown. Are we all then "risk adverse?" If risk means any unwillingness to lose, one would never invest, since in the investment arena only insured municipal bonds—even assuming the insurance backing is safe—are a guarantee. If risk means never starting out better than 50/50, then why bother? But it stands to reason you cannot earn from an investment without an attempt. And if after thorough planning, an initial entry transaction you are saying—and we all have—*"Well what if it doesn't work out?"* This kind of negativity can preclude objectivity, which can be a killer in trading or investing. It makes more reasoned sense after assessing all the vital information that provides you with an edge to accept the realization: But what if it does work? What if you're so right, you triple your investment intra week! If you had not done your homework and knew nothing, mere chance might mean you may start out at 50/50. Isn't all the planning and knowledge worth something? Of course it is. And over time it will benefit you immeasurably, if—again if—you follow successful experiences.

Unknown needn't automatically mean bad. If having information is synonymous with worthy, then placing the probabilities of an event based upon it on your side makes outcomes brighter and should transcend the fear of being wrong—since there is the possibility…you could be right!

Shift the focus from what could happen and "bet" on your ability to correctly assess how information will affect an investment response from all the knowledge and experiences you have acquired, and you will not be rolling random dollars.

There are so many times when markets seemingly move too fast up or down and investors lament, "Oh, I can't invest now, it's too late." If the trend continues despite your fervent demand that it not, do you feel less apprehension being out and earning nothing? Or might the same "stress" be present being in, but earning a fortune from it?

The point is you can feel anxiety being in or out of an investment—so the sidelines may not bring sanctity!

Assumptions about the future in the abstract—mere guesses—are tantamount to a dice roll. Those based on study and the best of reasoned probabilities, are worth pursuit! The focus on any win-to-loss strategy must be on a reasoned basis, thus coming from the history of prior experiences and your preparation.

The following hypothetical is somewhat analogous: most male readers can relate to the times they had to decide whether they should approach a very attractive woman they didn't know. If their fear of rejection—similar to their potential fear of losing money in placing a securities transaction—is greater than the hopefully welcomed meeting than the joy of holding the blonde etc., etc., or, as per investment—their potential financial success were the trade successful—then nothing happens. He never knows. Sounds familiar? Yet if the "playboy" engages her, focusing on her saying "yes" based on his prior successful experiences, strategies, "lines" etc.,—term those probabilities—rather than centering on her potentially saying "No," it is likely some success will result! Maybe not every time, but far more often than thought. And don't think there isn't a parallel. Financial and social counsel!

### Give Up Control!

Most of us, quite normally, love control over our lives and the things that we must do to function well in our daily activities. Most successful people require control in some degree. In the U.S. securities markets, this can be a devastating demand. When price movement is outside the analytical expectations that we have launched based on our research, we can become very frustrated. We may demand that price retrace to our normal expectations—immediately! However, the markets shall do unto themselves as they wish. The investor has no control in affecting price movement—none.

In his book, *The Day Trader's Advantage*—which is a misnomer for sure—author Howard Abell refers to an interviewed day trading expert, Bill Williams, who responds to the question of the psychological underpinnings of a trader…"good trading is almost like a religion, in the sense that you are giving up your personality to a larger, greater force, and that larger greater force is the market."

Since no investor drives the long-term fundamentals carriage for the companies they own, it is the best reason why great wealth can be created over the long-term period(s). Novices aren't running our investment companies. There are highly trained management personnel whom we "employ" to do it for us. Yet we alone rake in the chips from their labor.

We accept that our advantage—control if you wish—is to be in the initial planning prior to the securities transaction and with a very well chosen exit strategy. If those were completed at our intelligent best, then the perils or rewards that accrue afterward are just experiences we may <u>learn</u> from…and therein is a certainty of riches.

### Never Assume It's in the Bag…This Is Easy Money

Whenever you invest and are having a series of consistent successes or, as some might say "are hot," is the time to alter the discipline you have learned, to get loose with ideas, or to "take a shot" at something. The true "probabilities" of the next strategy succeeding don't change despite the last several triumphs. They more typically are systematic of the dress rehearsal when doing investment planning.

A few repeated successes are great, but they offer no automatics for the next transaction. Respect what it takes to properly sequentially plan a strategy. Don't get lazy while in a "good streak." It may be you were somewhat lucky and that's about to change. It's quite easy to give away hard fought monies when becoming complacent— work hard and <u>remain</u> disciplined.

### Respect, Respect the Trend in Place!

In the prior and subsequent chapters, there is much devotion to the trend, but it would be worthwhile to add the following: were the entirety of this writing to be of no value, then adherence to the following would easily justify its purchase.

**An existing price trend is more powerful and likely to continue than any external opinion, and most events and news that might be reasoned to affect its continual direction. And for those intent upon investing contra its direction, the usual reason for almost each of their failures.**

An example of this phenomenon is when markets move very quickly and in large magnitude and one wonders if it's too late to get in? Generally, it never seems to be. Why?

The sheer momentum force of strong price trends with the quick sentiment change they induce will totally dominate any logic-based rationalizations as a cure to their directional move. Their rapid course will "capture" more and more observant players, more will witness, and still more who refuse to be left behind will enter, while those who just can't stand being out will jump in, to the traders who sense momentum, and, to finally, to those who just plain throw in the towel and jump aboard.

The trend can take price to areas that common logic would never believe possible. An example: the rise of the internet sector 1997–2000 and the decimation of the internet sector 2000–2001. Our thought processes as to what is supposed to happen, isn't what brings a trend to its knees.

If it's upwardly strong enough, a trend can get very overbought of its own nature, yet still continue advancing or, if having become oversold, still continuously fall, and fall further still. This means in practical investment application that you should not try to intellectualize the start or the continuance of powerful price trends by reasoning "It can't keep rising/falling," "It needs to pause for a least...," "Logic says a bad (economic/company) event or report will halt the move," etc, etc.

Remember: The question as to the market's "why," is always less important than the enduring reality of price. So long as you can still participate, the price action is the sufficient "why."

In most experiences, one has been better being in, and being attentive, and not standing silent from the sidelines, forcefully demanding that this can't keep happening! Whether it logically follows that an ongoing move is in fact in progress, or has moved too far already, is irrelevant. Of course, at times, price shouldn't be where we think it is, but if it won't stop trending so, why fight? Engage the game of investment reality! Follow price...and profit for it.

We don't know how fast or in what proportion buyers and sellers will come around. The prudent investor allows the sentiment buildup to take price wherever it is ultimately headed. Virtually anything can happen for a few days to a week or more. Our logic isn't going to derail it! We are always intellectually and prospectively behind trends. We are led by them, not the other way around.

Juniper Networks (JNPR) and PM Sierra (PMCS) in early April 2001 led a remarkable NASDAQ advancing spurt which drove both of these issues to over 100 percent appreciation...in seven to eight days. That's illogical—for sure. But with a powerful technology price trend suddenly apparent, it is something one does NOT want to miss by being "too intellectual" as to why it is occurring. You simply don't know when investors will move in mass. In PM Sierra's case, the public didn't want the stock to plunge from 280 to under 20! Strangely, 11 days later they couldn't buy it up fast enough as it crossed 42! Very doubtful that logic was the root cause for the doubling in value. And in short-term, it almost never will be.

It has become more fact than theory that, as the flow of information continues to become faster and more pronounced, beginning price trends will have the tendency to become more apparent than ever before, since almost everyone can almost instantly know what's going on. This means that their initial launch will tend to be more feverish than ever, and waiting too long will exact a progressively greater price.

When a respected investment professional, a Federal Reserve Board Chairman, highly regarded Wall Street research department, or the business press, or worse—the investor—assume, what <u>must</u> occur, simply remember the omnipotence of the mass of investor buying and selling and the consensus vote that it creates. Their collective buy and sell actions can create stunning directional movement—not statements of others, which are at best temporary and always conjecture.

An exception might—emphasizing might—be a meaningful external event of significance that will alter the corporate profitability equation for a lasting period such as a rapid increase in corporate taxation, or an unexpected but uncommon high interest rate hike. (This causes competition for equities since higher interest rate returns lure investors seeking safety without the perpetual risk associated with stocks. But a rate hike is more likely than not to be the death of a trend.)

The prior-mentioned, trader and author, Jake Bernstein, was also interviewed in the Jack Schwager text, The New Market Wizards, and offered this advice: "Of all the common market principles, I put 'trade with the trend' at the very top."

E.F. Hutton had a well-respected "technical analyst," Newton Zinder, who often proclaimed in his daily message to the sales force: "The most authentic and enduring market movements come from out of nowhere." (Meaning in the absence of the short-term transitory effects that some sources may try to instill, the market will run its natural unaffected course, until it ceases.)

Put your faith in intermediate or any trend—the direction the market wants to go—and in the bias you are witnessing, not in what people are saying is supposed to happen. They may be right one time, but following price action is always right. Respect it!

Rational or not, trends do their own thing and often rise too far and drop too deep. Do not be immediately deterred. Rational is in the "wallet" of the beholder. The market is always "rational" if prices are allowed to seek their natural level. The market in the present is always right as buyers and sellers "mutually" agree on today's price. Price is the rational determinant, since it is the only measuring basis for investment. And a price now is rational; a lower price in six months would be, as well. Price is almost "independent" of everything else. <u>So where it sells, is where it belongs</u>, or until it changes. This is not double talk. It means prices reach the point they do by investor's actions—nothing else! Tracking price trend tells us all we need to know.

In his aforementioned book, Mr. Schwager interviewed various professional traders and one such trader, Jeff Yates, offered this thought: "It's my firm belief that the market's wisdom is far greater than mine. In my opinion, the market's pricing of an item is the best measure of its value." Would an investor feel better knowing his portfolio had a 120 percent, five-year earnings growth rate, but had lost money the past 12 months?

Ask mutual fund holders of most small cap funds, or out-of-favor market sectors, during the late 1990s. We should be always investing from the perspective of the dynamic of price movement.

Sometimes short-term investors plan their attack based on the fundamentals of their investment choice. They review the company's earnings, profit margins, revenue to sales ratios—any number of factors—and at times assume, since they use the company's products and they find satisfaction in doing so, that the company is a "good investment." They often confuse company product/service with investment merit. If they were planning on a takeover, the company internals would certainly be a decisive factor. But if not, "investment merit" can be a world different than "takeover merit."

Along these same lines, investors would be very wise to remember that Wall Street is not yet a philanthropic location. The stake Wall Street has in advising companies and the public and the fees they accrue therefore; they will rarely purposely put any investment to chance. This means a straight story regarding problems within their investment banking company client might not surface from a firm that has that lucrative relationship. (The notion that an employee stockbroker who is still largely compensated on the basis of the *quantity* of commission revenue they generate from their clientele or from activity, can then be truly independent—a detached financial advisor if you will—is an extreme stretch! Their "take home pay" isn't directly based on the quality of their advice, so much as the numbers of commission dollars they convince —or consent—to their clients to spend on transactions.) Do we really think a Wall Street firm, receiving tens to hundreds of millions from investment banking underwriting contracts, is going to knock, at least publicly, that same company and jeopardize its fee income? Not in this year.

## Ride with the Engine of Price Momentum

When investors start to push en masse for a security or a sector, they will almost universally do so from the point of price action and not from fundamentals. *"The stock went up (or down) today (or for the past week) so maybe it will continue, I don't want to miss it."* This is herd think. While fundamental factors are always on display, they are static figures throughout each year, except the four quarterly times they change. In between the stock's run—up and down—will be based on supply and demand and when it directionally gets moving, rational and fundamental thought processes aren't at work throughout the entirety of price movement and almost never toward the very end of trends.

"Thinking it through" isn't going to help since most investing in this area isn't being guided on that basis. For who is to know how many investors will yet pile in and no one knows at what price they'll stop. You can bet the stoppage will not be based on fundamental factors. It will be based on an overabundance of very willing sellers who are being dizzyingly rewarded and who are preparing to undress their gift! So a feeding frenzy can go on quite long…but just not too long. There are standards even with trends. They don't run forever, just as surely as a hyperbolic price rise always signals the near term end of these emotional buying tirades. However, when money gets thrown into areas, go be a participant!

It's the height of egotism to think one can predict human action and reaction with accuracy when the evidentiary component (human emotions) is still at play. Leave the reasoning for the talk shows and the press. Watch the price action for clues as to the continuity of the move.

Price momentum is just price motion. It is not in dissecting the logical mind to reason out why! As long as it's not yet in hyperbolic stages, it simply doesn't have to end.

Did the extent of the Internet sector price collapse in early 2000 to late 2001 parallel the same degree of failure in company and sector fundamentals? In almost all cases, the answer is no. Downside price momentum was clearly in front of the deterioration in earnings, specious business models, etc. If you could have pegged Yahoo's (YHOO) earnings in March 2000 as somewhat deteriorating, would you have also assumed its price would have plummeted 90 plus percent! Unless you were clairvoyant, of course not. Would it have mattered, if having watched the falling pricing you were soon persuaded to sell and thus retained maybe 80 to 90 percent of value?

It doesn't matter if the frenzy terminates—it must. It only matters that you participate first, and second exit long before giving back much of your winnings. When Merrill Lynch's security analyst Henry Blodget predicted in the spring of 1999 that Amazon would drive over $400 per share he was (if he was a really smart), basing his prediction on the price momentum of that moment. In retrospect it was an easy technical analysis call. The frenzy for internet investment was running...he capitalized and he caught the fury. Might it be asked that if fundamentals are so important then why didn't he—knowing of Amazon's corporate strength's etc.—have later predicted its price retreat (actually price slaughter)?

The Internet phenomenon was of the most lucrative examples of the value of yielding to price trend as dominant occurred with the ascension of the Internet in the late 90s and its demise into 2001. An enormous, frequently denied ballooning advance, occurring under slight logic, later transforming into still even greater downside opportunity as prices rolled over and down, shedding almost all value. Perfect examples of allowing price trend to lead. Entering into an advance based on price momentum, sans fundamental rational reason while later remaining silent and investment short, as prices fell apart. Unconcerned as to how fast, or how much, pricing evaporated. Having accepted that price momentum isn't governed by anything other than mass investor bullish or bearish sentiment consensus. These lessons should never be forgotten. There were <u>fortunes</u> offered for sale <u>twice</u> within a time interval of just 48 months!

## Anticipate the Obvious after Placing any Transaction

The fresh instant after a position is underway will probably have you up or down. You are making some money or you are losing some money—at this first instant, a 50/50 proposition. This we call normal.

But, if thorough planning proceded the trade—and of course it always should—and if your investment is with the trend in place, there is no way you have not given yourself a big edge. If this is the case, then you are never starting out at only 50/50. You have a huge advantage, since the price trend already in place with your well-designed investment is suggestive of the same assumed continuing price direction. Revel in this fact!

If a fast profit appears, it doesn't mean you were right—not ultimately. You haven't sold the position. There is no consistent method capable of knowing where the next price will be after your entrance, or where it might be in four minutes. Let's see an example:

You position a strategy to purchase call options at 2 with the stock price at 75. The execution goes well and you purchase at 1 15/16. You did a bit better. The first stock trade is at 75 1/ 4 then the stock runs a shade higher to 75 1/2—*you're already waiting for Dick Clark and Ed McMahon to appear!* Hey, you were right!

The option begins to have a mild upward bias—it now trades at 2 3/8. You look up and the stock is trading at 75 1/8. You then note a 74 3/4 price and the option selling back at 2. A few minutes of back and forth trading, and the stock sinks to 74, down -1/2 point for the day and your option is now underwater at 1 3/4. The next trade is a 10,000 share block at 73 7/8 and the option moves down to 1 5/8. Now you try and reason where the next trade will be. You assume the stock will bounce up a little more, since the market is getting stronger. But do you have any further basis for that prediction? No! You cannot predict in that new instant any better than four hours prior where the next trade is destined. Maybe you wait a little longer and perhaps a few hours go by and the stock recovers to 75 with the option moving up to 2. Where will it trade next? How can you know? Hours pass and the stock, near the close is back down below the prior lows and hits a 73 1/8 price level. What's next? You can't know—not with assurance.

The point above is that at any point during the day, there are very few hints as to where the very next trade direction might be! A falling price, from two minutes ago, provides no more ammunition to know where the next two minutes of trading will price an issue—could it be lower still? If it is lower, will the next series of trades be even lower?—It's somewhat fair to say with the probable exception of technical price factors and maybe an accelerating up or down market as a whole, that each subsequent trade is truly independent of the last. Ergo, in that next instant, you just cannot know. Unless you are out to become a day trader, it only matters where price is when you sell, days to weeks to years out—not minutes.

## Be Practical & Realistic

What are the reasonable odds that as soon as you enter your order, that all hell breaks loose? The market immediately goes against you, war begins, the position never again provides another chance to recover, your picture and street address will be splashed across the papers as the assumed culprit for a change in market direction—come on! If you have prepared properly for the trade—slim and zero.

Most investors already know that when you make an investment, there will never be a point in the future where you can be <u>positive</u> your intended sale price is at the high-water mark. If you guess at where a price top might be, you are using very little except "luck" to exit. But if you wait to see a decline in progress, you cannot (at that point in time) earn the high price, because prices will have already marched downward. So you have the never-ending conflict of processing information with the acceptance of the unknown, along with the agitation of never knowing what to do for certain. Trying to make sense of the investment dictum, "Don't guess at price tops and bottoms," with the common sense maxim, "Don't allow your equity to melt away," to still another, "Be patient, you don't want to sell too soon." Can an investor do all three on the same trade, at the same time? No, No, and No. They are mutually exclusive.

Think about how this affects a short-term trader who needs to be right—right now. No prizes are given for guessing out of a trade that runs wildly days later; or witnessing a once small decline turning into a murderous one; or holding the 5,000 shares of stock and never knowing where it will stop falling and damning yourself for having waited. It's tough. And it's why the tax returns of traders run hot and cold, mostly icy.

When you buy at the very daily low, or at the actual bottom of a trend, if you hit the top price in selling perhaps a few options contract(s), you got in or out just right—you were near perfect. The market said so. Rejoice! This once, the eyes of fate smiled invitingly upon you. You were partly, maybe totally, lucky. It wasn't so much a skill that can be consistently executed and there needs to be an acceptance of this truism.

You never buy enough when your stock rises, and you won't sell enough at the top. Forget acquiring perfection or joy with every position; in a very imperfect business it isn't going to happen.

As any investment position ages and if you are profitable, you should never assume you have "made enough" and therefore, arbitrarily sell "before it all vanishes." This is the classic "scared money" belief. Without evidence of a price direction moving against you, no one really knows where the ideal exit point will be until well *after* it's happened and then, usually, only for a temporary period of time.

### If there is <u>no</u> evidence, why assume there will be the instant you <u>submit a sell order</u>?

Or had you planned to purchase, that the security will fall precisely as you gain confirmation!

### If there is <u>no</u> evidence, why assume there will be at the moment you execute a <u>purchase</u>?

And if there is contrary evidence, always delay positioning the trade!

Give yourself the chance to witness your profitable positions taking off. Refute another of Wall Street's dogmas, "…that only pigs get slaughtered" and that greed isn't worth pursuit. If prices aren't changing direction adverse to you, don't assume they will—until they start—then act. You are entitled to earn as much from your mental toil as possible. The markets aren't keeping score of your successes. They don't try and curtail your good fortune.

Here is excellent proof. During late Fall of 1998 and into early Spring of 1999, the Internet sector soared. Rational or not, it exceeded all types of price targets. The chatter heard from so many of Wall Street's old guard was that the current sector price rise made no sense—meaning intellectually—and as we have learned and now hopefully accepted, it didn't have to. The word was, the rise was a reincarnation of the 1600s Holland "tulip bulb" mania…"the jerks who think to invest in that nonsense, flimsy metrics…." But it made investment sense to those who grasped that you <u>make money from price first and not the business model</u> to have followed that price trend for that period of time. The pros focused on the wrong issue—the trend followers posed the relevant question: Can I make some money long before, and if, they fail as ongoing businesses?

Since price momentum was on their side, why fight the obvious? Would they really care if the sector might ultimately "crash?" They exited 50k richer by practicing the "greater fools theory." They were practicing being price dependent… and they were being rewarded—then!

It is customary with manias to almost universally end badly because there is eventual Wall Street insistence in some type of fundamentals reality at some point! "Will these guys even make a dime?" While the efficiency of the Internet is bringing together parties and information as a consumers' panacea, it may never be for marketers who crave pricing power, since the buyers ability to shop for price is now uniquely unparalleled. Making money is more likely to be an exercise in business volume than from fat company profit margins, which now must remain tight since Internet competition is just too intense.

Nonetheless, there was nothing wrong with participation in the upward momentum for as long as it might have lasted, since these types of huge lasting trends never end overnight. There is always sufficient time to exit when any trend that becomes that pervasive, strong and enduring finally concedes to the ultimate buy/sell dynamic and stops.

145

More proof: was the NASDAQ right in March 2000 at the 5,000 level high or in the spring of 2001 at sub 1,700? Yes! The marketplace is right and is reality every time it places unrestricted prices on assets. Whether it makes reasoned sense at either level is irrelevant if that is where investors, at that time, price assets.

Again, this is evidence of how the human condition needs rationality and how Wall Street wants/needs to have rationale and price direction be coincident behavior. Yet they are different.

We have learned that prices over short and intermediate terms are not guided by logic—they work unto themselves. How dare anyone stand in the face of a bullish ceaseless trend trying to "impede" its relentless ongoing direction by going short or selling—sans any evidence of a top? Perpetual "bears" that stood in the face of an obvious torrid bull market lasting trend. Many lost their livelihoods, their clients, their employees' trust, and their colleagues' intellectual respect. A "trending price song" is often played and a party has started. Attentive investors need only hear the effect.

## Never Allow One Position to Affect Others

Sometimes investors allow a poor current investment to dominate other opportunities. They become fixated on reducing a loss or rallying a profit, at the expense of concentrating upon other ideas that can prove profitable. This is wrong, irrational and may cost you twice.

One bad investment doesn't mean the next will fair poorly. And wanting to overly focus on the problem investment in the hope undivided attention will resolve it usually results in missing the *next* better return opportunity.

Any investment is only one of a portion of an entire portfolio or potential number of alternatives. Devoting all of your energies into one, at the expense of all, must be avoided. If another well researched alternative is being considered, only its potential should be the basis for prospective purchase not clouded by a recent failure. Another alternative can make up for the prior loss very quickly.

## Decide How Much Minimum Profit Out-Weighs Further Potential

There are times when becoming "profit hungry" means frequently having sold well below a high price. This is frequently done so as to "book" the gain and to enjoy the feeling of just being correct and not wanting to lose the advantage at that point. Great in concept, but it can be very costly in practice.

Prior to initiating strategies, some degree of expectation should take place whereby a designated level of minimum profit should be considered before any selling takes place. This amount might be $100s or $1,000s but it's the investor's call. Equally important is what stage of overbought or oversold the position is in. If the stock or sector has been badly hurt and well due to rebound, selling out after a small $200 to $300 gain might make little sense with vast upside potential looming from the oversold condition.

For example: a position is put on and a short-term profit of $300 appears, but soon price evidence suggests as to the position going against the investor. Should they sell, keep the $300 and run the risk of losing a far greater profit? If the goal were to part with not less than a $500 minimum profitable amount, the answer is yes. The $300 should have been allowed to stay "up in the air"—be risked—since a $500 position goal wasn't met. Here, the downside potential loss of the $300 would not outweight the potential or the planned minimum profitable amount.

## Agree to Get Rich Slowly

An investor isn't likely—and shouldn't expect—to make a significant profit any sooner than he would expect his employer to have paid out their full annual salary...on the first day of each new year. We earn our livelihood over time and in the same manner we should not expect to reap profitable investments that turn into sizeable sums with the passage of days.

Accept that building asset wealth almost always takes years. Taking too many chances and feeling that need to "have to be in" isn't necessary and leads to taking too much risk.

Remember, there will never be a headline.

### "No more profitable opportunities on Wall Street."
### All the good ideas are used up. (Wait...about four minutes for the next.)

## Take a Refresher Course in Self-Discipline

Be keenly aware that the decisions as to when, or *if*, a strategy should be undertaken, can be completed very easily and often too easily. There generally aren't any dissenting parties present. The investment decision can be from no more an instant computer keystroke. If there is no discipline present prior to entry, positions start on "a whim," such as "I've got a feeling this is going to work." This is not a wise basis for risking money.

The mechanics in placing a trade can involve mere seconds, so after the "buy button" is pushed, the consequences of the decision are going to be played out. Therefore, the undisciplined...be forewarned.

All the work and time you expend is useless unless you have the discipline—some might call it courage—to put into action what you have learned. There is a mature willingness to re-travel correct paths and to have learned not to replicate unsuccessful tactics over, and over, and over. Our markets aren't outwardly parental in voicing their lessons. You must learn them...then remain always directed toward the correct, profitable actions that experience teaches.

You might call this requirement for discipline the ability to control yourself; doing what has, and is, working, not what you simply want/should/hope plays out. And there isn't an investor alive who hasn't violated this trait. Worse still, it is a personality characteristic you either have acquired at this stage in your life or maybe you might never acquire. Hard as it might be, consistent discipline is one more important psychological asset along the direction to acquiring the best investor mental state.

In most of life's experiences any learned lessons are not usually brought to play very often, hence we make repeated mistakes having forgotten the lessons from our past. With investments, we are tested, often daily and decisions—even to do nothing active—are thrown upon us. So the learning to travel correct roads is often demanded upon us. It follows that those lessons had better be learned or repetition of errors will be nonstop. It's played out in life just as frequently.

Be guided by the multitude of experiences that have led to knowledge and are more apt to be consistent with this latest market experience than not. In other words, in refusing to be guided by what you know is usually correct action(s), you are reducing your profitable probabilities to straight chance. And it further means that intimating whatever might have taken years to learn, now, at this point in time, is to be discarded. Would you then believe you have increased your chances of success? More likely than not, you have reduced them to about the same level as a novice—one with no experiences and no knowledge. Whereas following the rules increases your chances of far greater probability.

Trust what you have learned through your experiences before second-guessing the next event

## Patience

In a society that craves for the immediate, instant gratification from one's toil, the patient few can improve when trying to tone down this ever-so-common modern trait. Yet when investing real money, there are times when doing nothing and waiting is best.

Investment information that we already know of, is of little use if we don't act, and unless we allow some time to play out…to have all investors ultimately discover our brilliance. Perhaps this is not true. If we have done our homework and our investment expectations eventually were indeed going to produce a large return, then selling prematurely to satisfy the impulse to "feel rewarded," our results will produce substantially smaller profit and very hollow victories.

Information we may have just come across, a piece of news, a research item, a technical analysis factor, and that we act upon in the assumption that everyone else will eventually "catch on" and confirm our genius—thus, we better be first and at this very instant—is of mild value if we too prematurely insist for "confirmation." This erroneous thinking suggests that investors follow us.

Investors act differently at different times for different reasons. What we know, even if we are better informed, still needs some time to play out. If we won't allow it, can only mean that we believe the investment world watches us for a first clue. Assuming the masses will follow us in and out of our strategies at just about the opportune time we are placing buy and sell orders, isn't reality. Investments should be put on generally slowly after fervent preparation. *Yet position exits should be immediate after price observation yields that the best of the once strategy, is now behind.*

## Our Timing of When to Take Action Is Always Subordinate to the Markets

There are times when the markets appear dull or rang- bound and it's easy to sit back and make the assumption that the market doesn't seem to want to move. This can lead to going on "mental" or "observant" vacation. A simple warning from experience: Don't.

If the time for perhaps a dramatic move is just about right, persevere through the waiting and the boredom. Moves off extreme tops or bottoms are often dramatic. You are more often than not, about to be very well rewarded for remaining attentive.

## Make Note: Our Investment Savvy Isn't Influencing Other Investors

An excellent example of this phenomenon occurred when technology companies in the Fall of 2000 repeatedly warned of softening business and the sector continued to drop and did so again with similar news from other companies, and then dropped yet again. Now at some point an intelligent, deductive view would be that investors should have accepted that this redundant theme is going to repeat itself and, since the repeated dim news isn't new, stop selling all tech companies in sympathy. But this needn't happen just when you believe it should. Bad news will eventually be absorbed and when it is the stock's pricing, being negatively impacted with the disappointing news, will cease to plunge and maybe even start upward. When it does, this is when you line up to start buying, but no sooner. In simple English: be patient and observe. Other investors' timing and ability to reason isn't necessarily similar to ours. Let the evidence of price be the teacher.

## Investment Decisions: How Often Is Enough?

The frequency of your investment actions should be predicated upon the type of investment strategy you are intending. Be but forewarned: the more you do, the not so merrier, and probable failure is looming.

If <u>long-term</u> driven, it may behoove the investor to purchase, either one time or dollar cost average—the same dollar amount consistently applied at specific calendar periods, throughout a bull market's duration—and retain positions throughout its entire duration assuming—and this is key—that the market retains its long-term bullish slant. A wait-and-hold tact throughout eliminates effort for sure, but truthfully subordinates the potential of higher investment return to the strength of the market's move entirely. *(Watching industries and individual company's stock prices either plummet or soar to unsustainable price levels by over-reactive rushes then sitting back to allow "fate" to remedy these gyrating monies, is too removed for this author's liking.)*

If <u>intermediate-term</u> prone, decisions might be made a few times per annum if the markets or specific industries yield very overbought or oversold status, and where investment can then take place in anticipation of the beginning of a 2 to 3 month consistent directional move.

If <u>short-term</u>, and depending upon whether it's day trading or "lengthier," decisions and activity need to be made quite often with the accompanying stress and the randomness of result being accepted. Waiting—and too often just hoping—to be bailed out isn't a good option.

## Come to Terms with Having Knowledge & the Discipline to Use it

From our earliest years, we have all too frequently been told to never repeat past errors or, more conventionally, "learn from our past mistakes." The act of investing might be the best example of how we practice this attribute. People who never learn from error and repeat bad experiences are not rare. Most of us are somewhat guilty. It might be said that a sign of mature intelligence is having the will—again, the discipline—to follow our learning and not simply what our immediate desire wishes would occur.

All the hopeful education that you as a reader may take from this book or from prior experiences is only as good as your willingness to follow their repeat lessons and those from past experiences, actively practicing that knowledge. Repeating mistakes is a very expensive investment lesson and an unenviable character flaw which keeps people from attainment in all areas of their lives. Discipline is vital.

## Understand the Distinction between Technical & Fundamental Deterioration

Since Wall Street seems loath to downgrade a public company based upon fundamentals deterioration, blind following of their shifts in company research can be disastrous. There is a distinct difference between a company losing market share, or a wrong product cycle introduction, or its stock price sitting on a technical cliff. Fundamental recommendations rarely take into account the technical state of the markets. And while fundamental recommendations can ultimately prove valuable, they shouldn't have to be from a starting price far below where first touted.

Observation over many years tells us that Wall Street virtually never recommends a "sell" on a stock. This is primarily because their investment banking business is frequently too inherently a part of the companies they research. With "buy" suggestions not just the norm, but as, an expected source for stockbroker commissions, it's not a terrible stretch to see how fundamental recommendations are not as helpful as they might otherwise be. When we couple this with most fundamental analysts' avoidance of a technical view as well, it makes for shaky investment opinions.

A simple case in point: on 11/29/2000 with the NASDAQ hitting daily repeated lows, Merrill Lynch comes out and recommends Veritas (VRTS) on, of all markets, the "in bloodied play" NASDAQ. The stock promptly drops 5 points with the power of their suggestion. Two days prior, Sun Microsystems (SUNW) was another of Wall Street's "winning" ideas—the stock promptly rising 5 points over two days; then as the NASDAQ carnage escalated, SUNW dropped about 10 points into the high 70s— still a 5 point loss from the date of the fundamental recommendation. Goldman Sachs was the "town crier" that time.

And were we to base an investment decision to hold a stock in a falling market upon the words, however honest, of the company's CEO, you would be better advised to understand from where he or she sits. CEOs are responsible for running the inher- ent dynamic of their businesses, not dissecting the price message or volatility of their stock. They rarely comprehend the nature of price movement and almost exclusively "cheerlead" on the basis of the fundamentals expectation. They are generally not good prognosticators of the securities markets or their own company's prospective price action, any more than most.

Yet fundamental deterioration isn't useless info for everybody. For long-term investors, it's their most persuasive element and what justifies an exit. When the most important of these—unexpected high percentage earnings growth rates—level off, or becomes lukewarm, expect selling.

Companies starting to crack internally tend to relatively under-perform on a price basis over long time-frames. Yet for all other investment periods, it is a secondary issue. However a <u>technical price breakdown</u> hurts no matter whether the company is in good or bad financial condition. Mind the technical first.

## Curtail the Notion That Paper Profits Aren't Real

Countless times when investors enjoy a paper profit—one not as yet realized, since a complete sale hasn't taken place—they tend to become more "charitable" with these unrealized gains, often very slow to sell and protect what had been earned. Their sup- posed logic would seem to be…"It isn't real yet, so if a bit's lost, so what, since I still have profits." Wrong!

*All value, at all times*, is real. No different than were the investor to die with a "paper profit." (Estate tax valuation, and due tax is based on the value on the date of death.) Unrealized, as yet "paper," profit is as much authentic, and as much your enti- tlement, as are your losses. Change the thinking that you can afford to part with some investment gains. Grab all that you can. If the investment price action looks weak enough, the degree of profit (or loss) shouldn't impede a suitable sell discipline.

## Accept the "New" Investor Attitude toward Securities

*Once upon a time in the era when price changes were reported slowly and the world was still very distant, investors bought stock and held stock—often for generations. Not only was it customary to buy and hold, it was remarkably expensive to buy and sell. The 1975 NYSE decision to allow member firms to abandon fixed commissions, and the discount commission industry it created, has allowed the cost of transacting securities business to be virtually inconsequential.*

Where once 300 to 500 share purchase orders might have meant $200 transaction expenses, orders can now be executed for 1,000s of shares, at 1/15th to 1/20th of the former cost. Options trading costs were about 10 percent of the money involved just to enter that arena. It is commonplace today to find $5 to $10 charges on stock regardless of the numbers of shares being traded, and near $20 to $30 options costs. It has truly meant that the transaction expenditure in making decisions are a non-factor. Once the entire buy and sell decision might have been predicated upon the execution costs in and out. Today, it doesn't have to be a consideration; consequently, share volume has exploded.

The confluence of these factors and our generation of investors who hold nothing sacred—hardly a stock—and who have been spoiled over the past two decades of bullish moneymaking, and who also revel in instant fulfillment, has meant that fast investment decisions are here to stay. The resulting effects—namely, rapid price gyrations—are more apt to be the rule rather than the exception. The result is an investor who can exercise a wise sense of when to act and will be far more proficient in acquiring, and maintaining, investment wealth than maybe at any other time in our history.

## You Still Are Profiting in Taking No Action—Remaining Sidelined

Take a bow when you are right for having done nothing, avoiding what would have been an investment disaster. While not measurable positives, it should count for confidence building. And naturally, you do retain monies that would otherwise have been lost, at least in the short-term. So good investing means not just taking some affirmative act. Avoidance in missing the tragedies, in remaining out when no firm direction is in evidence, is nonetheless an "incalculable profit."

Investment is not a singular street. You surely make zero profits when entertaining the sidelines, but you retain 100 percent of monies. When the urge to "get into something" comes along and is not balanced by some trend in place wherein you can derive a good investment, stand idle. Doing nothing won't cost you any capital. Wanting some investment "action" because you can't make money unless you are invested in something, can cost you plenty. Stay out, unless you have strong conviction. In today's markets you can make more in a few chosen weeks than one could have in years in the past. Pick your spots carefully.

## Is the Age-Old Investment Wisdom, Buy & Hold, Really Always Preferable?

For decades, investors have been bred to accept that buying for the long-term meant one purchase, nary ever a sale, and holding through thick and thin. As we learned earlier, this buy and hold technique has worked so well over the 1980 through 2000 period, which was an historical anomaly, that any argument with its acceptance was apt to be weak. Results have been grand. And there have been numerous investment studies that have alluded to the idea that remaining in the market through all kinds of periods has provided an investor with a superior return versus attempting to "time the market," or to choose consummate enter, exit and reenter periods.

One example, completed through Ibbotson Associates in Chicago, tells us of $10,000 invested on the eve of the 1929 Crash and left "unattended" over the ensuing 70 years had grown by a factor of 841, in recognizable math, to $8.41 million. This 70-year period contained many wars, recessions, bouts with great inflation, assassinations, and on and on. Yet rather remarkably, very little print exits as to where these assets were placed and the <u>crucial</u> inference.

First and foremost, these long-term buy and hold studies tend to focus on the Dow Jones Industrials, since the Dow has a multi-decade history, and also, when available, the S&P 500. Yet, neither is some random construction of diverse long-term held portfolios. Both of these indices by their construction are a diverse mix of equities, and, not unimportantly, the biggest and nearly most financially sound within the U.S. securities markets! Why this is so relevant is because artful diversification permits far less risk entering the portfolio and consequently during sour market periods these indices, almost always, rarely plummet to underwater price levels greater than negative 25 percent. With this as historical fact, it's rather easy to understand how the long-term buy and hold mentality results in having these indice's price levels remain so upwardly biased.

**There is virtually no <u>significant</u> downside price action in these indices because of their inherent diversification, as often as there would be in an individual's portfolio.**

If the most price carnage one might experience is in the 20 percent range or maybe the occasional 25 percent area, it would be folly to even try to exit, pay taxes on any gains, then reenter. The "20 percent" window—in and out, tax liability consequence, and back in again—is simply too narrow. While a $100,000 portfolio in an S&P 500 type investment might dwindle backwards to maybe $75 to $80,000 perhaps every 5 to 10 years, later upside price trends far more than make up for any 20 percent bearish periods. To no surprise, being in this "market" works without any real possibility of serious 30 to 50 percent corrections taking away large portions of asset value which would otherwise take many normal years to recover. (And not to mention the market doesn't have an income tax liability; investors always do.)

There exists a very serious illusion what always being "in the market"—as represented by the Dow or S&P 500—actually means.

Unless you have made investment selections in large part uncorrelated, meaning the portfolio does not move price directionally all at once or close to it, you must then be prepared to exit positions prior to large sector/industry bearish periods. Otherwise, long-term buy and hold may not protect against major loss if the portfolio components are too similar.

Of course, a significant question remains unanswered regarding portfolio selection: if a portfolio of stocks outside of the large Dow type, and S&P 500 type issues, if held forever, would, even if adequately diverse, provide protection against swift, meaningful, downside price action? With precise studies in this regard very scarce, it is an open question. One would assume so, since there are plenty of academic studies which summarize long-term investment records of growth versus value, and large cap versus small cap type strategies from mutual fund results, whose portfolio components are much smaller.

While sector/industry diversification alone might be sufficient, it would be additionally advised that all of the stocks chosen within the portfolio not comprise too much of any one style type—all inclusion of small stocks or all mid cap stocks of a growth investment style only. In other words, diverse means a true unique complexion of equities, so when one investment style or perhaps sector or market is in serious decline, there isn't material impact upon the total portfolio.

In sum, we know diversity within the Dow and S&P 500 works over long periods to ensure good long-term investment return; whether it works elsewhere, over multiple decades, is of debate.

One last warning regarding long-term holding: there can be danger in permitting portfolios to dwindle in sour environments even with the common theme espoused by so many—"They'll come back eventually" and "I don't need the money now anyway." Yet these are flawed beliefs. They presuppose that the time value of money—that is, value that either falls or is allowed to migrate year after year—has no real monetary impact from interest loss and that investments always return to former highs, and that the near peak value that may become realized exiting somewhat near tops cannot then be used to short stocks where investment profits can pile up when prices continuously drop. In each of these assumptions the "sit and wait" investor is making scary bets that their assumed diverse portfolio can insulate against falling prices.

## Does the Briskness of Investment Activity Even Allow for Learning?

Investment activity is really very different than what we find in most professions, since we can have multiple experiences during the course of days and even hours, the outcome of which can be better to educate us for future guidance. Compare this phenomenon to a doctor who might lose a patient, then not see like circumstances emerge for many years, the experience from which should serve as a guide in not rehearsing mistakes, incorrect procedure, miss-diagnosis and so forth. But wouldn't this assume the doctor would remember the original situation after the extended time lapse? In most professions, second chances are infrequent; in our securities markets, they are the rule.

Depending upon the recurrence of your investment activity, you may be given steady opportunities to learn from error. Your ability to remain disciplined is terribly important, because you <u>will be</u> tested again...and likely very soon.

## Prepare to Give up on Capturing the First & Last 10 Percent of Price Movement

In as much as one can preach not to be too assumptive as to where prices might find their way, in reality no one reaps <u>all</u> of any movement. In practical continuous applications, this is because it is an impossibility.

Minus guesswork and luck, there is no way to know when tops and bottoms will occur with precision or where to enter or exit at perfect price points. This is Investment 101. Consequently it makes for a calmer and more practical investor to plainly accept that the last and first 10 percent of price movement isn't consistently going to be had. Capitulation here decreases our frustration level and increases investment maturity.

Try as one likely might to catch both ends, but accept the fact it will be luck—never skill—if you get the best of either ends of a transaction. And even when done, it is almost always a transitory win. Because sometime—generally fairly soon—a new price will be found higher than where we exited.

## Be Very Conscientious of Investor Behavior— Is this Period Normal or Abnormal?

It will be vital to recognize if the period you are in is normal or abnormal. In abnormal times (prices at extremes, panic price reactions, 9/11, etc.) old rules don't work and time-tested techniques can be battered.

For example, in severe downturns, price support levels which may have held for long periods, and at which point previous buying would have resulted in upward movement, may now give way. Consequently, prices can move far more than normal expectations and our investment experience will have less importance.

When investor sentiment appears to go to an extreme in these times, be careful. What looks so inviting may not be! Rapid price rise can stop abruptly while declines seem to never want to end regardless of reason. These would be times to be very careful, since little can guide us.

## The Luck Element

The times when you purchase a security, or already own it, and you suddenly receive exceptional news sending the price skyward, are simply periods of good fortune which you didn't predict and should not take seriously as testimony to your investment acumen. Alternatively, the periods when you may have just purchased and are immediately greeted with an earnings downgrade, etc., are similar uncontrollable acts.

If you have no control over the news or an extraneous item which affects your investment, how can you punish or reward yourself upon its delivery?

You were lucky; you were unlucky. Wise investors wouldn't base decisions on elements of luck anyway.

Forget these times—for they are normal uncontrollable occurrences within the investment arena and generally over time play themselves out as does your share of good and bad fortune. And it's why there is so little devoted to this area of investment within this text!

## The Greed Element

Since we know the markets are under no one's control and, at least in the short-term, might be random, it comes as little surprise that obtaining the most from a trade isn't going to happen except in rare times.

Were we to purchase just prior to a market launch and our position(s) become instantly profitable, we would undoubtedly still complain, since we probably didn't buy enough. Naturally had the position gone against us, we'd lament why did we buy any!

When a sale is appropriate and as we sell the stock immediately sinks, we are likely bitter because we didn't get completely out. We simply wanted more. More at the bottom and more from the top. With this type of common investor mindset, frustration will be your constant companion and happiness always illusory.

The truth is that perfect execution pricing is "unattainable" in any period. And luck always plays some part in the timing of executions. It is no more under our province than is equity price control. Why then frustrate and second-guess a well planned timing decision? Over many years, investors have gained their share of good fortune. If it's meant…so will each of us.

## Why You Must Try to Give Your Strategies Time to Work

It has been stated ad nauseam to slash losses quickly; yet this means actual loss. It does not mean exiting from as yet profitable or typically neutral situations. Being too brisk to liquidate means a concession to haste which should never be welcomed.

It has been repeatedly spoken that short-term activity is too random to be taken as a steady diet. Yet placing a position today that has cost the investor nothing, but which hasn't moved to the desired level of gain, is not a rationale for liquidation, only an obvious facet of Wall Street normalcy. It isn't supposed to in a day or two...or maybe three.

## Could This Time Be Different?

Central to successful investing is learning the rules of Wall Street and then consistently following those "disciplines"...tendencies...probabilities. While there will always be exceptions to long-held beliefs, the reason why we follow the Street's "rules" is so we get the chance to <u>replicate</u> profitable strategies, price expectations and so forth, and to view them working out again and again in the future. And...not assuming this one time, your intellect at this moment is greater than all the prior knowledge you have amassed from multiple similar situations.

The likelihood is that this time will be no different than a prior similar situation and that results will occur as they had in the past...that's why these disciplines became "the rules of the game."

## A Time to Roll Dice: An Example of Almost "Easy" Money

Broad overall markets cannot directionally trend indefinitely. After too many consecutive days, at some level, overbought/oversold conditions always surface to the extent that they cause, at minimum, a retracement and perhaps even a major trend change.

When these conditions are close to occurring, the markets being very overbought/oversold anyway, and presumed market moving news is about to be released from a very well known company with those many eyes focused upon it, it can pay to assume the result of the news release.

In May 2002 the NASDAQ was down five straight days with a few technical indicators signaling a possible short-term, very oversold bottom. Our friend Cisco Systems (CSCO) produced a decent earnings quarter and coupled with its broad appeal and renown, caused a major instant move on the opening the following day. The prior day was an instance where making a bet on a good CSCO release had minor risk—especially if you were in it. The stock stood at 12 and change, and even with a downbeat forecast, how low might it have gone? An optimistic outlook surely would have helped it, and its market, the dire NASDAQ.

## How to Handle Positions When the Trending Party Is Almost over

As sensible as we would think, there indeed comes a point in which as trends mature, we should decrease exposure, since forever enduring isn't reality.

With positions already held, it makes sense to "take money off the table," to lighten exposure, as the trend ages and we start to see <u>price evidence becoming contrary to expectation</u>. Since trend profitability is logically reduced as it ages, limiting exposure minimizes probable asset depreciation.

For intent to place new funds after a long trend has been in place, the same advice would stand: limit the amount of monetary commitment. If the duration of the trend to date wasn't sufficiently compelling to prompt positions to be taken, there is even less profitability as the period advances.

## Is It a Bargain?

The bargain price you might feel you are grabbing is <u>relative</u>. Someone who bought shares at 50 may have felt that it at the time represented good value, then idly watched as you bought at 30, and you now might feel you have the bargain. However, if you are wrong and allow a subsequent falling price to impede you from action, and an additional 10 points evaporates, the bargain purchase isn't yours either. It may only become so for the brave at 20, or at 15, or at maybe 10.

The evident point: a long security becomes a bargain only when it starts up and then only if your purchase price is fairly close to that origination price level.

When an alternative surfaces from which you will perhaps be capable of regaining lost monies and probably composure, the vast portion of the money, if having been removed, can be put to work quickly. In the interim, sideline monies earn some interest and you still keep a small tax loss while awaiting another day.

*Summarizing: investing is an ongoing process – not a once in and out. Never allow the single trade to affect your objectivity over everything you have learned to that point. Learn from ALL of your experiences and be biased by all of them. First and foremost though, learn the real rules, and act in accordance with their probabilities, not conjecture. Investment in this arena is about "odds" management— you will always be rolling "probabilistic dice" to some degree.*

## Conclusion

*Forget a drive to investment perfection—you won't enjoy one. Making money shorter-term isn't about smarts; it's about discipline! When you win, it means you were disciplined, not necessarily wise, too. If you lose, you might well have been frivolous or stubborn, but not stupid. Your intellect isn't at risk when you invest for 48 hours. You are intelligent or you aren't, and your past is the standard of measure, not a two-hour or two-day stock or option trade. We measure intelligence in a wide variety of ways—stock market profits and losses isn't yet one of those yardsticks.*

*Investment success is not the sole province of intellectuals or the professionals, but those who wisely practice discipline. Those that learn from experience how to reason and exploit opportunities without improbable assumptions. The savvy folks who have the courage and conviction to take a well-planned stance and move to action, knowing from studied experience and learned relevant information what to expect in terms of the probabilities. Having the monetary and psychological strength to wait and allow profits to run. The smarts to cut losses fast, admit when an idea failed and prepare for another day. It's not really gene sequencing.*

*When the fear of losing money isn't as great as the potential of winning, well-thought positions can get put on. Short- and intermediate-term investing and to a reasoned extent, long-term, as well it is not played cerebrally as scientific thought-invoking expertise; it is played with discipline—the discipline to find trends and to stay aligned with them as long as they remain. To accept our rational sense is generally secondary to experiences, since investment result is not a consistently deductive process. This does not mean that intelligence is useless. It means, in fact:*

*Price momentum and directional trend are almost all that ever counts over almost all investment horizons and singularly what investment decisions should be predicated upon almost every time.*

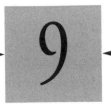

# Loss Control

## Handling Yourself through Expected Shorter-Term Losses & Loss Generally

What about losses? Since we don't invest to have less, this aspect of investment is always far more trying.

Sensible buying discipline demands that prior to a purchase, an intended holding duration be set. If the intention is to hold a stock for many years during bull markets, and perhaps make periodic "dollar cost averaging" investments, then sitting through 4 and 5 point <u>immediate</u> losses having nothing to do with the specifics of the company—a very bad market day, etc.—might not cause a fast exit for some, since years will be available to make it up. Yet, for all other intended holding periods—minutes to months—calmly watching monies evaporate with only hope as your strength, is flat blunt ignorance right now, and will parlay into stupidity shortly. In this area, patience often has zero virtue.

Countless investment books on investment and trading all resound to one dominate chord:

### Never Allow Small Losses to Become Significant
Curtail the amount of dollar losses quickly—on stocks for certain, a bit less so with options, since huge percent changes occur frequently and are really non-controllable, (with options, we use time maximums to help us decide exit points,) and…

161

> - You can always return and buy it back!
>
> - You can always return and buy it back!
>
> - You can always return and buy it back!

It costs but a single commission…at maybe $8.

The procedure to repurchase after any type of loss would be no different than with any initial purchase. You follow the same buying discipline.

The market has infinitely greater affecting ability than does an investor's urgency that price moves as they might wish. We do not reason for the market; it reasons for us. Trends going against you in a "hard" environment are destined to get only worse. Sell out and protect what you have. Respect the power of a trend in place; its dominance is vastly greater than our intellect to change it. Please…buy into this investment reality.

### Can You Truthfully Expect the Following Legacy to Play Out?

- You research thoroughly, and initiate a $50 purchase and the strategy immediately backfires.

- You are losing…and not happy.

- You sell at $48—proving from prior advice you are a quick learn—albeit a poorer one!

- At the instant you see the sell confirmation; the price starts upward, for a few points back to $50.

- Not wanting to be left out—in case it takes off—you hand in another buy order.

- Again, consistent with your purchasing, the stock starts downward.

- Not wanting to throw away yet more money, you liquidate at $48, still again.

- And once more, upon receipt of your sale confirmation, the stock starts back up.

- For one last time, you buy back in, now at $51.

- And finally, the stock—actually the marketplace "watching" with pleasure at your every frustrating move—begins massive selling and the price closes at $45, as you head out for the nearest tavern.

The odds on your being that wrong, that short-term—repeatedly failing—is nil. And the above series of transactions is the worst that could happen if you sell and buy back and sell… Investors often don't sell because as they are losing, they reason, what if they just liquidate entirely and the exited position then begins to work out. They would have to reenter with fresh anxiety and hope they would be correct this time? (They forget, remaining in losing positions brings on zero comfort—it creates further anxiety!) Other than being incarcerated, if all the original justification is still valid, and the stock's momentum starts to trend as originally planned, and assuming you are content to first trade short-term, and then simply reposition the strategy.

Remember the most recent high—for bullish scenarios—will provide some resistance, and expecting a rapid turn-around to take out that old high might be too much. But since an investor was likely prepared to part with some portion of retracement (10 to 20 percent) anyway, why not force the stock to get above its prior peak before repurchasing if the intent is to treat the transaction as one of intermediate term. If the price direction thereafter still can't continue, exit finally and say goodbye.

Even piles of online transactions commissions when getting back in and out are never as expensive as capital losses. Commissions are dollars lost, not thousands. It is precisely for this reason that being adequately diversified means not becoming "whipsawed"—selling out and then having positions turn against you. We know that very diverse portfolios are perhaps similar to the broad market indices—the Dow, S&P 500—and rarely should suffer greater than 20 percent declines in ongoing bull markets. Therefore selling out no lower than somewhere near their downside 20 percent target, say at -15 percent to -20 percent, would limit further harm, and probably means if the market were to fall lower still a bear market would begin anyway, whereby the investor would be sidelined or maybe engage the downward bias. If the market turned upward, the investor could reasonably go back in, knowing that in not breaking beneath the -20 percent threshold, the next trend of significance would likely be upward.

Note the following 14 S&P 500 Bear Markets since the Crash of 1929:

| Period | Duration in Months | Per Cent Loss |
|--------|--------------------|--------------| 
| 2000 | 28 * | - 48 percent |
| 1987 | 3 | - 34 percent |
| 1980 | 20 | - 27 percent |
| 1973 | 21 | - 48 percent |
| 1968 | 18 | - 36 percent |
| 1966 | 8 | - 22 percent |
| 1961 | 6 | - 28 percent |
| 1956 | 15 | - 22 percent |
| 1948 | 12 | - 21 percent |
| 1946 | 12 | - 29 percent |
| 1938 | 42 | - 46 percent |
| 1937 | 13 | - 54 percent |
| 1933 | 20 | - 34 percent |
| 1929 | 33 | - 86 percent |
| * as of 8/2002 | | |

If you have watched your position go against you maybe several months—or more commonly—many consecutive and painful days, you may yet be reluctant to sell, because you expect a due and deserved turn-around. And, as always…"it can't just keep falling"…"there has to be some price at where they buy." Say you bought at 45, three days later it's 39 and you reason it's already down 6, there can't be much selling left. The fallacy in this reasoning is the misguided assumption that investors purchased <u>after</u> your acquisition date (in other words, lower than you), so they have no urgency to sell. But this assumption may not be even close!

What if they had purchased <u>prior to you</u> at 50, or 60, or higher? <u>Their</u> extent of pain is far greater, and investors will tolerate punishment for only so long. In these cases, they have plenty of ammunition to justify selling, and selling more as price spirals downward. This is one of the best reasons to limit your loss quickly, since far greater losses might be very near. It is with little doubt that sometime an upside day will arrive, but when? Two points lower at 5 or at 8? What if the company concedes it's having trouble? Do you think a plurality of investors will rally to support a falling price? Well you needn't wonder if you were out!

If watching a position nosedive costs you $2,000, it really means you have momentarily $2,000 less worth. To use a glass as being half full analogy, you are $2,000 less rich. And the vehicle (position) that controls the $2,000 lesser amount is really irrelevant after the unrealized loss has been accepted. Therefore, can it matter if you had sold quickly and transferred that smaller amount to a potentially more rewarding investment if the "second choice" then runs on to a huge gain? Do you ultimately care which horse wins you back your dough?

The lesson: having a position at a price disadvantage means an unrealized loss within a portfolio. It isn't important how you retrieve that "unrealized or realized loss," only that you do, and that you not become "original position paralyzed."

Had you sold early and even gone back into that same issue, and if a second time it didn't immediately move in the direction you expected, could you not instantly, and finally, liquidate, having given yourself the stubborn opportunity to recoup again? Of course.

Don't be seduced into passivity by the market or by your negative position alone providing you what a "failed" idea has already initially cost. It might even get worse. New ideas flourish almost daily.

### Always Protect Your Investment Capital

Here's a short example why quick selling at a loss carries some advantage.

Assume an investor has a choice of keeping his recently purchased shares now sporting a two point loss or selling completely, since it appears the stock isn't likely to do as anticipated. If a sale is completed and an alternative stock chosen is dissimilar to the one having been sold, the investor immediately has a lasting advantage and isn't in violation of the IRS "wash rule." (After a sale takes place an investor must wait 31 days before buying back a substantially similar stock and still be able to retain the tax loss.)

The 2 point loss is a short-term tax loss applied against any short gains to offset tax liability. If gains aren't present, the loss can still be carried forward up to $3,000 for that year. The investor having sold and hence limiting downside exposure, has still earned the luxury of substituting a new asset that presumably will reacquire the 2 points of loss, and while awaiting being made whole again still earns a 2 point tax loss, which, had nothing been done, would have been forfeited.

More justification for adopting a practical sell discipline prior to initiating any purchase…

**Investors erroneously reason that taking a quick loss to protect capital has lasting implications and that by remaining in the original issue, it alone brings them back whole, that there is no other alternative to recoup their quick loss?**

In taking quick losses, do we feel better if we lose money over six tortuous weeks as opposed to losing the same amount in 20 minutes but with a potentially immediate second chance to regain with the large bulk of the transaction?

Investors reason that leaving the dying position open will bring them back—that it, the position already at a loss—is the one, <u>the</u> only one, to revive them back to whole! If they don't sell, they haven't lost. Maybe they'll get back to even, from, of course, that already <u>floundering</u> trade and no other. (Doesn't this sound like convoluted thinking? You bet it does.)

We know that the broad market or sector temperament will make or break most short-term investments. If the period you are in is sour, the near term might remain quite poor for long positions—it no doubt will depend upon the severity of the mood. If your long investment is falling and the broad environment is not difficult, a bit of patience can be smart unless what has put your holding under water is something very company-specific and very meaningful. In that instance, you are better to be totally out, hunting for other options.

When you start out under water, the degree of anxiety that you can stomach is really individual, but the cure for taking a quick loss shouldn't be. Once again, if the short-term loss is related to the investment alone, then a quick sell trigger is recommended; if related to general market deterioration, then slightly more leeway can be allowed—but not much. What good would there be if the loss, manageable at two points, is allowed to broaden to 15 with the narration…"But it's a weak market."  If it's that weak, then being long in anything is a dead mistake.

A quick sell, however painful, saves both money and nerves, and the capacity to continue investing and so forth.  A preset 2 point downside limit means a major loss cannot transpire—assuming immediate liquidation occurs. And while it will be no laughing matter to give up 2 points on perhaps 300 or 500 or, worse, 2,000 shares after all of maybe two hours of ownership, the balance and bulk of the money is "side-lined" awaiting the next investment choice, from which the loss can be regained in the best available investment—maybe even the one you just exited, but with 95 percent of your money from that position still available.

Don't get dragged through trending enduring losses, because any one of the surrounding events that helped intensify your losses—you can bet—are still present. If you could lose 2 points in ten minutes, why think it couldn't be made all back and more, in a subsequent ten minute period—maybe even that same day!

Markets and sentiment change very rapidly. If the unexpectedly markets took it away, can they not give it back just as quickly when mood, perception and sentiment change? They can, and do, every day.

In a grown-up world, we have all always sold too soon, bought at tops, missed opportunities, so why should a quick acceptance of a temporary loss be any different than we are accustomed to? We don't hit many short-term home runs, and life is not always a bed of roses. If we do things correctly, the singles and doubles add up to our winning much more than we might imagine. While far more trying on our patience, it is less than insistence that any one loss be recaptured from the original position.

Now options losses are a different lot. We know that as options age, they lose value and at some point they expire, so we must plan on exit strategies on the basis of how long the investment should be held. (There is a distinction between allowance for any options position to run away since we can't really know how high "high" might become, or in our knowing how much money we permit to escape from our initial dollar outlay. We can base the exit decision on how much time we allow before liquidation, since exits based on percent loss can come about all too rapidly and force us out just before any price turn around.)

The investor should accept that curtailing any option loss quickly through firm action, and not in idle viewing and hope, means that the valuable equity left, will be allowed entry into another, perhaps superior, opportunity that can make back what was lost.

At a time when transaction costs, commissions, are so low—of no consequence really—correcting errors should be an easy given. Note the following series of examples that argue for curtailing losses fast; statistics here don't lie:

| Losing Percent | Percent Gain to Break Even | Estimated Probabilities for Recovery in 3 Years: |
|---|---|---|
| 10 percent | 11 percent | A given |
| 20 percent | 25 percent | Almost an assurance |
| 30 percent | 43 percent | Very likely |
| 40 percent | 67 percent | Maybe |
| 50 percent | 100 percent | Unlikely...unless you study this book |
| 60 percent | 150 percent | Slim |
| 70 percent | 233 percent | Very, very doubtful |
| 80 percent | 400 percent | Two chances... |
| 90 percent | 900 percent | Take the write-off now! |

An early exit with almost all of our capital intact allows us to earn from a money market account while awaiting a superior investment.

Having invested in the broad index of NASDAQ in March 2000, and ignoring the message of falling price meant in the summer of 2002, that same $100,000 portfolio would be worth about $80,000 LESS, or valued at a scant $20,000. To have this amount reach the same $100,000 would require a whopping 400 percent return—don't bet the farm on that occurrence! You'd have more temporary enjoyment, and probable odds recovery, rolling shiny dice in Atlantic City.

A much smaller recovery percentage is preferable if having first taken protective action rather than just watching...and frustrating...and praying.

### The Easy Message:
### If we allow asset value to continually melt away,
### the road back to equality is virtually an impossible event.

And one added point: investing in an index such as above means virtual certainty some value always remains, bleak as it might get—all components can't all go bankrupt. Compare that to having regrettably owned World Com, Enron, Tyco and even once mighty Polaroid—individual debacles du jour.

### The Easy Lesson:
### Never allow losses to ever get out of hand! The road back is
### much, much too hard.

### Be Careful with Percentage Losses

Still another caveat regarding taking a loss: percentage losses can be misleading and alter the perception of the degree to what constitutes an acceptable loss of equity value.

Take an investor who starts with a $50,000 account and through shrewd selections manages to rally the account to $250,000. If the entirety of the account was to always remain at risk, and a nasty bear market/correction began, the investor might suffer a greater than "100 percent" loss of their original principal amount. How?

If the market or invested industry sectors were to repeat October 1987-like declines and drop 40 percent, the above account would be worth $150,000, amounting to a $100,000 "haircut." Although this represents "only" a 40 percent slide "from the top," it is more than twice the original account valuation: $100,000 versus $50,000. If our investor valued a 50 percent loss from his original as the most he would tolerate, here is $25,000 absolute dollars, and the $100,000 paper profit loss is four times that maximum sum! It is better to understand keeping all monies at risk, at all times, and might mean a far greater loss in actual dollars than the original actual dollar amount once thought to be a maximum allowable downside. The markets care not as to your tolerance for financial pain and might make you pay several times what was once thought as enough. Be careful with percentage numbers.

## Negative Investment Mathematics

We have already learned that the "winner" regarding investment returns is the one with the greatest <u>percentage return</u> over a measuring period that the sheer magnitude of dollars gained is secondary to percentage returns. We also know that attention to price occurrence is far preferred to guesswork for citing when and where price tops and bottoms might occur. We have also discussed that diversity is always a two-way street. The greater the margin of safety in having many also means lesser the potential overall return, since money is being spread rather than concentrated.

In elementary math we also learn to understand that percentages above 100 percent are possible, and below -100 percent aren't, in almost every measure. Investment history tells us having investments run out to 300 percent and 700 percent, or even multiples of 1,000 percent gains isn't impossible, albeit unlikely. Sitting "silent" through these types of advances certainly allows for the occurrence of extreme percent returns mainly because we cannot know just how high "high" might get. And we do want to be around if the price of what we own ultimately races for the stars. Just how high will investors in a panic bid our holdings? Therefore, presupposing where a top might be is often a foolish and expensive exercise. Simply wait for the price evidence to appear.

But a curious thing takes place when discussing investment loss. Investors appear naïve as to just how <u>devastating</u> very small percentage losses on very large portfolios can be, even through they are removing many years of totaled 200 percent, 300 percent, or maybe 400 percent plus profits under various meltdown conditions.

All of the total monies that percentage advances may amount to still represent no more than 100 percent of a current portfolio value. That is to say, you don't have a "450 percent" portfolio to lose! It remains 100 percentage points and that's the good news. The sour news is that if all those monies remain actively exposed to the market or if they always remain invested someplace, the small 15 and 20 percent sector or market "hits" brutally expose the dollars built up during those previous huge percent returns. It means a profitable particular portion of your portfolio that may have taken years to develop, can easily be shred many times over by frequent small percent losses, since there is but a single 100 percent figure to work against. (It's the real reason why portfolio diversity is so profound working over many years: significant individual issue losses cannot impact the portfolio, since the assets would be non-correlated — that is, have but slight price co-movement characteristics.) Note these next two examples:

*In fiction: suppose an investor starts with $25,000 and through some luck, skill and market timing has the good fortune to see that amount balloon to $200,000 in a decade's time. Now the $200,000 figure still represents 100 percent of what can be lost—not the actual 700 percent appreciation figure. A potential 30 percent bear market removes $60,000. The new 100 percent total is $140,000. A few small mistakes or one large one might remove another 25 percent and our new 100 percent total figure is now a bit over $100,000—granted still over 300 percent appreciation from* commencement, *but with only two sizeable losses. What if there was a third? What if a wrong sector bet was placed and a large portion of the original high at $200,000 was exposed, and -70 percent absorbed? One need only look at the internet from the late 1990s into 2000 to have seen this play out.*

*In reality: had you bought Cisco Systems on its public debut and held out against the urge to cash in for approximately ten years, and while the multiple thousands and thousands of percentage point profits you've earned, is very, very enviable, from only mid-March 2000 through late-March 2001 you would have passively also lost nearly 80 percent of all those ten years of gains. In a 12 month stretch—one significant bearish technology period—more than what "12,000 percentage points" of gains amounted to were next lost on a real -80 percent price plunge. Why would one expose that much prior success to obvious downside momentum? Why ever! We're not gene-splicing. Take protective posture always! Protect your wealth with potential liquidation at downside limits of perhaps -10 percent to -15 percent levels!*

Suppose your Cisco holdings were being counted on to fund a comfortable retirement in the years 1999 through 2000. Surprise! Your nest egg is now 1/5 of what it had been—as of 10/2002, 1/10!! And while long-term holders might be bailed out—at least at some point—what if that "point" (time period) coincides with an urgent usage for those monies? What does the retiree do? Continue to work, live on less, and wait for another decade to recoup? Investors have come to accept that over the long-term all will be there when they are ready. Even our equity markets aren't that sporting!

The stock you own at 100 that drops to 50, an obvious 50 percent hit and 50 point numeric plunge, when next bought at 50 by you or anyone, and ridden to 100, means a 100 percent return for the same 50 point ride. Obviously, the measuring base number for tallying return accounts for the difference: 100 in the first case, 50 in the second. Don't miss the important inference: the same point's movement when falling robs you far greater in percentage terms, than when rising. An investor is hurt twice as much under the same numeric price movement with prices falling, as compared to rising.

The Cisco drop in early April 2001 to about 13, about an 80 percent falloff from its 82 high, could have still provided another 50 percent to short investors with only a 6 numeric point fall! (When stocks reach very low absolute price, with almost all the numeric price risk removed and assuming the company remains viable, they present enormous upward percentage potential. Cisco at 6, would need just a 6 point upward move to yield a 100 percent return. Bet they indeed will be around for many years; CEO, John Chambers, is just too skilled.)

The point is that "downside math" can rob you far more quickly of the years and decades of investment gains if the monies are always 100 percent exposed in "bearish" periods or if you allow small losses to become significant. Regardless from where you start, the entirety of what you are left with is still only a 100 percent figure, and a few 30 percent surprises are worth dodging.

**Avoidance of the Downside Is the Compelling Lesson:**
**Always, always, limit our downside exposure.**

## Trying to Balance the Tradeoff between Quick Liquidation & Loss Control

We cannot control how soon Wall Street will see our reasoning for a transaction—we can only control the extent of our willingness to bet they will. We really do this by controlling loss. Yet if we liquidate too soon we give up the judgment for our initial purchase; waiting a bit too long can be ruthless and unforgiving. It seems the market's influence on all of this is where our edge is.

For example, if we think our short stock might sink and it doesn't quickly, a new tear in the overall market probably will revive us. So before starting liquidation at a loss, sense how close the market, or our investment's sector, might be to helping us. It is the very best of an investment situation to be firmly within a fast trend and on the right side of it; it's not something you want to see develop after having given up and sold. Worse still, at a quick loss.

# Why We Base Sell Decisions on Price Alone & Not Always on Time Held

As you might guess, basing equity selling decisions on the length of time we hold an investment has dire consequences if the markets play havoc with normal expectations. In other words, if the market deems you incorrect regarding your price assessment and you have "owned" the stock four minutes and are already losing enough to cause you pain and anxiety, it means you should exit the position.

**You do this because the market, the sector, or security itself, can bring on far more pain; and if you do not control the selling function, the market will dictate an exit option for you...that isn't advised.**

And if you have held a position for many months or perhaps years awaiting redemption and have experienced no positive return, then, at minimum, the time value of money was your loss.

Final points: there are few things within the investment playground where we enjoy control. We determine a buy point and we later decide the selling area. Between these two sole acts, we are nothing but observers at the will and whim of momentum and little else. You have to agree that your reasons for price movement under your time parameters can't possibly be the same as all the owners of the very same position. How could they possibly? They why expect and probably demand prices to react as you fashion? It makes NO sense, nor should it. Trending price makes sense.

# Positioning for the Opening Transaction— Initial Strategy & Selection Process

## Preliminary Pre-Transaction

### *Practical Money Mindset*

Returning to prior chapters, we know that investing with monies that are deemed too precious, too important, is not a reasoned choice and is not advised. Utilize a 10 to 15 percent exposure, based on the entirety of your investment assets, for investment other than long-term, until experiences command a differing policy!

Depending upon your monetary investment goal for a particular strategy, or perhaps as a general guide, might determine the amount of money invested in each transaction. For short-term type thinking, the $5,000 investment with a correct 10 percent move might throw off $500 in hours or even minutes. The same 10 percent on a $1,000 investment "yields" $100 <u>and</u> means if the profits goal was to liquidate when any $100 *was* available, hundreds and hundreds of ideas and commissions and anxiety would be demanded to earn a sizeable amount of money. It's *a day trader's delight*. At $10,000 with 10 percent success will bring a return of $1,000, but naturally the dollar risk, if wrong, proportionately increases. It is necessary to determine what the goal of each investment is, prior to its initiation.

The following could easily be a real world example:

Assume we intend to utilize investing as the core of our annual income. A yearly goal of $50,000 is desired. Let's see at what levels of <u>activity</u>, and <u>proficiency</u>, we will need to fulfill our goal.

> If investing $5000 in each transaction,
>
> earning 20 percent once per month = $12,000 annually
> earning 40 percent once per month = $24,000 annually
> earning 40 percent twice per month = $48,000 annually
> earning 40 percent weekly = $100, 000+ annually

We actually see in theoretical money terms, if these <u>short-term</u> investment results are <u>always</u> correct—*an impossibility*—and by investing $5,000 every other week, with a 40 percent net return factor, we meet our monetary goal of $50K per year. This is a doubtful likelihood!

Losses do need to be factored in and repeated. Forty percent returns are more storied than played out. Even our practical sense tells us there are very few full-time investors—heaven forbid, traders—that can truthfully say, "I made $50,000 last year from my investments." How many can you name?

In sum: intending to earn a living—never mind one substantive—from our investment skills is for most of us impossible, unless the amount of money we begin with is large, or we are creating a day-to-day to weekly series of ideas and short-term exposure and being correct very often. So let's change the assumed all-positive results to average and smaller net results, and let's start with a fatter bankroll:

> If investing $25,000 in each transaction,
> earning net 20 percent once each month = $60,000 annually
>
> If investing $50,000 in each transaction,
> earning net 20 percent once each month = $120,000 annually

Now the possibilities certainly appear more promising. But don't yet resign!

As we visualize the various changing elements, it becomes apparent that money grows exponentially as the initial "bet" grows in size, but large dollars also turns into hard losses when wrong—not the few hundred that we might easily stomach. The moral: invest enough to make "winning" appealing, but not so much as to cause emotional turmoil. This balance can only be individually determined through experience.

The above numbers will not lie! If an investor required earnings of $100,000 each year from perhaps their investments, or from securities investing as their full-time employment, it would mean nearly $2,000 is being consistently averaged each week—quite atypical!

The worst thing that can occur is the dollars illusion when an investor doesn't recognize the financial "formula" required to seize financial goals and simply invests with nary a plan—the *"We'll see what happens" approach*. What you first need to know is how much money you require and then what that respective level of success demands before attaining your financial goals.

## Trade on Paper First, & Don't Cheat with Yourself

Until you can get very comfortable with the ideas contained within this book, it is wiser to trade on paper using real-life pricing and reacting as if it were real money. This way, you see how pricing and trends evolve and affect results, without any expensive ramifications. Make your mistakes on paper. However, the missing component of anxiety, and its effect, cannot be induced if the transaction is one of just "paper tests." An alternative would be to agree to do something difficult if you lose some amount, or reward yourself above a certain profit. At least then you are accounting for results in some way and the missing component of anxiety is a bit introduced.

You should firmly agree to the supposed price you are buying and selling at, without the temptation of changing. Allow the transaction to be priced just as you would have to in the real world. For a prospective practice purchase, write down the time, and the ask price, and assume you bought the security there; for sales, use the bid price. Even through you might be capable of shaving a little from either, for the "make-believe education" use the actual bid/ask prices.

Just do everything as you would, as if it was real money. It may be impossible to actually emotionally recreate the actual transaction, but if you are willing to penalize and reward yourself you might get close to replicating real emotions from the hypothetical results.

## Putting Emotions on a Realistic Foundation

A reread of Chapter Nine should suffice...focus on pre-position realistic probabilities. Keep assumptions few! Monitor what is occurring from the evidence of price and invest consistent with that movement.

## Juggling Investment Alternatives, Setting up to Begin

Thankfully, since the mid 1990s, there have been hoards of investment software programs providing an almost limitless number of stocks and industry sectors that we can follow. Most have an automated type of screening analysis following pre-set criteria, so that manual review of each stock, each night, isn't necessary. When following thousands of companies, computer automation isn't only helpful, it's essential.

Regardless of which software you choose, make sure it can capture industry and market charting track an unlimited number of the individual stocks you might wish to follow, the extent to which should be limited only to your willingness to input the initial information and subsequently monitor price.

Before actual trading takes place, it is recommended that any serious investor keep a running diary of all transactions containing: the date and reason for the initial execution, the purchase price, what occurred during the entirety of the time it was held, the date of the exit and the reasons why, the price received, and what happened shortly thereafter. Also include the broad markets response during all the above. Maintaining this discipline for years as to what had been done, why it did or didn't work, will provide superlative insight into what can be done to improve. We do not want to <u>retry mistakes</u>—ever; we do want to recreate our successes. Each transaction, and especially each losing transaction, is supposed to be a lasting education, unlike practical life, where it often isn't. Duplicated investment mistakes will hurt just as much the second time. We must learn from all our errors and repeat all winning strategies!

### Try to Initiate Positions of Some Consequence

Whenever an investment idea is brought into reality should also have an accompanying degree of confidence proofed by the placement of a sufficient enough of a position. When correct, it is quite worthwhile having done so, yet not so large as to cause overburdened anxiety. The idea of a small get-your-feet-wet trade is too indicative of a lack of conviction and should be avoided.

Another reason why consequential is preferred, is that if the position is profitable but then starts to wane, there isn't the tendency to <u>avoid</u> selling the otherwise too small position or "How bad could it get, I only have 100 shares" mentality. Realistically, much can happen; it is still money at play. We simply should not permit even a seemingly small position to inhibit a normal investment philosophy. This means when it's time to transact on price, do so. It is too easy to psyche yourself out when owning "just a few shares."

Lastly, placing transactions should never be done just to be "in the market." If there isn't sizable reward in front of you, avoid doing anything until your conviction is improved. Investment is purposeful activity. It shouldn't be lightly treated where simple participation becomes a need, which often invokes less, or no, discipline.

## The Intermediate/Long-Term Investing Sequence

If you are intending that a presumed transaction be for intermediate or long-term then examine all of the following. The probable extent to which you are successful will depend upon how many of the following elements are <u>favorable</u> before you initiate a transaction. With more than 6,000 actively traded stocks, numerous indices and sectors, and with 4,700 stocks having available options, and the computerization of investment software, running low on potential strategies isn't going to happen.

Insist all of the following factors be favorable or find a stock where almost all are, or patiently wait. In today's markets one large successful transaction could yield annual income magnitude results depending upon the original amount invested.

## First & Foremost...Determine Trend Formation/Direction

The price action/direction of the market and industry trend you intend to be investing in will be crucial and a defining initial step to your ultimate success.

We know that most stocks, and therefore most industries, will follow the broad markets as a whole.

We look first to find what trend the market may be in, or about to be in. If it is definable—that being unmistakably upward or downward—then we always want to be invested in a similar direction.

We don't allow our usually <u>bullish</u> preoccupation to cloud evident bear trends and sectors. Examples: Internet blowup and NASDAQ falloff March 2000. Huge money was there for the taking in harmony with that very bearish and lengthy classic trend—Internet stocks crumbling 100 and 200 points! That falling price trend and the loss within the S&P 500 as well, shouldn't have been missed. There was a seven trillion dollar loss in equity value! (In the third quarter of 2002, mutual funds had less than <u>1/10 of 1 percent of their holdings short</u>, and only about 60 out of 8,400 mutual funds made any money, as stock prices plummeted!)

Did they have to guess the top? No. But they had to stay awake as prices cascaded downward and seldom stopped. Whether we could have estimated the timing of when the markets would shun those lofty valuations and puffed stories was irrelevant since most investors just watched it continually play out and down. Most of us—at times to a fault—are too bullish; you can generally make money far greater deeper and even faster when stocks plummet as compared to when they advance.

Investors need to remember that intermediate price momentum by its definition has changing patience and after a period of calendar time—that being about perhaps four or six weeks—a trend that can't reassert itself, may not be able to, and has changed its direction. Rather than looking to buy the dips in assumed continuing bull markets, might we not observe the <u>evident pricing proof</u> of the advent of a bear market's beginning or intermediate change of direction? Wall Street's roads are not all directionally north.

A maximum correction in an ongoing bull markets tends to be at 20 to 25 per cent declines from highs. Regarding the NASDAQ, that meant the 4,000 level found in late March 2000, only a few weeks after the 5,000 plus high had been seen. If falling prices fall beneath this 20 to 25 percent area, it is probably indicating a long-term trend change, one from bullish to bearish. Similarly if a strong upward bias cannot restart after two months of neutral price action, is it possible the upward bias has passed? The point is you have to be sensitive to price and calendar changes if the prior trend is now reversing! The last tact is to be looking for price points at which to be buying when the overall sell dynamic is beginning to emerge as dominant. You need to focus on the current state of pricing and become objective and determine market trend direction.

Evident enduring price action that is unmistakably bullish or bearish and not as yet in any extreme price formation should give us an easy direction to follow. We merely observe the trend direction and accept it as lasting until change is in evidence by price. However, there are times when price gives us less of an obvious tip as to direction.

## Has a New Intermediate- or Long-Term Trend Begun?
## A Huge Money Question

This is often a period after protracted advancing or declining markets when everyone wonders when the next trend direction will start.

We have learned that we will only measure the extent of a trends move into history through rear view price observation. We know that if we do not make an educated guess as to a true move after an apparent beginning, our waiting will have cost us potential profits if we thus insist upon apparent "certainty" before acting. *(Naturally this certainty can only be measured from an assumed prior point to where you are.)* It is a true catch 22 problem. If you wait too long for trend certainty you do potential; if you act too hastily to capture every available investment point, you do so impulsively, with guesswork, without any of the required pricing evidence that the trend is yet real.

The *preferred and ideal* time to initiate a transaction to parallel the expected markets movement during the intermediate trend is certainly coincident with the market's start, but rarely is this done. When it is, it is an example where the randomness of short-term movement was met with a fortunate investment that coincided with the market's new longer direction. As we already know, the skill level in calling the start of trends, be it up or down, is very suspect. *There is slight evidence to suggest a skill level is at play in calling turns or some deductive element. We seem to feel everything that happens to our investments needs to be explained on a rational basis.*

The mere application of an unbiased view as to what is occurring to price and not what might or should is the wise approach. Only after the fact, can we know if there is a new trend in what we would assume would be of at least average duration—but that, too, we cannot know until its history has played out. Our markets do not have to move in any direction at a specific time, and can stop their thrust rather abruptly. But this does not mean that they reverse direction in great magnitude on a dime—which they rarely do. And the trend stoppage might mean only a sideways move.

It is very important to note the slope from a price graph, that being the intensity of optimism or pessimism of a price trend. Entrance or even continuance in one too overbought—maybe hyperbolic—or too oversold, is prescription for failure. You cannot expect extremes in trend to last very long—days, maybe a week. We would prefer moderate trending, for enduring normal trend continuance.

Then what are their hints as to a true beginning? Our challenge is to find out if predictable information is attainable and, if it is, are we as certain as to its usefulness that we will dare lay out our investment dollars for that presumed ten week or so average duration? How do we know? Do these trends begin internally based on price or externally from news? At what point is it real—at two weeks, at four? Will this move be of typical measure? Is there an always answer? The answer to these questions is in...probabilities, tendencies. What a shock!

The impetus for the start of these trends will almost always be from technical factors—a double bottom or top, a breakout of a prior resistance level, a nasty correction or lengthy advance coincident with a longer-term support and resistance areas. Or, they may start from very consequential fundamental and or economic factors, but usually don't. Maybe the Federal Reserve has reversed years of tight money posture. From whatever the cause, they become genuine only with one continual directional trending price action—from either advancing market price action alone, or naturally, if pricing is becoming murderously sour, declining market price action.

A great advantage for determination is that we can start with no more than three key market indices and then look at our intended industry, rather than reviewing hundreds of individual stock charts which, together, don't portend what simple S&P 500 or Dow Jones 30 Industrials or NASDAQ price observation does. The market where you intend to invest is where you more narrowly focus for market trend insight. *(Even though when viewed over multi-year periods, these market indices will tend to have price patterns almost identical, they can deviate from one another for shorter periods.)*

When these broad market averages have been very badly hurt, it almost always requires a fair amount of time before investors feel enough confidence to en masse begin a sustainable rally. This period is termed "base building." Emotionally, it's confidence building. It's time for investors to buy a consensus before believing the prior trend action is complete. *The human psyche can tolerate missing opportunities far better than losing money, so they tend to err on the side of caution before dynamic decisions get in place, leading to lasting moves.*

It's also fact that depending upon the **severity** of any prior downside period, the bloodied market may have very little downside exposure, even if it can't quickly rise. Conversely, the NASDAQ in March 2000 could have been reasoned to have very little <u>upside</u> strength, even if it might not immediately fall apart. A short position or puts exposure at that period would have entailed really only mild risk.

Since we never know for certain when major advances at bottoms are in fact starting, and if the downside had been extreme, when the advance does come, it can catapult pricing very quickly. Especially when the prior trend had been brutal, since investors impatiently awaiting and assuming new bargains often jump in unison even when they only suspect <u>the time</u> is appropriate.

A compelling reason after the first several days of upward price action (most especially when the plurality of market breath—advances over decliners—is vast!) and coincident bullish technical chart action, and having had some time pass from the low point, is that some bullish exposure is warranted. Why?

Primarily because trend is then behaving upward, and only the degree of proof is important. It might just take longer than a few days to induce a real rally. With no exposure, you might dearly pay for being too careful, because downside potential is so limited in extent, and upside surprise is potentially so potent. Admittedly, the catch

22 paradox is always present in the early stages, but immediate exits will result in little negative effect if a move is <u>still not genuine</u>. If it's not the "real deal," you simply sell and sideline your investment capital, but still remain very attentive. Your attendant loss is very limited, since so much prior selling had already preceded it. History in these instances might help us.

### The Key:
### What maximum percentage appreciation from a market bottom, or depreciation off a market top, would have signaled that a new trend, in fact, was in place?

For example, does history show that after every 30 percent advance off the prior low point, a new bull market was ultimately to surface? The answer is yet to be known but these are areas worth pursuit since they add to our learning the correct probabilities of price action.

All right, but if it's starting—up or down—how do we know how long this intermediate move will last? Is there a point in time at which, if passed, more upside/downside will continue? And can we know by how much it might become an ongoing historically normal advance or decline?

The respective answers are:

We don't, not exactly, and no. The prospective durability (in calendar time) of a move will only be known with certainty after its occurrence. It is also reasonable that the degree of the degree of <u>magnitude</u> and <u>duration</u> that preceded the new trend will lend some evidence to new expectations. Two examples:

Markets that have been red hot and have the potential of becoming vastly overbought would be assumed to give back <u>much more</u> in a bear market decline than if the prior advance was very mild.

History has taught us that the longer—in calendar passage—the advance (or declines) can last after initiation, the more probable they will endure—that is, become genuine; simply trend continuance. If 15 percent had been added on in the past three months from the low point, and if that advance can muster another several weeks of strength, then maybe a bit more upside, investor disposition would be increasingly more bullish. Even though time passage always mutes memory and the belief that more of the prior trend is still to come, it is wisest to be less concerned with defining a market trend than participating in it. If it plays out as not being a new major trend, is it not worth capturing some portion of any lasting move, even one of retracement? There isn't a one perfect rule to signal continuance or duration—we learn through monitoring. This really is good, because if blind acceptance of old rules were always followed without demanding they maintain their prescience, we would be more apt to be unpleasantly surprised during the times they don't work. We are always better prepared remaining attentive and not too assumptive.

It would be great to say after 15 days of upside trading with an eight percent S&P 500 advance that the suspected bottom was in place, an all-clear flag is raised by the folks at Merrill, and we then back up the truck and buy with both hands. Not in a real investment world.

## Based on Directional Outlook, Choose the Strongest or Weakest Industry in Price Direction Similar to the Market

We next look to position ourselves within industries that technically parallel the respective broad market's trend. (This should be simple; most security firms that provide research as well as retail investment firms will have nearly 100 different industries. It is also exceedingly beneficial!) You want to invest in industry price trends that offer evident price conviction. They are trending up or down parallel to "your" market choice and not yet either extreme in price momentum or aging of the move. The 17-day RSI of the industry chosen isn't much greater than 70 for upward trending continuance and less than 30 for downward, and is moving in an even more significant direction as the market. *If the market is headed down we find industry groups falling even faster on a relative basis choose those weaker than the respective market. Relative strength/weakness works here as well.*

Being in the right industries is easier than choosing the right stock, and industry trends have more directional staying power. Investors may switch between hot sectors/industries very frequently but once in motion, they tend to remain. It is termed "sector rotation." To take maximum advantage of where the "momentum money" is headed requires, at minimum, intra-week monitoring.

If the market's direction and the prospective industries are moving in opposite directions—and remember depending upon the market's fervor, not very typical then choose an alternative industry and stock where the price trends are the same. Or, invest only with a very short-term period—no exceptions.

If the market's direction is quite evident and the prospective industry is neutral, or vice versa, you might still try and select stocks from that industry, but first observe they are in a parallel trend with the market. *The reasoning is that a neutral or market price direction will not impact its sister component.*

The power of the market's direction if it is strong or weak enough will become the catalyst which will ultimately make almost all industries, and then all stocks, side with its broad advance or decline. We simply never want to be in an industry (no more than in a stock) that is trying to buck the broad market's intermediate to long-term direction.

* An important caveat when using markets as a price forecasting guide, is apparent optimism or pessimism by way of their actual price index compared to what unweighted members of those markets might be doing. In 2000 and 2001, the NASDAQ index fell in a big way. It did so because the most significant portion of it by

the computed method of market capitalization was technologically driven. Yet the average of NASDAQ issues did rise! How do we look to the market, the NASDAQ, for direction when its price level is falling because of its cap weighting bias favoring technology? Do we just forget about acceptable non-technology opportunities which might be rising, if the index—the NASDAQ market—is falling and bearish?

The answer, as it generally is, will be found in more keen observation of the sector within NASDAQ where we might wish to invest.

If we wish to purchase a paper company trading on NASDAQ as the index sinks, we can do so provided it is in an upward trend and possesses the other necessary considerations. While this violates our premise that we allow the respective market index to guide us, when an index such as NASDAQ is so affected by one segment, such as technology, we can still invest if where we intend to place capital is itself strong in price trend, and preferably, so too is the true average NASDAQ issue. Hence blind guidance on the NASDAQ market index when investing is too simplistic.

Other examples: you intend to buy a tech stock on NASDAQ. If the overall NASDAQ is making lows, and a NASDAQ technology index is as well, then do not purchase a technology stock on the NASDAQ, expecting a long upward bias...unless you enjoy losing a lot of money.

You believe a large S&P 500 rally is likely and maybe has started. You cite the pharmaceuticals industry as where you want to invest. You see its trend is neutral. You can still look within that industry and select the best price-performing company, since the industry component isn't bearish trend was that the case, likely to hurt the buying of a pharmaceutical stock by a negative industry effect.

Reason suggests the Dow will continue falling and the financials already looking weak will remain so. You investigate within that industry and find the worst—the weakest—acting stock and either short it or purchase puts. In this manner you are investing consistent with the current market, industry, and stock trend, are all bearish.

You love small stocks and you watch the Russell 2000, its typical benchmark, for clues. If that index is very strong, it's a fair bet that most small stocks will also be in bullish trends. The correct strategy: you would invest on the long side—purchase stock or call options—assuming a continuing upward price momentum for both its industry and the single stock.

If an intermediate trend has been in place for months or a long-term trend for perhaps four to five years, both by historic average aging, the best investment tact at that point for initiating new positions, should be more short-term focused. Try to trade in-between short- to intermediate-term moves, since most of the price dynamic may be history. (Yet in trying to obtain as much as possible from each upward move, exiting when due, intending to buy back, would be pure short-term strategies by definition—and by now, as we know, tough to master. Contrast this with remaining mostly passive throughout the entirety of an intermediate or long-term duration—with the few exceptions of severe overbought/oversold periods—having arrived on the scene early. This is where the big money is to be found. It isn't on short-term trading floors!)

# Sequencing Your Opening Transaction for the Specific Investment

### Only Invest in the Current Directional Price Trend That Is Now Evident for This Security

Confine your choices to two: Clearly Upward Trending and Clearly Downward Trending. Insist that the specific investment also parallel the direction of its industry and the broad market. Trends not too steep or too shallow for advancing, not declining too much or too downwardly meek for declines. In this manner, the trends move unto themselves and invoke no notice, nor demand investor reaction, and can continue their natural trending pattern. *Compare this to a very influential rise or fall, which would probably provoke investor action and perhaps significant enough to alter the existing trend.*

The modern investor has at their arsenal a vast number of choices that has no apparent end. Investments can be made in indices representing almost any industry or market, as well as a lone stock selection. An almost pure investment trend will always exist someplace. For example, if it were assumed that technology were to advance, rather than selecting an individual stock issue, an investment could be chosen in an index or exchange traded fund representing all of technology, like the Morgan Stanley High Tech Index or, in semiconductors, the SOX Index. If gold were thought to represent opportunity—maybe an index comprising gold stocks. This should mean that if a subsequent price trend consistent with what you expected did materialize, the potential for profitability should be realized.

### The Stock's Current Technicals & Indicators Favor Right Now!

The RSI isn't too high greater than 70, signaling overbought. For upward strategies, it's too weak if below 35, or too oversold, for bearish ideas.

No more than four consecutive days have gone counter to the assumed trend we are intending to invest in—*and consider the magnitude of absolute price over these periods.* More might prove beyond just mild and expected "retracements" of the current trend. If it's five, and clearly six days or longer, watch out—a trend change for that particular stock might be brewing.

The investments price trend isn't immediately approaching strong technical price resistance for upward, or strong support for a downward-biased investment strategy.

Price isn't too far above its 200 DMA for upward (maybe 70 percent, yet this varies); or less than 25 percent for downward.

The last day or two haven't risen outside the range of normal in chart pattern terms. Or today the investment hasn't already experienced a price move well above/below the prior close, which might indicate at least a fast counter-move to normalize this day's abnormal action. Really check the investment's technical picture closely.

### Specific Company, or Eventful Market, News Isn't Imminent...Know What is Expected from Your Investment & from Industry Leaders

Research or trade reports, conferences, potential news and expected EPS announcements are all likely to have at least transitory influence for upward/downward bias. If you cannot know for sure what effect a due event might have—and you almost always cannot—it might be wiser to wait through the event or news dissemination. While you can witness the trend in motion, expected news when viewed by investors unfavorable to your anticipated response can destroy even any short-term profit.

Consider announced earnings: if they are good, the stock might sell off in the anticipation. If they are bad, there could be punishing downside price action. Here you could be reducing investing to a gamble. The warning label: don't—or try not to—initiate transactions with EPS announcements pending, and never when the market's psychology is very unforgiving. Your investment's sorry story won't likely be spared. (When the market is very healthy, a poor news item will have much less effect so holding off until the announcement isn't as important.)

## Move to Initiate the Initial Investment Transaction, Either:

### Initiate an Investment Position Outright or on Margin

If you have completed all the above steps after thorough research, place the transaction order. You cannot earn an investment profit without the courage to place the securities transaction.

### Select the "Probabilities Best" Options Strategy

Select the right security, with the best option series, to ride the anticipated trending wave to prosperity.

You know when to initiate a security transaction and we have learned that with the markets in gear, the probabilities are overwhelming; their leading wind will hasten our trending stock and following option. Now let's confine our search to which option series and how much calendar time we should pay for.

### An Options Selection Process Checklist

Our choice can be in-the-money, at-the-money or out-of-the-money. Each has advantages and disadvantages. Of course, options have unique pros and cons. In short, where possible, invest in stock, or short stock, positions. It's safer, purer, less expensive and time isn't an issue—and you may enjoy some profits.

### In-the-Money Options

When the stock price is above the chosen strike price, in the case for call options, or if below the chosen strike price with put options, the option is said to be in-the-money and has immediate "intrinsic" value. The <u>deeper</u> in-the-money, the more an option will act like its stock price, moving in about equal proportion and in far smaller percentage terms. The more you desire your option to act like its stock, the deeper in-the-money you go, but more than one stage (the next series above/below the current price) isn't necessary.

The advantages are a direct, virtual one-to-one, option-to-stock price relationship and any adverse stock price move represents much lower percent loss on these types of options. Here you needn't pay for calendar time, since any movement in the direction you expect should result in immediate profit.

The downside for in-the-money options is the opposite of the advantages—when correct, you don't have significant upside percentage profits, and you always pay for more significant premium, $5, $500, or better isn't abnormal.

### Out-of-the Money Options

The more common tact—and far more mistakenly—is to choose an option series where the current stock price is below the exercise price in the case of calls or bullish intentions, and in instances where bearish movement is expected, it's where the stock price is above the exercise price.

The largest percentage gains occur with these types, since the base price from where one price begins—the options initial acquisition price—is so much smaller than with in-the-money positions. When correct in significant ways, these "long shot" types will bring about very large percentage returns; when wrong to any degree, means parting with substantial portions of options capital. These option types are best utilized when you are the seller, not when you are the owner.

If you input your option choices through the Black Scholes Model for estimating returns for some anticipated price movement, it will become obvious which selected option, in-the-money versus out-of-the-money, for the same expected point movement would yield the greater return. Going home with some options money is preferable to succumbing to the lure alone of potential high percent returns.

### At-the-Money Options

These occur when stock price and options exercise price are almost exactly equal and they are a compromise of the other two in price action and potential.

The curt answer as to the ideal of the three choices is of course to buy the lowest out-of-the-money calls and puts the most conservative—but—only if you are going to be right. The frequency of success is higher with in-the-monies; the potential is greatest with out-of-the-monies. Actually, the element of time enters as well. Never buy out-of-the-monies if expiration is very close, for obvious reasons. The more conservative method is to purchase in-the-money…also, over years this should prove far more lucrative!

## Determine Probable Future Options Pricing

The best use of the Black Scholes Model or similar options pricing models, is in their providing what the likely price of any option should be, based on the investor expectation of a future stock price. It is very essential to have the model compute estimated options pricing for your many alternatives <u>before</u> you place a trade, so you will know how to handle the "what ifs."

## Strike Price Determination

The more confident you are, the more "venturesome"—maybe even want for greed is correct wording—and the more time you have, the more out-of-the-money options become appropriate selections—yet don't, don't, don't try and go more than one series away from current price. Keep the expected stock price movement to the exercise price level between 5 and 10 percent. Do this so that if the stock price performs as expected, the option will advance in value in some <u>close approximation </u>of a one-to-one stock price move.

In any event, buying options at a distance—out-of-the-monies—from current price necessitates too much stock price movement which will never be reflected in the <u>options price</u> to the extent it should, even when you are correct. We already know that if you were wrong and the stock ran opposite where it was expected to go, or stands silent, or moves far too slowly, you risk large percentage losses.

Examples using the Black Scholes Model:

*Stock price at 70, volatility of 30 (average), expiration in two months; using in–the-money and out-of-the money call options.*

| Assumed Price : | + 20% | + 10% | 0% | - 5% Movement |
|---|---|---|---|---|
| **65 Series     IN THE MONEY OPTIONS** | | | | |
| STOCK/OPTION PRICE: Beginning 70/6.48 | | | | |
| After 30 days | 84/19.20 | 77/12.2 | 70/5.48 | 66/1.30 |
| | or 196% | or 88% | or 15% | or 80% |
| Intrinsic Value | 19 | 12 | 5 | 1 |
| Time Premium | .20 | .20 | .48 | .30 |
| On Expiration Date | 84/19.00 | 77/12.0 | 70/5.00 | 66/1.00 |
| | or 193% | or 85% | or 23% | or 84% |
| **75 Series  OUT-OF-THE-MONEY OPTIONS** | | | | |
| STOCK/OPTION PRICE: Beginning 70/1.50 | | | | |
| After 30 days | 84/ 9.33 | 77/ 3.49 | 70/ .53 | 66/ .00 |
| | or 522% | or 133% | or 65% | or 100% |
| Intrinsic Value | 9 | 2 | 0 | 0 |
| Time Premium | .33 | 1.49 | .53 | 0 |
| On Expiration Date | 84/ 9.00 | 77/ 2.00 | 70/ .00 | 66/ .00 |
| | or 500% | or 33% | or 100% | or 100% |

The above illustrates the more correct you are in terms of the stocks movement, the more advantageous out-of-the-money options may become. Of course, the element of time—when the stock price makes you correct—is a major factor. After our sample 20 percent advance and at the end of 30 days—about 22 trading sessions— the 75 call series yields a 522 percent return as compared to having purchased the 65 series, returning 196 percent. *(Conversely, being even slightly wrong—stock moving—5 percent or doing nothing [0 percent column], can mean eventual complete loss with the 75 series, the out-of-the-money choice.)*

Next, compare the two at a 10 percent stock price appreciation after 30 days: 133 percent to 88 percent. Why the percent falloff if it's still the same 10 percent move? Simply because the 75 series with 10 percent stock movement is but two points above the strike price and the possibility always exists that the stock might fall and the option become eventually worthless. Of course, never forget that the amount the stock price is above the call strike price (its intrinsic value) hence in-the-money and must be reflected in the options price. This higher value, when compared to the lower base acquisition option price, reflects in much higher percent appreciation.

Note the change in intrinsic and time premium value between the two series. The higher the stock price becomes, the smaller the 65 series calls time premium is. Again, why?

Time premium or "the overvalue" is the amount of excess option premium bullish traders are willing to pay since there might yet be a higher price. However, as any stock becomes progressively deeper in-the-money, the smaller the probability of their paying for time value is, since the very deep in-the-monies are so expensive anyway and higher strike series might still be rewarding. On expiration, options cannot have a time premium...they expired. As time advances and the intrinsic value is expanding (the stock point movement in-the-money), fewer traders will pay the time premium for very high-price call options. In theory, the time premium should remain fairly consistent until expiration when it would have to vanish. In reality, it doesn't.

### To Be Volatile or Not—"Paying for the Ride"

One of the major components that affect the pricing of an option is its volatility, its "snap." There are differing methods to compute the level, but the standard deviation of price movement over the past 20 and 50 day periods are normal computational approaches. Note, however, the absence of long measuring periods or any market or industry effect and response—a number of missing elements. In purchasing a stock with high volatility and higher respective options series prices, you are presuming it will maintain its "quickness" and its price direction will continue to align the way you might hope.

It is known that in most cases, options with a high volatility component are not worth their "excess" pricing for a purchase strategy. To paraphrase author Bernie Schaffer in his book, "The Option Advisor"..."the best option trades are on trending stocks whose options are priced cheaply by the options pricing model relative to their true potential." The lesson then: choose lower volatility and always run the Black Scholes Model or one similar before initiating transactions to know where the options price should be if the underlying stock price moves to a specific price by a specific date. As already learned, this is the model's best use.

A common options term, implied volatility, is "new" volatility just factored into a stock whose investors anticipate great price variance, maybe just before an earnings release or significant news announcement. This is where the stock's normal volatility and direct reflection into its option series is suddenly higher so that one purchasing at that moment is paying far more in premium for acquisition than normal and, worst of all, that excess premium tends to wane almost immediately after the significant event that caused it has gone. The lesson: try and determine if a stock's normal volatility has been altered within its price by using the models—simply track its volatility—and, if so, always wait until more normal options pricing returns. *There is enough options risk without volunteering to take on more!*

It's fundamental to grasp that any stock price amount above the exercise price—regardless of effect—has to reflect itself in at least similar number in its call options price, since it is then in-the-money. This must mean that a lowly, staid, slow-to-move stock priced at 30 that gets dragged along in a bullish intermediate-term rage and hits 45, must have its 30 series call option worth 15, its then intrinsic value. This is far from "so," since that same 30 series call, with the stock having such low volatility, might have been priced at 1 the day the move started. Using the same circumstances, a high-volatility stock would have priced at 3 3/4 or possibly 4 3/4. The eventual percent appreciation is then very different: 15 sale price – 1 1/2 purchase price or 900 percent, or 15 – 3 3/4 and 300 percent. O.K., you would take either one, but the base price you start from has very sizeable ramifications for options than with stock, since with options pricing, one stage out-of-the-money is usually just 3 to 8 percent of the stock price. The point is, it tends to be low in price; subsequent higher sales usually represent a high percent return.

A stock with low volatility moving to 56 with a 50 strike price, will be worth at least 6 or more to maybe 1/4, with the added value of the time left until expiration. The same stock with a high-volatility element, might price its option at 7 1/4. The issue as to which is worth retention and or initial acquisition, is firstly, technical condition: which might advance the most, the quickest? Second, is the greater time premium, here 1 (7 1/4 – 6 intrinsic points, and which we know will eventually see zero), still to be maintained in the options total price if the stock moves upward? We already know it ultimately won't—because it can't. The more volatile issue <u>acquires preference</u> only if it has better price <u>potential</u> to make up for its higher initial cost. Unfortunately, you'll know on expiration.

Simple graphic or tabular proof—"price intensity"—can denote trending strength or weakness and measures the percentage return a stock is showing over some period of time. The inference is that price will continue to trend about the same amount over the same duration. This may or may not happen, but you should know how quickly it has moved during a trending period because it probably will maintain that pace again, absent some abnormal or company-specific effect. Examine the VRTS example in Figure 10.1 (next page).

The starting price point, Point A was near 88, and through the mid-October highs at about 167, Point B, the stock advanced almost 90 percent or about 30 percent each month. Veritas, you might guess, has very high volatility. Knowing of its 30 percent per month movement might tip a "short seller" or put buyer that if a bearish posture is warranted from price action, that extreme price movement could occur, and were one desirous of purchasing puts, a strike price even 20 percent out-of-the-money, or 30 points, might not be beyond reach in a downside charge. It's exactly what happened.

Now we know a 10 percent per annum is an average, start-to-finish yearly equity move, and less than 20 percent standard deviation. In no instance would 30 percent recurring monthly plus or minus moves ever be anticipated for any stock. Yet under market conditions, prices can roll. You want to know what price expectations are odds probable when assessing which stock with which option series. Hopefully, now you have a little more ammunition to make that decision and by using the options models you will.

Summarizing—buy options with expirations two to three months out minus the

## Figure 10.1

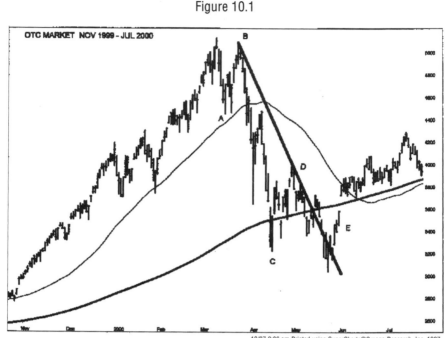

12/27 9:06 am Printed using SuperCharts©Omega Research, Inc. 1997

intermediate trend time already lost. *If the intermediate move is already aged one month, buying options no more than two months out would still capture the average duration of three months, without overpaying for probable unnecessary time.* Price potential being the same, it is recommended to buy options with <u>low volatility</u> levels and make sure implied volatility hasn't just been factored in.

For an <u>conservative—more likely successful—option investment</u>: buy slightly in-the-money (the delta will be somewhat high) or maybe at-the-money (the delta will be slightly less), so as the stock moves, so too will the option. Since the option price is apt to be high in price, were the position to go against you, large percent losses wouldn't occur as quickly as they would have if the option had been priced at 1 or 1_.) *A .50 option move against you wouldn't represent too great a percentage, compared to a $1 or $2 out-of-the-money option wherein a 1/2 point move is a <u>measurable</u> percentage change.*

For <u>aggressive option—more risk/reward</u>—option investment: buy the closest out-of-the-money to the current price, if you have calendar time, at least two, preferably three weeks, and if you can reasonably expect a move of magnitude, 10 percent at minimum. Yet if correct in a significant way, out-of-the-money will become superior to in-the-money. But remember out-of-the money is *statistically inferior* to in-the-money—i.e., the frequency of losses are multiple times greater.

A true story might best prove the latter example:

I had been a broker a few years when a young man came into to our E.F. Hutton office and wanted to invest in, at the time, red-hot gaming stocks in Atlantic City, and Ramada Inn (RAM) was his interest. To "bottom-line" the story, he would later bring me a few of his friends, whom I equally convinced, as I did him, to purchase out-of-the-money calls and await the expected casino approval. (I recall RAM sold about at 14. I suggested they all buy the 20 strike price, out-of-the-money calls.)

With the frenzy of casino gambling very new and companies already there having huge stock price movement, this RAM strategy seemed reasonable. As it would turn out, we were all correct—on paper—and naturally not the <u>only</u> place you might want to be—since the stock did indeed march upward in gaming tandem with its sister companies. Yet as the time for options expiration grew near and the stock still not beyond 20—I don't recall it even having approached 19—their joint investments were essentially worthless. It was a rude awakening to the true crapshoot that out-of-the-money options can be <u>if too distant</u>. The statistical frequency of price movement isn't sufficiently that great over short periods of time, or enough to often "win." When you are investment correct you are always supposed to make money—some or a lot. When you don't, it means your strategic planning needs overhaul.

Let's take an actual 2001 Merck option and prove the points more so.

| In-the-Money Call | | Out-of-the-Money Call |
|---|---|---|
| Start: Stock price 59.625; options one stage in and out of the money. | | |
| Strike Price | 55 | 65 |
| Option Price | 5.10 | .39 |
| Delta | .85 | .16 |
| End: Assume a stock price on expiration at 70 with a +16 percent return in one month * | | |
| Option Price | 15 | 5 |
| Percent Return | 194 | |
| Actual earned profits using even $5,000 invested *(using theoretical <u>portions</u> of an option)* | | |
| Calls bought: | 9.8 | 128.20 |
| $$$/Expiration | $14,700 | $64,100 |

*\* If Merck's stock price had advanced 8 percent, to just 65, the chosen out-of-the-money options would be zero; yet the in-the-money would have still fetched $10 or $1,000 per call option, hence $9,800.*

In summation:

> • Determine the broad market's (Dow, S&P 500, NASDAQ, Russell 2000) price direction for where you intend to invest. You want to invest in price trends that offer evident price direction and not extreme in price momentum in either direction or in duration since their inception.
>
> • Locate industries and their sectors that are moving in price tandem to that market and that are not too overbought or oversold.
>
> • Choose individual investments that evidence the strongest price action (for a bullish trends) or the weakest price action (for a bearish strategy) with respect to their own industry affiliation and that have technical – price – characteristics that suggest now is the appropriate time to initiate the transaction.

In an ideal investment climate, the broad market, the industry and, of course, the place where you place your money—the individual investment—are all in the same price direction with their momentum having just about started.

## The Short-Term Investment Investing Sequence

*You didn't think there would be anything for the gunslingers amongst the reader audience? There are times when knowing how to navigate the short-term will help—somewhat. But once more: these are minefield areas. (Dreaming <u>what could have been</u>, and capturing good results, is very different.)*

*You will win some and you will have to lose some if you play herein. Try and make the winners "larger" than the losses cost you. That is, be more dollar-correct when right, than dollar-wrong when wrong. Capture any potential two and three times profits being offered almost immediately, unless price appears much more favorable to you; you can't expect much more in one to five days of "investing." And always nip the losses very fast.*

*Maybe one last time: the more instant you want reward to be, the more the probabilities for success revert to the proverbial "coin flip." You should not delude yourself into believing that there is sufficient time or hidden intellect to "winning consistently" in the short-term. At best, you should align yourself with enough of the "right" tendencies to "tilt the table"—but don't wager the villa.*

### Only Invest in the Short-Term Directional Trend in Place

If but one central rule of investing could be had—long- or short-term—this one would stand first. Invest—up or down—in only the short-term parallel direction of the security, since there might not be time to recover from a diverting price.

Were an attempt to be made to invest opposite the dominant price direction (during a common price retracement) or when a trend isn't present (a lateral market), then a realization must be accepted, the security's holding has to include a close braking of shown losses, since on almost any day, the dominate trend can reassert itself.

### Watch the Stocks and/or Industry's/Market's Five-Day RSI

Surprisingly simple, yet at extremes—above 80 as an overbought indication; under 25 to 30 as too oversold—it so often proceeds opposite trend price movement. This indicator tends to be stock, specific and works great with some stocks but and not with others, yet, very worthwhile watching closely for price hints as to very short-term overbought/sold indications. Its only usage should be from <u>extremes</u> of sentiment levels. If it's not above 80 or in the 25 to 30 area, the indicator just isn't useful.

### Repeat Only Time-Tested Strategies You Know Work

Institute strategies that you know work and not those that you hope work, since time will not be your ally. There are certain stocks that you may have followed that you know are more probable than not to rise in quick market moves and so forth. Those are the ones you transact with. Don't go outside what you have learned works. *If the market is due to rally, you will learn that the brokerage stocks tend to get hot quickly, so you would buy Merrill Lynch (MER) because it's more than probable that it will work again this time.*

Don't try to out intellectualize your past experiences—they are a far better instructor than our moment-to-moment ideas!

### You Must Devote Total Time & Attention

It is far more essential for short-term transactions since they are so random in nature, to be extremely attentive and virtually commit to entire days of watching price action. In this way you tend to get a feel for an investment over the short run. How far and fast might it run intraday? Does its price pattern early or late intraday and so on. Watch the support and resistance <u>intraday</u> levels. Total concentration is required dealing short-term. In the shortest of time horizons, merely noting only closing price, with occasional intraday glances, is very inefficient and means daily lucrative patterns go undetected, as well as ways of minimizing incorrect strategies.

### Get Extremely Price Focused & Pass on Hitting Home Runs

Since price movement in today's era is so fast, large intraday price swings open up for the possibility of making a nice gain, even intraday. Remaining very focused can mean the two point opportunity that appears quickly can and maybe should be taken. certainly if the position suggests a reversal, since it can just as easily disappear by the close, and you are not trying for continuing days of price movement. Short-term trading means you grab for any large profits while their being offered! You are not intending to be around for a "grand slam."

### Buy Larger Positions & in More Volatile Issues

This may seem counterintuitive at first, but holding enough of a position in a stock that "travels" means that being correct with a small price movement leads to worthwhile profits and justifies the initial action. Obviously, it adds to larger losses if wrong, yet we don't plan on being wrong in the onset. The point is, buying 100 shares in most companies, for short-term potential, is too little to have meaningful profitable impact unless you receive large intraday(s) point movement; and in the short run, this too, is too hard most times. All things being equal in directional expectation, search for issues with higher volatility—not necessarily with high volatility levels.

### Try to Acquire Real-Time Intraday Graphics

Being able to watch and review price to know where prior resistance and support occurred intraday, how fast the stock opened and so on, means not having to recall all the intraday swings and prior moves. It means you won't have to guess where price levels were. It's added cost but usually worth it.

### If Purchasing Options, Utilize In Priority: in-the-Money, at-the-Money, & If Extremely Comfortable & Ample Calendar Time Is Still Available, 5- to 10-Percent Maximum out-of-the-Money

In this sequence, the higher delta associated, when options are in-the-money, means those options will move approximately on a one-and-one basis with the stock—that is, the correlation between stock and option is much more acute. The "deeper" in-the-money, the greater the delta and higher one-to-one correlation. This is absolutely essential since you do not want the "lag effect" you always have to overcome with low delta options—perhaps a stock's actual two point move bringing the option along at a 3/8 to a 1/2 pace. *This options "lag effect"—delta far less than 1.00—means a purchase at-say-the ask side and with a customary sale at the bid side, translates into the difference, the spread, having to be made up by the stock price movement before you can make any money. Yet, for those correct price movement, you should rightly be <u>immediately</u> profiting from. This is a give up, of two of the stock's point movement before you are even! Consequently, for very short-term trades, this is another impediment you should try to avoid.*

If you are right regarding the direction of the stock, and had you purchased options, you should design your option purchase series to make just as much as you would have had you purchased the stock outright. This is best done by buying in-the-money. The deeper in-the-money, the more the option acts like a stock moving lock-step, its delta approaches 1.00, and there is less time value being paid for. Of course, this relationship works against you when wrong, because the stock price movement will reflect almost an even loss in options—because there is no "lag effect" to benefit from when you are wrong.

The upside is that the percentage of original options capital being lost is much smaller using in-the-money positions. On balance, therefore, there is more advantage than not in purchasing in-the-money versus out-of-the-money options positions. And the importance of immediate profit when being correct, which in-the-money movement should provide, can't be dismissed. It is too necessary when investing short-term. Paying for "time," then—buying out along the calendar—isn't necessary unless a huge move can be expected and there is sufficient time to capture some or all of it.

*Unfortunately, this found wisdom was acquired at a "cost." At the expense of yours-*

*truly and options clientele, when ignorance and naiveté, even coupled with honest expectations, could not overcome practical options reality. It's a long way of saying we all pick up expertise with our experiences. For those inexperienced in this area, it is aggravation in the extreme to have been right, maybe 3 points on the stock, yet to have purchased options that barely move! If you are to be proven right on calling the stock's direction, expect and design your initial strategy to make money immediately.*

Here's an example of the investment math with respect to options and cash and a margin purchase of a theoretical stock:

Investor desires to purchase 1,000 shares of a $50 stock intended to move higher; the investor is bullish.

|  | Capital Outlay |
|---|---|
| All Cash Purchase | = $50,000 |
| 50 percent Margin Purchase Buy 10, 40 Strike Price | = $25,000 |
| Call Options @11 | = $11,000 |

For each 1 point upward movement in the stock's price, the investor should see a $1,000 increase in their account. The stock purchase, either way, will reflect an immediate profit, and so should the deep in-the-money options. However, the lower capital commitment with the options purchase remains a two-way street. Although the investor need to place only 20 percent of the money required for an outright stock purchase, they forfeit the luxury of time, since options always have a limited life, where stock is a perpetual equity right. If it doesn't advance right away, it may in weeks or months. The options player must be right—more or less—right now.

### Focus on the Broad Markets & Their Intraday Multiple Pricing Trends

Since stocks play follow the leader mentality, strong market moves, up or down, will dictate stock prices over multiple minute(s) and hourly periods. Being very sensitive to these broad moves makes profitable probabilities more likely than not. *It would be highly improbable to witness the Dow up 2 to 3 percent at some point during a day and not have most large cap stocks and call options moving quite significantly as well. A market starting to make a move must be watched carefully and then followed as to its price direction, since its effect will be felt almost immediately, depending upon the intensity of its movement.*

Therefore, it makes equal sense that a stock looking weak, very overbought, and crying out to be shorted, may not fall as anticipated amidst a strong market—albeit temporary! Perhaps delay the short sale. Watch the market for clues as well as the specific investment since market moves dominate the short-term effect.

The market will tip you for intraday clues as to where most stocks will wander—stocks seldom run counter significant market moves. Example: a NASDAQ intraday downward reversal probably tears apart almost all NASDAQ individual stock intraday gains, and as it expectedly should.

Read the Sections on Intraday Pricing and the Dynamics of Price Movement In the Following Professional Ideas/Strategies/Concepts Area.

### Prepare Yourself to Know & Understand the Volatility of the Security You Are Interested in

A stock's volatility determines its usual reaction to market moves. A broad market rally will light a fire under most stocks, but their maximum intraday move will tend to remain connected within their internal (individual) volatility. Average intraday price ranges (high to low) tend to be about 7 percent: 3.5 percent above and below the prior close. A stock of average volatility up 5 percent for the day without specific impetus from something peculiar to itself, accounting for the move, might—might—have run its upward intraday course, and warrant a sale that day. A highly volatile issue might move twice as much and not be a sale candidate. You must learn the unique characteristics of how your positions might react to market movement and news events.

PM Sierra (PMCS) enjoyed a rather high volatility reading. On October 31, 2001, with the NASDAQ up 40 points and that stock having been down three consecutive days, it shot up a shade above 11 percent at its intraday high. This is far in excess of the average expected intraday upward advance of 3 percent. Yet it illustrates how much more we should expect when our holding is a volatile issue. Without a formal study placing stocks in various volatility grids and then measuring their intraday price movement, one can only estimate what various volatility levels can be expected to produce in percent price movement. Yet suffice it to say, very volatile stocks can double normal intraday maximum average percent moves. So average 3.5 percent moves can run to positive 9 percent as well as negative 9 percent and, as we see with the PMCS example, even more.

---

**Average Volatility:**

3 percent moves on $30 stocks amount to about .90 to 1 point
$40                                     1.20 to 1 1/2 points
$50                                     1.50 to 1 3/4 points
and so forth....

**High Volatility:**

9 – 11 percent moves on $30 stocks amount to about 2.70 to 3+ points
$40                                     3.60 to 4 1/4 points

---

By now, the reader should know that simply because a stock rises significantly intraday, as did PMCS at an 11 percent clip, you do not automatically sell. This would be too price presumptuous and not suggested, and particularly if the price response was not attributable to the company from a news event, etc. At +11 percent, the stock is well above its expected one-day intraday high, and on any start down below maybe a half a point, we would surely consider a quick exit if trying to maximize that single day's move. *(But nothing prevents a sale with a subsequent repurchase that same day if, as expected, the price falls to a more normal upward percent advance.)*

Naturally, if the market and/or stock remained strong throughout the following days, the temporary "high" felt in exiting near an 11 percent gain would be lost, as well as equity value, if the stock marched still many points higher. It may well climb higher because sellers might equally pull their offers awaiting what might yet be higher pricing to come. We can't forget that upward price is not a cause from just buyer's bullish conviction. The seller's side of the equation has equal merit—at all times.

An additional consideration in intraday timing is the time in the day when the stock might move toward a "maximum" based on volatility. If it's on the opening, maybe in a mini buying rampage, the stock will have six added hours to fall back toward normalcy. If the drive to the maximum expected high shows at day's end, there would be little or no time to retreat. In this later case, it might be a sensible time to retain the stock until the following morning—at least.

Still another factor is price. Low-priced stocks have far less trouble gaining expected intraday percent moves than do higher prices issues, although they don't capture large point moves. But there is investor resistance to fast point movement. In a strong advance, investors might step in with a stock up two points. Far fewer will show interest after a four, five, or greater point move. They would logically reason it was too late, etc. See below:

Two High-Volatility Stocks:

At $15, PMCS would have little trouble moving up or down 1 point or 10 percent.

A $75 stock probably would have trouble moving 7 points, the same 10 percent.

The advantage in knowing how volatile your holdings are is that it offers you at least the chance at exiting at intraday maximum moves and not watching price values sink away when more normal pricing occurs, as it always must. And, thus . . .

**Prepare yourself to know and understand the volatility of the security you are interested in.**

**Accept the Study of the 50/50 Probability That Trending Stocks over Many Consecutive, Up or Down Days, Can Easily Continue That Same Direction— They Need Not Automatically Reverse. Be Prepared to Sell out Losing Positions Adverse to You No More Than 2 Points Away from Your Entry Point or, at Any Monetary Level Where Pain Is Felt**

This is one more way of providing the discipline to exit after giving up but a small portion of price. This automatic sell trigger is <u>regardless</u> of where your entrance price was. A stock you bought at 32 and is now at 38 then starting downward means at 36 you sell—you do not watch price movement to 30, then a full 2 points below your entrance price, and 8 points beneath the 38 high price. Similarly, losing $4,000 in four minutes might be reason to exit if that amount of loss is upsetting—and why wouldn't it be?

The market can't know where you entered, so opt for control when you decide to exit. In this manner, you keep the vast portion of short-term movement that might begin going against you. Particularly when trading against the dominate trend for the "assumed bounce"...it may well come...but from a far-away price level, and many days, if not weeks, later. Don't wait to surrender your capital; if you have to short-term part with any value, lose small, and lose quick. Don't drag yourself through tortuous days of worry. Here's a few hints as to what might cause sudden short-term movement and how to react:

> • If the individual security has moved significantly 8 to10 percent intraday and the market and/or its sector hasn't moved significantly, and the company has no news to account for, it might mean the buy/sell balance had tipped too far to one direction. A more normal price action pattern should be expected later or the following day.
>
> • If the markets are moving dramatically, they will meaningfully influence the short-term price action of most stocks on normal days and always when the stock isn't very overbought/sold. Appropriate action might need to be taken since the markets may move even more dramatically, causing more short-term stock volatility. *It's not opportune to be shorting stock if the Dow is reaching for highs.*
>
> • If the stock's fast movement can be traced to itself as a lone cause—provided the price affect isn't too great—probably means remaining consistent to its short-term trend already in place.

*Remember: the market and stock movement short-term is very random. The sale you execute limiting yourself to a 2 point maximum loss is transitory price action. This means being prepared to buy back the same position if the overall strategy still warrants and if the stock begins to move in the manner you had originally expected. We don't just give up forever if the investment <u>initially</u> works against us. It may work out significantly—later. By selling out after a minor loss, you cannot sustain large equity damage and you will have an opportunity for another day.*

### *Ignore All 50/50 Short-Term "Opportunities"*

Since the short-term requires being correct almost instantly, trying to invest in advance of any unknown news event or expected type of information is akin to reducing the ultimate probabilities to gambling...Roulette 101. Short-term focus means being right—right now. If your "bet" is wrong, losses result. Investment has to be more than a coin toss. Without the successful probabilities of an intended strategy being much better than 50/50, <u>do nothing</u>!

*In March 2001, Wall Street awaited the Federal Reserves interest rate cut and upon receiving a less-than-expected figure, promptly sold off. Investors having gone long and purchased in anticipation, were rudely stricken with steep losses within two hours of that announcement.*

*You have a fair profit already and are awaiting the outcome of influential news. Should you sell? Since we cannot know the investment reaction until after the news release and if the current profit is substantial enough, it pays to exit before the news release to ensure retention of the gain. One added consideration is the investment climate at the time. If it is very favorable and forgiving—when companies recently announcing sour news the investment reaction was insignificant—you might tempt fate and chance the news item; if not, don't!*

### *Capturing the Very Short-Term Bottom or Bounce*

Whenever the markets become <u>very deeply oversold</u>—NASDAQ March, 2001 qualifies—there can be the enviable time when volatile stocks react extremely quickly, returning 15 to 30 percent in just a day or two in a quick upward eruption. With the dilemma of waiting to see the bottom before buying—compared to having many frequent short-term losses mount up when presumed bottoms were bought, but didn't materialize—is confounding, frustrating and costly. Even small losses add up. It's a gamble and there's no way around it. We cannot know if the markets truly bottomed in one day, since true investor sentiment, conviction, isn't found daily it takes multiple days, usually weeks before we can be sure.

For most investors waiting for "the ideal bottom" probably isn't worth the effort, since it's very difficult to be nimble enough to exit with monies made when possible, and as well, yet exit and contain losses, if the short-term "pop" isn't lasting.

For those brave few, trying to capture these infrequent, potentially lucrative periods always seems worth the effort on paper despite the fact most investors simply love to shoot for apparent bargains. The almost random nature of calling the market turn makes it difficult. Here are a few ways:

1. Wait for the specific marketplace you wish to enter, the Dow, S&P 500 or the NASDAQ, to advance mightily on the day you wish to purchase, since <u>it is the</u> cause for bottoms and rally configurations, not the verbal or written opinion of anyone. If that market can advance perhaps 2 maybe 3 percent with good market participation, and very heavy volume. This suggests strong bullish

sentiment, participation, and conviction. This type of market lift-off can break the back of bearish sentiment for the very short-term, if it's beyond a one-day event if that at all.

Demand it be well up or well above a very low intraday bottom, before entering, but don't wait too long, since too high an entry price always means less potential if the rally is not the real thing. Invest about half of your normal short-term monies.

If the market moves _very significantly_ over the day—a 6 to 7 percent NAS-DAQ would qualify and about half as much with the Dow and S&P 500—it might prove to be no more than a one-day "flash in the pan" type move. Here, very extreme bullishness could cause hesitant buyers to hold back—with too much upside was seen too soon—and still bearish investors/traders as likely to restart their selling, shorting, pushing prices downward. *This type of price action is often termed a "V" bottom, down then right back up, and is seldom sustainable.* In other words, too much too soon might be as bad as nothing or too slow. The way to handle this explosive move is to watch the 3 to 4:00 p.m. closing period, and if the markets appear to want to close 5 and 6 percent or more, sell out most of your hopefully then profitable positions, retaining maybe 25 to 30 percent, so that if the rally continues into the following day(s), you still are participating.

Measure the extent of gain in the market after any initial early morning positive from about 10:00 am. This tips you as to how much follow-through is occurring after any large opening. Fake outs occur frequently. Participants often get in on the opening, only to see the market move laterally. A probable continuation rally means investors are buying throughout the entire day with the market closing well up, but not extreme; the bullish hope that it leads to further upside into the next and following days.

You might just bracket your days of purchase. This means you believe Tuesday might be the short-term bottom and you purchase. If it's proven not to be the real thing, you wait for at least two days, at Thursday, or even three, before reinstituting a bullish posture. This prevents getting in, out, back in again, and then out again—a too-frequent almost gambling mentality in trying to seize the advent of the expected short-term move. In this "bracketed" manner, if the move is real, you are already positioned and enjoy quick profits rather than chase price. And for all the time you may have remaining patient, you want, and deserve, to be present if an important low price does get placed.

In the end, if it's not a bottom, you do not want to be around waiting to fish for a new one—wherever lower it might be!

2. Try and hold positions more than one day unless the price direction appears capable of going much below your downside limit. Doing this will give you

several automatic next day(s) chances on any upside participation that might develop, without having to buy in again at inflated pricing after, say, a strong market opening. *In severe bear periods, you should expect that most of the downside has already occurred, so there really should be limited downside at, or quite near, a suspected short-term bottom. If you are a day or two premature, it should not cause too much harm.*

3. Stay with what works—buy the prior strongest (bullish) acting stocks or those stocks that always seem to advance first in market bullish periods—e.g., usually brokers. Don't go on a bargain hunt at presumed short-term bottoms. Play probabilities for the moment, since you can't know until well after the fact whether this rally is a real two to three day mini advance or one that might just be the beginning of an intermediate advance. *The strongest stocks/investments tend to retain more of their gains the next day, even assuming the expected advance doesn't materialize. Therefore, it is more sensible in either case to get into the strongest of investments.*

There is a very important reason why when attempting to transact for the very short-term we do so with stock first. The spread—difference between the bid and ask, the "cost" to chance playing in the arena—is always far greater with options, often 30 cents. This means even a 10 option purchase representing 1,000 shares has you down $300. Were you to have to sell quickly, you would sell 30 cents lower than where you had bought maybe minutes earlier. There may not be the time to make up for the 30 cent spread.

Buying stock with the normal one or two cent spread means that almost any upward movement when bullish covers the spread, and invites at least the possibility of even the shortest of quick profitable exit. *(If the short-term turns into more, then options can be utilized—they probably should not be before you know for sure if you are seeing a real bottom, first.)*

4. Ignore unspecific company news that might conflict with a purchase. In the very short-term, fundamentals and continuing downgrades, etc., etc. have nothing to do with how stocks will move in a mini-rally…nothing. Don't get taken off track. A very hard short-term advance will take everything upward with it, virtually without exception. And a fundamentalist or a technician's opinion isn't that exception.

On 4/5/2001, prior to the market's opening, a technical analyst stated the semiconductor sector looked to be weaker still, having made a new price low the prior day. However, at noon, it was the second most advanced market sector, with the markets well up, and at 3:20 p.m., up 13 percent. Why? The market—here the NASDAQ—had made the profound impact; always greater than any individual's opinion. It might turn out to be a good fundamental call, but the markets and their ability to trend are ALWAYS the dominate force for all periods.

5. Where possible, try and initiate positions in <u>more volatile</u> stocks, assuming all other aspects of the proposed purchase choice are acceptable. The reasoning is that at true bottoms where little downside is assumed left, the most volatile stocks should advance the fastest; they were likely the leaders to the downside, as well. Hopefully, that prior downside direction is short-term completed. But—and it's a huge caveat—these stocks can retreat very quickly, giving back any short-term profits if the bottom is not yet really in place!

*The following four stocks all possess high volatility and all suffered savage selling pressures during the NASDAQ technology sell-off in late 2000 and early 2001. They are typical of what can happen when a short-term bottom appears to be in place. The date was April 5, 2001:*

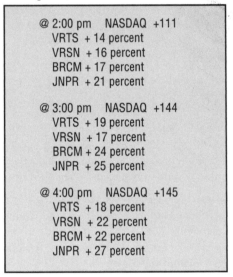

```
@ 2:00 pm   NASDAQ  +111
    VRTS  + 14 percent
    VRSN  + 16 percent
    BRCM + 17 percent
    JNPR  + 21 percent

@ 3:00 pm   NASDAQ  +144
    VRTS  + 19 percent
    VRSN  + 17 percent
    BRCM + 24 percent
    JNPR  + 25 percent

@ 4:00 pm   NASDAQ  +145
    VRTS  + 18 percent
    VRSN  + 22 percent
    BRCM + 22 percent
    JNPR  + 27 percent
```

**It can't be forgotten that despite a market's continuing gloomy dive toward a pricing floor, the greater the ongoing magnitude of that fall, the more likely ensuing rallies will prove sustainable.**
**Why?**
**Because at some point the bargain created by falling prices proves too tempting...and they can't all—the index, the market—hit zero!**

In April 2001, the NASDAQ composite was off 68 percent from its March, 2000 high and were that to become a MINUS 78 percent and possibly a MINUS 88 percent, any bullish attempts at short-term rallies would have greater probabilities of lasting. Entire indices don't fade to nothing—companies do, but never entire markets.

### Understanding the Difficulty in Not Assuming Yet Not Waiting Too Long— The Critical Decision

There is no argument in always accepting that short-term price prediction is very tough. And waiting too long to be sure before acting runs counter to the precept that being assumptive is equally wrong. However that is one short-term price reality: each time may be quite different. Unless the trend direction you are in continues unabated, wherein you should assume no end, all other short-term moves are fraught with peril. You never know.

Be premature about your entry point and you <u>will</u> decrease your profit potential. Similarly, if you merely assume a price cessation that isn't being proven by price action, you decrease reward. Can you both wait for assurance yet act decisively—of course not.

It might take perhaps four to six months of contra price action to be "sure" that any "new" trend is a lasting one. So waiting even many days before trend entrance— to be "very sure"—isn't going to help us know if the "new" trend is real!

The best transactional advice is to ensure you enter and exit trades from proven successful experiences. But capturing the <u>timing</u> to obtain the most of these positioned trades is never going to be near perfect, never easy, and much too often, almost always results in much less than hoped for. *There just aren't many traders driving Mercedes.*

This section also gives rise to the idea of guessing entry price points. Nibbling in the short-term is risk any way you can define it, and to add to it, might seem less than reasonable.

You are bullish, but wait to be sure, so as you wait for a day's price pullback, price drives up five straight days. Do you chance on obtaining a position during day six? Who knows if days seven through ten continue higher.

Conceptually waiting five days for only a *short-term* payoff is senseless. By definition, you are more prone to have exited before a fifth day. Watching first, for even two days, then entering and chasing price, isn't good probability either.

*You assume your stock can advance to 45 from its 41 level. In order not to just guess its start, you wait and watch it hit 42 and then you purchase. Let's agree that the ultimate short-term move is to have been to 45, and as it passes 45 you watch, then patiently wait for more, but finally exit as it drops back to 44. A potential 4 point move—low to high— in real life terms, becomes a 1 point profit (44 to 42) times your number of shares, minus the IRS portion, and minus a few commissions. The question being asked, at the wrong time, by everybody: Was the result worth the effort?*

*Short-term tends to always be less than fulfilling and leaves you scratching your head.*

**The aggressive conclusion has to then be, to guess that the first proof of your being correct will be continual, despite the risk in not waiting for further pricing proof.**

This way, you maximize reward even though risk is heightened as well. Yet if you don't guess a bit, you are certainly destined to give away profitable points. It does make short-term sense to chance on correct trend continuance by commencing the position with a normal number of shares.

A lesser aggressive plan would be to transact a smaller-than-regular purchase amount to at least participate at some level with the same timing caveat for the entrance of the position.

**If you are apparently right by perhaps 3/4 of a point direction, get in quick...or don't bother chasing price too much, short-term, is a pathway to loss.**

Watching a declining broad market and an intended short, sink for four straight days, having wanted to short the overbought equity, which wouldn't rise even one day to allow for your entrance, and then finally giving in and shorting it on the fourth day—investors might do this so they can find some satisfaction—and money—in benefiting from having being proven "paper" right, despite their delaying. They reason: shouldn't we earn something for being paper correct thus far? Yes, and they would have, had they entered with the strength of conviction early on. They didn't. Short-term probabilities over three and four days change. They are unquestionably less. It's not far removed from buying lottery tickets and arriving the day after with changed numbers.

And don't get trapped into thinking, "The trend I had forecast right and didn't get into won't stop now so I'd better get in." Place your best bet, it will...the day you finally concede and then get in!

Is the short-term for keeps? No. Is a sound mind at work expecting day after day after day after day that there is still short-term gold awaiting us? One can find reward at any time we choose? What odds would still favor the short-term continuance of that move? We can't know with precision but they aren't great. *They certainly aren't as great as four days ago!* If you wouldn't, or couldn't, muster the courage of getting in early, why then get in at all and likely late? Is it probable that three more consecutive down days, then adding to seven, are immediately ahead? Is this sound logical thinking? Is the short-term that forgiving?

If the short-term is to be an expected three to five day holding period, and you sit on your hands for the first few, and would have been proven right, what sense is there in entering on day three or four? To then succeed, your initial short-term expectation, as to expected duration, would then have to be wrong. It's betting on your late entrance day, number four, that you are now going to be wrong as to the length of the original expected move. Does smart investing engender this kind of action? Let's hope not.

If you think about the psychology of an investor watching price trend the way they expected, but as yet haven't participated in, there would seem to exist a number of successive days where they might refuse to get involved, where the trend momentum would retard demand. "It's down three straight days, I'll wait for an up day before shorting." Similarly, the demand from others to short is probably less as the stock heads down; they've already "missed some of the boat." So to a point as a price trends short-term, demand for its continuance should conceptually lessen...to a point.

At some point, though, if the trend appeared non-stop, that driving momentum would enhance demand. Where the logic is, "I might as well get in now since it'll never allow me an opportunity," this is when having been correct, but still not a participant, causes unbearable frustration and the investor just commences the strategy. This might be after six consecutive trending days and more, which are examples of high-trend conviction. As we usually understand after the fact, for short-term "health" this isn't recommended.

**Merely wait for the next short-term cycle to begin—up or down—
somewhere...and it might take all of a few days!
Don't chase price short-term. There are always other and better times...
there are always second chances.**

If the short-term is where you think you belong on occasion, your results are always going to be tough and frustration will be a constant. It's not any area where pure mental acuity makes for too consistent a difference. There is little room for mistakes it's why "don't" is usually the happiest advice.

### How Do You Know When It's Best to Liquidate a Short-Term Position... after the Fact

Throughout this book, there has been repeated mention of not being assumptive when trying to assess where price might go. The general idea is that without some evidence as to a stoppage of a trend, why assume one and blindly get out? Yet most of what has preceded us was regarding more time available to launch or curtail ideas, where a few technical tools might hint as to a trend's termination. The short-term doesn't provide too much in the way of measuring whether a technical indicator is flashing an exit light, since the intended duration is rather short to begin with and is random. So the guidance expected from even technical factors won't be great, and shouldn't be expected to, since the measuring period from start to end is likely to be just two to four, maybe, five days, maybe at most two weeks. That is to say, if some indicator was signaling it was OK to initiate a trade, how extreme could it have gotten in three days to be a reliable prophet of an exit suggestion?

A compelling answer to short-term timing help is always less then hoped for.

Excepting running into known resistance/support price levels, there isn't going to be too much precise guidance. Major help always comes from the <u>broad market</u>, which can push individual equities further then we might imagine. But in the end, it is apt to be a sense of how the stock simply reacts during a day. Does it bounce back after a decline? Is it very market sensitive? Maybe it advances time after time with the market falling? Does it have intraday repeating patterns—rise in the mornings and sell off late each day? Is the amount of earned price movement enough to simply satisfy the investor? *(We know you cannot get rich over three-day holding periods.)*

And the questions above should not be broadly assumed to be pertinent for all stocks. Like our Five-Day RSI technical indicator, some stocks react well and some won't. It will be on a stock-by-stock basis, and all the more reason to know the price characteristics of what you are buying as much as you can.

As ill-thought as it might seem, trying to buy for the short-term in the face of a nervous falling price environment—yet assuming only a retracement of a bullish move, not an out-and-out correction—carries with it potential less downside risk than buying after multiple day or weeks of advance. It's counterintuitive, but for prices to run that far down and allow for a bearish comfort to be felt, the downside—what's really left at that point—is probably limited. When we are most certain, it's because price has gone our way. However, at that moment and at that price level, probabilities would not favor our being short-term correct too much longer. This sets up even more confusing possibilities.

If price has moved up for many consecutive days, whereby very-near term potential would be expectedly limited, do we just sell and violate the basic premise of allowing trend to play through? In the short-term, we don't enjoy the passage of time. From the beginning of a short-term strategy, we are proposing a fast exit and shouldn't therefore ever witness a short-term move extending into an intermediate one. We should be out—by our own hand.

This whole idea sets up the premise that we should sell when we are most comfortable and purchase when we feel the greatest anxiety. Since for us to all feel these respective mindsets, price would have driven short-term about as far as it might be expected normally to go. And this is not too likely off-base. It's fair to state short-term ideas always sound good on paper. But being too philosophical isn't a final answer by any means, since there is always a difference between what should happen and what is happening.

If the position advances to some level where an acceptable profit has been earned, some near-term exit consideration. Yet what constitutes the specific price movement one should leave behind—part with from an intraday price top—and not risk further asset depreciation? Might it be 1/2 point? A full point?

You won't know beforehand unless you're trading short-term with the goal of a specific profit in mind—and when having reached that level, you exit in whole or in part. If you make the exit price amount large enough, you run the risk of both being taken out too far down and suffering, or running up against the potential that after price has retraced, it then retraces some of the move against you, right at your exit point. Retraces the retracement! It is commonly referred to as being "whip sawed."

The theory behind placing portions of intraday point exit levels is that after some degree of point decline, if demand doesn't come in, it may not. The surge might be just over. Buyers might not be sufficiently seduced after a .50 cent intraday point drop to halt the slide, but they might. It isn't to hard to argue that after maybe a 2 point daily reversal, they more likely should if the stock is really headed upward. Maybe their ideal entrance point is in between. We don't know beforehand, because we can't. Excepting slight help by keen observation, you'll never be positive in the short-term before or after actions.

When you opt for exit after giving up a specific level of deterioration, you sell if that price point is met.

*Example: your stock has risen to 67 and you have a 4 point profit. You also know in the short run, the 4 points can be lost. You have agreed before that a 1/2 point, .50, retracement from some intraday price is all you will chance. Let's say the stock has hit 67 and then starts dropping with a falling broad market and quickly hits 66.75. You now have both the market working against you and the stock may be falling close to your exit price of 66.50 (67 – .50). If the stock trades at that level and you sell out, you retain 66.50, but there isn't much preventing the stock from either stopping its fall there, then rising, or falling beneath 66.50, then rising to 68. But yours is a value call and one where you control price at least in this limited way. And the above might take place in 30 seconds. If you hadn't pre-planned for the .50 point stoppage, you might not have time with prices in motion to both watch and calmly think.*

It is no laughing matter to see an intraday Dow fall apart, and with it, your short-term profits. Worse is that as it falls, we probably haven't a firm hint as to where it might end. Somehow having some control over retracements would seem to resolve some of the unknown.

Would a .50 move against you, in dollar terms, be meaningful enough that it might force your hand, your willingness to give up versus the intention to stay invested? If you made a decent profit already, the "point level" at which you will tolerate giving up value, should probably be small. If you've made very little, it might make some sense to remain positioned a bit longer by extending the level of point going against you. But we do know one thing for sure: There is nothing that can guarantee us consistent exits at near ideal pricing. And there won't be anything in 20 years.

A good argument is to exit entirely if a short-term goal had been originally set and was then realized. Since you should always try and estimate to what level short-term price might get to when originally purchasing, this would seem a simple and a fair method. If your goal is completely met, why not exit at the first instant of retracement above your goal? You've accomplished, you've won.

If your goal hasn't been met, if you didn't have a clue as to the extent of a potential move, define the amount of money 1/4 and 1/2 point retracements mean, and exit if the price moves to those levels, so ulcers don't become part of your daily existence.

Short-term is never played with precision, it can't be. The short element of time makes it that way. But don't make it any more difficult. Be disciplined with the degree of retracement levels that you set. If they are hit, exit. At minimum, this way you control, in some limited degree, your investment fate. But this is much better than watching the random vagaries of price dictate your returns.

Your idealized but realistic short-term investment scorecard would show a plurality of wins over losses since your short-term odds—if you learn not to redo mistakes—should gravitate well above 50/50, and the winning times would be maybe three times the magnitude when losing. *You lose $500 this time; you make $1,500–$2,000 the next time.*

The ultimate trick to short-term trading is to "come home"—get out—with more than you got in with. If that means you lose in frequency more than win, fine. Just come up roses on balance. If you can do that year-after-year, you will be in the very elite of that investor category.

And for the twenty-fifth caution:

**Do not make the short-term a *constant* emphasis.**
**Our markets really offer far more monetary and emotional appeal...**
**if we only lengthen our viewpoint.**

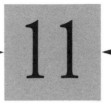

# Professional Tips:
# Miscellaneous
# Ideas/Strategies/Concepts

## Preliminary

*No investment strategy, no rule, always works. Nothing largely unscientific, which is what securities investment ultimately is, can be infallible. All the following equity pricing examples are lessons from experience, and any new experiences to be retained, are to be tested repeatedly first, and then learned from. The majority of our investment history that proves to become better examples should be played through over and over until they have shown to have no predictive merit. Only then do we discard their lesson and hunt for a new rule or standard to be adopted after practical testing, with it being continuously monitored for lasting value!*

*All of the following concepts should be considered education in and of themselves, for they all come from the lessons of years of actual Wall Street transactions. They all can provide invaluable price direction and can <u>save</u> or <u>make</u> you a good deal of money. Treat them as "free" experiences.*

## Calendar

Yale Hirsch, the editor of "The Stock Traders Almanac," was the dean of market movement based upon time periods. While generalizations, they derive from factual occurrences over the decades, to wit:

Stocks fall most often on Mondays and rise most often on Fridays. This is consistent with medical/psychological observation. *Most heart attacks occur on Mondays. If depression across large groups was measured, it is probable that depression is highest on*

*Mondays with the start of a five-day work week and lowest on Friday, in anticipation of a weekend full of enjoyment. But notwithstanding, any calendar period is always <u>subordinate</u> to the trend in place.*

Stocks rise most times on the last two and first two days of any month. *This is because institutional money is more at play at these times.* It is also believed the third calendar day of each month is when institutional money managers make major purchase decisions. They can always set their own purchase timetable, but cannot quite as easily for liquidations, where action may have to be undertaken.

The month of September has a historically more inferior bearish cast than does the more commonly believed month of October. (October being when most market bottoms have so frequently taken place.)

Stocks generally rise before the seasonal holiday periods, such as July 4th and December 25th. *Possibly due to the same reasoning for their rise on Fridays—the feelings of mirth that lies ahead!*

Be conscious of the last week of calendar quarters when that quarter's stock stars are apt to be bought and the losers dumped yet again. Wall Street terms these periods "window dressing"—where mutual funds which have to make quarterly reports public, each try to have in their portfolios the best performing stocks and sectors so current and potential investors note their talents in the most favorable light.

Most mutual funds end their tax year in October and liquidate their unwanted securities for tax loss, which fuels the ancient suspicion why so many Octobers and Septembers are so difficult. *The result: stocks have poor after-Labor Day through mid-October periods, and may invite a sideline position if wanting to be long. As recent eye-opening studies have suggested that the bulk of profits in the S&P 500 over many decades has occurred between mid-October and early spring, March/April. Investment during other calendar periods returned very little over the same decades! (It is known that most of the technology sector follows this pattern; an annual reoccurrence.) Note the eye-opening study below:*

*Monies invested each year in the S&P 500 from 1950 through 1999 at the beginning of the following time periods and withdrawn at the end, grew as follows:*

| | |
|---|---|
| Started with $10,000 | |
| October – May | to $363,353 |
| June – September | to  $11,138 |

*Need one say more! The advice: investment vacation throughout the late spring into early fall.*

Few follow it, but it is historically telling.

The Santa Claus rally generally runs during the last five trading days of a year and the first two of the new year. On average, the market is up 1.8 percent during this period.

210

The first five trading days of the year, if upward, have a remarkable forecasting record of portending that full-year result, about 85 percent of the time.

Since the current IRS "wash rule" prohibits taking a loss on a stock and then buying it, or one similar-back sooner than 31 days later, the last few trading days in November are periods where investors might be selling their "loser" stocks to capture tax relief; here, some added market weakness and stock opportunity could be seen.

If there is a consistent meaningful time period in the market, it is between 3:00 p.m. and 4:00 p.m., and maybe a bit more between 3:30 p.m. and 4:00 p.m. This might mean a stock breaks out of its intraday range during this period. If strong throughout the day, it gets stronger still; if weak, maybe weaker. As the theory goes, the "pros" are at work juggling their positions and strategies for the following day.

In March of 1999, in 14 of the prior 15 quarterly options expiration periods, prices advanced in the week preceding. They are periods to pay attention to.

If a market or industry "bottom" coincides with an options expiration week—and they are frequent, since we must have 12 expiration week periods per annum—the profit (and loss) potential from options movement is huge, since there is so little time left for ownership in the near month and prices are inexpensive. This is one time each month when options really might be worth a good look. *If you do enter during these weekly periods, and options are your preference, purchase in–the–money only!*

The latter two years of a presidential term are generally far more investor favorable than the initial two. This is likely because a President will take corrective measures early in his term.

The early portion of the year is when most retirement funding tends to take place; a reason for the usually bullish period.

The third calendar quarter historically tends to be poor for technology companies.

## Volume

The only degree to which intraday volume appears to matter—that is affect price—is if it is huge in relation to its recent history, perhaps four and five times. The idea that a rally in a single stock or the entire market isn't a real one unless the volume is heavy hasn't followed, no more than with declines. Peak relative volume (percent change in volume)—especially at presumed tops and bottoms—opens eyes and does have predictive worth! *Many down days on less-than-normal or low volume with an up day of heavy volume, suggests investors may have new added buying interest. But stocks still trend very nicely on very common and even low volume levels.*

Wall Street loves the "washout volume" phrase. Its press suggests a real bottom for a security or market requires great volume—"capitulating volume". Experience suggests otherwise, although vast relative individual security volume can signal a top or bottom.

Waiting for huge <u>market volume</u> to signal an all clear before an investment isn't necessary.

On days prior to holidays, when far less than normal activity is expected, it is often preached that the volume will be light; inherently, nothing meaningful occurs. Wrong. *Stocks will move on one share. Do not delay decisions because of an expected "slow day."*

Very heavy option volume <u>relative to its normal options</u> trading may provide an important signal for impending news—e.g., a takeover, news release and so forth.

Measuring incremental intraday volume in-between rallies and brief sell-offs can offer some insight as to what might be behind movement. For example, if at 12:30 p.m., a stock has traded 12,000,000 shares—roughly 100,000 per minute—and in a quick advance of 3 points over maybe four to five minutes, the measured volume from start to 3 points later, is only 10,000 shares, this may indicate the upward spike is on very weak relative volume, and maybe holds no real promise for price continuance.

Large institutional volume trades, generally the 10,000 or more share blocks, offer no added predictive value as to lasting price direction—perhaps a little as to very short-term movement. *They are known as "smart money" trades, yet are very suspect. You can lose plenty following institutional decision making.*

*To digress a bit: TV financial reporters frequently talk about how often the small investor remains calm in the face of declines-as in October 1987. "They stepped up to the plate the day after the market crashed and bought," seemingly paying homage to the small investor for their unemotional ways. The other side is that institutions and mutual funds might own 50,000 shares of a stock and obviously are motivated to make judgments which could affect hundreds of millions of their clients, dollars. They should be reacting—it's not a 200 share block they have concerns over. It's no major call when 143 shares are at risk. Try it with 100,000 shares!*

## The Dynamics of Price Movement

### *In General*

Investors should not confuse company quality with investment quality. There can be a marked distinction. A company may have great products and services and be the pinnacle of its industry, yet be of little interest to Wall Street, so its stock price just languishes.

Over the short-term to medium-term, price pattern is everything. It is assumed that as Wall Street's informed "professionals" buy, investors should follow. (This isn't to be confused with insider buying which has a glorious historical record.) The pros more often than not buy on the basis of fundamentals within their target companies and not on the dynamics of price. So while "insiders" have been historically proven right, it is because they are long-term holders. Unfortunately pricing does NOT follow fundamental valuations except over long periods. As an example: the former

Resorts International's Chairman, Mr. Lord, immediately after gaming was legalized in New Jersey, sold the vast portion of his stake in his company in the mid-teens price area, well below its 150+ ultimate price. Here was a man with as much knowledge as anybody as to the internals of the gaming industry and prospects for his own company and yet...

Day after day, huge intraday price swings—highs to lows—is symbolic of great anxiety and a warning that price action may remain volatile with a possible turn in direction. These are periods where investors have little confidence and just overreact. Be very careful.

There will be times when you will wish to buy or sell depending upon how the stock closes for the day. It is better to wait until near the close to implement the strategy, to ensure you are seeing the kind of closing price action you wanted. Transacting at 3:30 p.m. means there won't be any time left for an unwanted price movement to occur. *Assume you think if your stock can get above a certain level that it will "breakout," entice more buyers and probably advance quickly the next day. So positioning to be in, or adding to any current position, should take place very late in the day to see if, in fact, the stock gets above this important price level. If you purchase at 11:00 a.m., as price rushes forward and get caught up in the bullish hoopla, only to see a late day downturn, you feel both foolish and frustrated, and, at least temporarily, might be poorer too. Be more patient in testing these periods.*

Sometimes a day will be of particular significance. Maybe your company is already doing well in price action and is about to break through price resistance, which would cause you to add to your holdings. They have a security analysts meeting, and if that goes well, you anticipate an upward pop in the stock through the long-held resistance level. The best way to play this event is to wait until day's end to see if the stock, perhaps having gone up and through the resistance—can continue and close above. In effect, <u>make the stock prove</u> it should be purchased. A random buy early on the day subjects you to less than hoped for price action—even loss—if the event goes worse than planned. *If the stock does as expected, the upside should easily make up for any price difference in having waited.*

Very few sudden short-terms, fast, movements, up or down, last, because emotion is governing, and it causes overreactions—we are all influenced by what we see. Your stock is perhaps falling trade by trade by trade, and you are induced to sell and not risk any more. Wait and step away. When the emotion for that period subsides, as it always does, more normal trading commences and a reversal of that prior trend is likely. It is classic investor emotional overreaction at play—don't fall for it. There is danger for an investor who wrongly assumes the investing public will react as quickly as he or she might. This is especially true for security industry professionals. Since the average investor cannot continuously monitor price activity, their reaction will naturally always be later and very often more pronounced than expected. So assuming that a stock's price reaction over a few hours is all that there will be, is often a mistake especially when price reaction is expected. Imagine a stock moves up five straight days and then the company announces worse-than-expected news. Investor's reaction can be swift, but even more pronounced later the following day after many more eyes have seen the event.

Be careful of pricing assumptions whenever movement isn't as fast as expected. There are times when stocks will advance too much, then seem price unaffected after a one day market meltdown. The thinking is that the stock is really quite strong—it can buck a down trend; "It'll never drop." It's usually only time before negative surroundings affect price. A stock that can hold up against falling prices—many days— is the true indication of relative bullish strength. A one-day non-breakdown isn't telling. *Naturally, the same thinking surrounds stocks falling continuously that can't seem to ever rise.*

To the seller who laments, "Whenever I sell, within no time the stock goes higher." It should not be for an unknown reason, or surprise, or cause torment, that after our sale at maybe even a day's or week's high price, that we witness within a few hours/days/weeks a higher price. In the real world, wouldn't you have ever expected to see the stock move above where you got out? If not sooner, then certainly later. It almost must happen, at some future time, if the company stays public! You can't in fairness believe your sale puts a permanent cap on price. After the sale, expect to put the proceeds to an immediate and potentially superior use. And don't continually second-guess an ultimately higher price—it's supposed to—someday.

Markets and sectors can remain overvalued, as in the 1996 through 2000 period, as well as undervalued, as did the Russell 2000 in the 1990s for years. Remaining on the sidelines for just the broad market averages to begin trends—decline in periods of extreme optimism or advance in periods of economic recession—isn't wise. *There is no loss in investing in a very beaten-up market, extremely undervalued, while awaiting its ascension. Periods where equities are "not being appreciated"—not advancing—should mean avoidance, since "dead money" earns no points! Shrewd observation of each market sector will always produce those in bullish and bearish trends—effort here will payoff.*

Equities demonstrating good price strength will have the tendency to continue; poor price action will portend continued downward movement. Trends in progress tend to remain as such, and overbought and oversold can get more so until extremes get reached. This means that during rally attempts, strong stocks will run up the most and those that have been weak will tend to advance the least. Simple justification: it takes more time to change opinion. Therefore stick to the relatively strongest, supporting the trend. If the trend is negative down, be in short stocks, those that have looked the worst in rally attempts. If a trend is bullish, choose the prior strongest. Don't try and pick the laggards, the bargains, that you assume will turn around and become the sprinters. If they had been inferior relative performers before, why after your purchase would they suddenly change? Simple trend continuance. It means if Wall Street's darlings are hot, they'll stay hot until their not. The underlying causes for trends won't cease overnight.

As simpleminded as it seems, the timing of daily transactions should always be considered in light of whether the broad market is in an intraday rally or decline. If you wish to sell and the Dow is soaring, wait a few minutes—maybe even hours. The upward mass of sentiment probably brings you better pricing. There is significance to the first 30 minutes of a trading day for a <u>directional carryover from the prior day's close</u>. *The prior direction will often tend to remain, at least through the very early morning period, the initial 30 minutes. A strong positive close will tend to bring in buyers early the following morning. Hence, if wanting to sell that morning prior to expected weakness, early morning might provide a good opportunity.* Price direction gaining momentum at the close tends to follow through the following morning, and vice versa.

As of January 2001, after-hours trading is still thin in volume but it can lead to interesting imbalances in the buy/sell tradeoff. Since so few players are participating, a limit order only—to buy or sell, even some distance away from the closing, or even the last price—can still become executed. Prices can have wild price swings since liquidity during those periods is generally very small. Prices can fall and rise much faster than normal. Caution is your advisor, but you may also get extremely good pricing because of these inefficiencies. For example, feeling a stock will open up strongly the following morning, you might buy the shares by placing a limit sell order several points above that day's close. Vice versa situations might have you pricing shares well below the last price. This occurred, in fact, to Novellus, NVLS, in the November 2000 technology sell-off. Yet, the caveat to trading off hours remains: do not trade with <u>market</u> orders, since you may be on the other side of thin order imbalances!

After the close, when most investors review their holdings, and assuming a stock might look vulnerable after a significant advance, it makes sense to not rush in on the opening and buy when the stock opens down, since inexperienced investors who had been delayed a purchase, might have promptly moved in to quickly support the falling price. Here, simply give in to the former bullish sentiment, and wait for their buying rush to abate, and reassess before purchasing.

Try and understand investor psychology toward price is that of a following mindset. This is where most of us want to pile into the positions and chase price. Stocks we want, that start moving, do draw us in. One reason is because there are so many investors focusing on stocks retracing from strong moves—those having being down several days running, yet who might have been in very strong intermediate directional trends. In these instances, be quick to get in and invest in concert with the assumed reoccurring primary trend. These little retracement steps that allow entry won't last too long.

The time to pay great attention is when markets appear to be getting very slow or listless. An old Wall Street maxim suggests "one never short a dull market for good reason," In the same manner, lull periods don't last long and usually when you are about to give up, they make a significant move. Don't, forget all investors eventually get impatient – just be wide awake when they do!

Be very wary of suspected investor apathy—then is no time to relax and vacation. Because the markets are more dynamic than static, change must occur, and opportunities soon will abound, regardless of transition market in-action, puny volume, and so forth. Half awake is not allowable. If bored, vacation, take the holiday…but get back quick.

For all the times stocks begin soaring amid "takeover rumors," and our intended short positions or option put purchases don't get initiated, remember, it can only happen once. If the equity is due to fall, buy the put, short the stock, and forget the noise. Think of all the money that may have been made had shorts on weak stocks or put options been put on, despite the bimonthly "takeover rumor" announcements. Once wrong doesn't mean you subordinate many potential downside strategies.

If the market appears to be ready to open strong and you cannot get in on the opening before any great strength appears, it usually pays waiting 20 to 30 minutes after which time the frenzy will usually retreat and normalcy will reappear, and the opening effect will have perhaps somewhat dissipated and true price intent shown. Once again, don't chase price early on.

Abnormal periods such as 9/11 require intense concentration with immense profitable opportunities; it's not a time to have your attention diverted. The worse it gets, the more likely it will turn; the better it is, the greater the probability a decline is near. These are very fragile periods with no firm investor confidence as to direction, and a quick trend reversal, if even for a few days, can have an attentive investor being handsomely rewarded. In sum: stay alert! (Stocks may easily move against the trend for brief periods—a few days. Absent a takeover rumor or the like, they rarely run counter the majority direction for very long. But, for any reason (often unidentified), they may for a few days…straight line movement isn't necessary to still remain in a firm trend.

A corollary to "panic selling" is "frantic buying." This means if your stock can drop into an abyss or soar without news to justify it, it might just run to the stars—or to the floor—when investor sentiment is in a trending rush. In other words, frenzies can act both ways for certain highly volatile stocks and can mean nothing more than fast buyers and equally fast sellers within those types of trading stocks. Lesson: know all about what you are contemplating owning…*before* you do so.

No one has perfect insight into short-term pricing—no one. Do not follow blindly any opinion as to what will happen. Observe what price is telling you. Anyone who really knew…wouldn't be employed, opinionating, for all of us to benefit.

A stock's unexpected reaction for a single day is not necessarily "proof." Generally, two days provides some "substantial" proof. This also means the stock that appears strong/weak may be so, for only a single day…don't try and build a trend from one day's price action. *(If the market or equity's sector is rampant, and the stock is flat—even down for that day—it doesn't mean there is anything wrong. If under the same circum-*

*stances, the second day brings the same unexpected reaction, then some concern might be warranted. All stocks don't have to move at the same time.)*

A stock holding up in the face of a downside avalanche has no lock on eventually missing the carnage. The next day or soon, they too often get hit. What all this really tells us, is that not all investment decisions, on all stocks, all get made, all at the same time.

If for a few days a stock resists strong market/sector movement downward, it does not drop or perhaps does so only marginally when it's sister industry, or the market as a whole, is being pummeled, this means it will probably rise quicker, when and if, a turn upward takes hold. The stock would be considered as having a relative strength advantage and, or as having been perhaps "sold out."

Waiting for an all clear message—all the financial press and Wall Street opinion in agreement—is not the way to commence a position when markets are nervous. Waiting too long—sometimes even hours—means significant loss of potential. The degree to which you can wait is really determined by the extremes of the most recent move which caused the nervousness. *Example: the NASDAQ mid-April 2000 dropped 25 percent in one week; the "snap back" rally started almost immediately and was upwardly dramatic. Any delay in purchasing caused much in the way of potential to have been squeezed. You don't have too much time to ponder a transaction move if it's close to a bottom after evidence. You might just guess and invest a little. Knowing it will eventually move above your purchase area, especially if the prior downside had been very steep! But if it doesn't exit immediately…and fast.*

Trying to mind reason very short-term pricing is generally wasted time. It seems better to take the position that the security is either fully sold out and due to rebound and/or too far ahead of itself, and due to tank and execute the trade. This is especially valid when trying to call very short-term tops and bottoms. Conditions change quickly—take the likely position and execute. Our "smarts" will not be very helpful, no more than patiently watching each tick for guidance.

It is the exception that stocks starting out weak, falling several points, then rallying back above neutral into positive territory by a few points, then falling back again and close down at a loss of two or more. Intraday swings tend not to have three back and forth and back, through neutral price waves of many points. They very rarely will have large intraday three wave patterns. While two are commonplace—maybe an up early, then down close. But, up, then far down below neutral, then back up well above neutral, isn't the norm. Investors usually don't have that flimsy a daily opinion on a security.

Avoid the purchase of highly volatile stocks—those with a high volatility number—in abnormal periods (e.g., when stocks are crashing or booming or under assumed market turns), if trading for the short-term. While they can run quick and hand you fast money. Their volatile nature means you lose the option of watching their movement first (since they move so fast). Thus, you feel the necessity to assume bottoms and tops, and when wrong, you may pay very dearly! It is more sensible to be patient or position very lightly, or invest in these only when the trend is decided in one direction or another. *In addition, volatile stocks are more commonly owned by traders than investors. This means they will fall and rise much more consecutively (over days) and, of course, in greater magnitude. They are often perceived as non-investments, some having little behind them—e.g., earnings, a lasting business model, etc. They are wonderful to own during glory periods; disasters in market routs.*

Trading on NASDAQ in pre-market trading, in advance of the market's reaction to news, carries a decided advantage. Since most investors will delay decisions until the markets all open, so as long as the stock doesn't appear to have fully reflected the event near its opening, it is where to tap the easy opportunity prior to the masses forming some consensus. *(In addition, strong price opinion before the opening tends to remain throughout until the actual opening.)*

There are many instances when stocks or industries get overextended and continue that way far longer than expected—"Oh it'll never fall (or rise)"—and investors give up. A word of experienced encouragement: don't. They'll have their selling or buying moment and patience will have been rewarded. Think of the Internet sector. How many times have they gotten hit to then come back—one day most of them won't!

Whenever there are many consecutive up days, as well as down, say five, six, seven or more, are significant examples of trend strength and a potential one-day move against that trend, is not worth following. Trend extremes, five consecutive days up or down, really signify one direction conviction, especially when coupled with greater than normal relative volume, and going against them is very unwise despite our inclination to do so. *If a trend were in fact to continue, then three or more days of countertrend and balanced with ample magnitude should be sufficient to cause the trend resumption. If there are more days—seven or eight—of countertrend movement, it might be signaling that a trend change is in progress. If you think about it, after a few consecutive retracement days, a strong prior trend really destined to reassert itself should.*

Occasionally stocks move unexpectedly far more than what would appear as a reaction only to the market's move. (It is learned—often the next day—that some news or advice affected the stock.) A warning: be suspicious of "out of the blue" large movement, up or down. You often find the following day that the "steal" you thought you found, isn't one at all, and there indeed there was a reason for the significant move.

When price trend is very strong, at some point the commentary is apt to be that the market is due to pull back. This statement assumes that investors will collectively vote to defer an intended purchase under similar logic, having acceded to the warning. They defer purchase and the market will then dip as foretold. But what often happens is that each individual's buying decisions are being formulated to allow "in their mind, only their entrance into the rally—no one elses'," and they and the "trend predictors" often foolishly forget that this overall persuasion—mass upward conviction – will still have effect. The end result: continued buying, pushing prices further and further. Sideliners awaiting their turn…wait more.

The following comments couldn't be stated more meaningfully:

**Do not stand in the way of price. If trending adverse to you—exit! Investors do not will price movement; we are always mere subordinates.**

### Downward & Bearish Periods

During strong downward price action, the most speculative, and the least unseasoned companies will move lower—fast and steep. After this period terminates, Wall Street will usually advance the biggest, oldest and most secure companies first. *(They are the ones that will be assumed to survive either the event or their shareholders' urge to continually liquidate, and they are the ones which have the greatest liquidity so institutions can get at them.) The corollary is that small stocks and the Russell 2000, which is the market proxy for same, will generally fall faster and deeper in an overall market slide. Therefore, puts on these types of investments are to be considered—or their proxy, the Russell 2000.)*

When stocks start to be routed, specialists may try and drop their bid pricing very quickly, so emotional sellers will liquidate lower than they might otherwise, and the specialists will be buying—filling their "required inventory buying" at the lower price. This measure coincidentally drags the ask price down slowly since the specialists might also have to provide stock. So why not at higher price for their retirement—and wallets? In, effect they widen the spread to take advantage of investors during emotional periods. *Proof? Watch how fast they drop the bid, and then raise it at the first sure sign of a firm rally attempt. If their stock is appearing to be rushed for specialists, they will bump the ask price up hard and fast, to induce buyers to purchase high so specialists and market makers may sell out of inventory at those quickly inflated higher prices. Even an added 1/8 on 5,000,000 daily shares pays the bills! Keep emotions in check when placing transactions. Try and be steadfast; it tends to be cheaper. Avoid emotional trades during the stampedes— up or down. (This phenomenon occurs in options pricing as well.)*

When declining phases first begin, the reaction for many investors is to "snap up" their perception of "bargains." It is not uncommon to see several failed rally attempts if prices continue to drift lower and lower again since the savvy will try and wait and then repurchase. Early on, investors tend not to believe the decline, what they are witness to—especially if the decline is very deep. Yet as that decline endures, there does come a point where losses are accepted, and rally attempts often seen before become rarer and short-lived. The smart investor is said to be selling into the rallies. This doesn't mean the selling never abates. It will abate when the <u>broad market</u>, either from some catalyst or its own internal changes, begins a sustainable advance. It generally does so when there comes an acceptance to the constant torrent of selling and lower and lower prices, and by the lack of any desire to start buying, since the bearish period is then seen as ceaseless…there it always ends. Be patient. Allow market psychology and price to turn up when it's ready.

An important question when major selling is occurring and individual stocks are going down, is to find if the selling is a normal action in the regular buy/sell dynamic, or is it something much more—perhaps an overreaction to overall market selling sentiment. If the latter, then emotion is the driving element behind the extremes in downward movement and almost anything can happen. Lower can become lower still. *This is noteworthy when selling is felt everywhere and all investors are on notice through the press and regular television coverage; a feeling of a need to act can occur. In these periods, rational price action isn't likely, and expecting abnormal price behavior is more likely—e.g., stocks falling far more than ordinary and illogically beyond expectations. In these periods, prices can fall very fast and things can get very ugly.*

When a true overdue correction first starts, it is more likely not to be a one-day event. If a stock is off that first day, the odds are decent that there isn't a need to act just then to snap up the apparent gift. *Contrast this idea with watching the stock fall for four straight days when the number of sellers is obviously active—those desiring to sell are doing so. We might assume the next day there would be fewer. The point: patience during minor declines can have sweet outcomes.*

Short-term tip: stocks do not lose their volatility overnight. $100 stocks cut in half in torrid selling periods will retain their sprinter status almost as much as when the stock had been 40 percent and 50 percent higher. This is likely, because as noted, investors in particular, and Wall Street in general, have a very short-lived memory, and repeat actions. If a $120 stock, now $65 maybe four weeks later, starts moving up as the market appears to be turning forward, the stock will tend to have point movement similar to when it was in the 120 area. This is a short-term phenomenon, and not lasting, but it means their volatility just won't vanish after either a split or a huge breakdown.

An aggressive idea is to buy the very volatile stock at a presumed market bottom after price evidence of an upturn. Since most stocks will follow the short-term trend of the whole market, and if the market starts upward or is about to, the most volatile will retain that characteristic and probably advance the percentage most in keeping with it's prior character. Here, quick profits of magnitude can result. If the market does not follow through—if it is not a sustained start upward—a preplanned one or two point stop loss curtails any otherwise deep loss in owning the volatile issue.

You must try to think like a realistic—not optimistic—investor during ugly declines. If your wanted stock has been going down and down and doesn't seem to have any sustained buying interest, why would it the instant you go in? Makes sense? Wait for a price trend change in the broad markets and pass on demanding that you get the bottom—since no one else does either.

Stocks always <u>fall faster</u> than they rise. Downside point movement can be ultra swift. Why? An investor almost must make a decision after they own stock—delay is not an available option. Since many investors would rather do nothing and avoid anxiety, they'll often remain in a present non-ownership position rather than accept the risk inherent in stock ownership. Even an advancing market might not force participation as might the instance when prices are dying. Since no investor sits and analytically tallies missed profitable situations to keep a running count of what might have been, being out means not paying too much attention. Yet being involved even when progressively poorer each day, means the market's dramatic periods force you take notice and, ultimately, action as you should.

During severe market pressure, all the fundamental company news that may have been so appealing will be forgotten, and the equity will fall anyway. In addition, there is very little fundamental effect in the short-term—it is almost totally technical, supply/demand reactions, price driven. And the corollary works as well. In a significant market or sector "buying binge," everything is rising—even the company that last week that had missed expectation etc. Wall Street has no memory—and that you can take to Fort Knox! *The Street rarely practices "equities discrimination" at forming bottoms or tops—moves will be uniform for price reasons alone.*

When the "pain" from falling prices is appearing <u>everywhere</u>—idle conversation, the cover of Business Week, the lead television news story, etc.—is just about the place for a bottom. *(Most of the selling that would ever be done during that period to arrive at that gloomy stage, has been. Then, when even the richest are feeling pain and start demanding explanations, you can almost bet the ranch the end is near—such as when political figures and major banks are questioning how long this might last.)*

When stocks absorb bad news and do not move lower, it typifies their (individual) bottoming processes and usually, but not always, their next advance. *(They might move first laterally for a time.)* There will be the periods when stocks have been weak and you are hoping you can get in at a bottom but you allow the dominant focus of continued downside to blur that potent upside potential. This happens when they can't seem to get going above their downward bias, and you just assume they won't, even as they move upward. Maybe you sell so as not to see a new loss or curtail more of the old one. It must be understood that at suspected lows, the upside is far greater than the downside, and selling prematurely so not as to lose more means forfeiting any quick upward price action which is probably long overdue. It means not surrendering too soon; maybe it was an excellent reason you placed the position on initially! Don't assume what isn't there. Keep the probabilities toward success and failure clear.

After very broad and bloody market declines, be ready for any entrance into any apparent strong market rally attempts, since the most volatile stocks will run 10 to 15 percent in a single day. Even if the rally turns out not to be lasting—the start of a true significant advance—even these huge "fake outs"—failed continuing rallies—can still provide extremes of profit to the nimble investor. Of course again, the clue as to whether it might be real, is the broad market and not our individual choice.

When there is major downside price action on the opening from very negative news or from a carryover negative session, the opening pricing through 10:00 a.m. will tend to be the low for that day, and this follows for entire industry sectors as well. Why? The psychological tendency for investors is to be too emotional, to sell first to "beat" others to the downside during the first 20 to 30 minutes. And remember six hours (10:00 a.m. to 4:00 p.m.) is a long time for continual selling pressures to continue to have their way. A shrewd investor can capitalize on the emotional concerns of others. Here's how. *Specialists will open stocks very low, since there must be large buyers' interested in their holdings in order to maintain their markets. With their _very_ low setting of the opening, which becomes their purchase price, they have already factored in a small cushion should prices later move lower still. So following them, hence buying on the opening, will make sense even though it is a "blind buy"—at an opening unknown price and with an assumed later day upward spike. Don't forget, you cannot know the low for the Dow until all their components open up for trading, so be patient before buying. (Another hint in this example is to buy puts on the Dow or its equivalent since not all of the Dow 30 will open at once. With lower openings likely to come, an early put purchase has an almost "win" built-in with probable lower opening prices pushing the overall Dow lower, and thus reflecting higher put pricing!) Conversely...*

If it appears that unexpectedly good news prior to the markets opening will cause most underlying stocks to hit their high on the opening—although this is not nearly as often the strategy. Again, be patient. *Because the specialist or market makers will try and take advantage of buyers' enthusiasm and open high, then distribute stock—their inventory—hoping to buy back lower, later in the day. Their opening price might be set artificially high, higher than it might otherwise. A smart countermove is to wait after the first half hour of trading and note the percent the stock that might have risen, and either sell shares you might own or, if its price is up 5 to 10, possibly 15 percent, that is far likely to be the high for that day. Therefore, waiting throughout the day for a lower price should get you a lower purchase price, and assuming that you believe the stock has the legs to run further over the next several days or weeks anyway. The point being, too much early enthusiasm should not deter you from being patient and later that day getting a better purchase price.*

If the market has had an extended down period and then an apparent extreme sell off day (a climactic day), it will probably make sense for short-term decisions, to even a "guess" that an actual market start upward will have some legs, since most of the selling will have by then been completed and the buy/sell dynamic will apt be to the buy side—most certainly if it can be with long-term intent. True market/sector bottoms in <u>bull</u> markets will get noticed—very fast: e.g., 4/14/2000. *(Contrast this tact with an individual stock getting whacked 25 to 50 percent–those you stay away from!) The advised strategy is to try and isolate the bottom as likely (use the RSI as one help) and then purchase with the knowledge that even if the pricing was to head lower still, it is also probable that the final low is near to try and to wait for a de facto bottom, and then react at a likely higher price. Our markets move just too fast.*

In nasty market periods—and not bear markets—broad markets rarely can suffer in excess of 20 percent losses and then move sideways for extended periods, being they are more destined to pick up bargain hunters. All that turmoil will always invite volatility and investor interest. An individual stock is very different. There is almost no downside limit if the news, or investor reaction, is bad enough.

Sometimes after a major market sell-off, buying a <u>market index</u> is safer and more rewarding since if it moves, you must profit. If you had chosen the wrong stock, you might not. Yet a stock's demand can get very extreme, since only days prior, the stock was 10 to 20 points higher and in an emotional buying surge, where fear is not quite as present, stocks can get overbought very fast yet can remain so far longer than they normally do.

If the market and or sector—and mainly the former—is being hurt badly, even an apparent low RSI or bullish chart will usually not be enough to start a sustainable rally for an individual stock if the surroundings are getting constantly hurt. Wait for the market or sector to turn up. A stock is almost never a steady island in a falling environment.

If a stock had been down many consecutive days, do not purchase until, and only, after a closing price advance presumably indicative of the breaking the downtrend. (If the magnitude of the down move is very pronounced over a day or two it might also be sufficient and can mean not having to wait for an up day to purchase.) The best way to ensure an up day is to buy late on that day, 3:00 to 3:30 p.m. or after. (If the stock is up that late in the day, odds are it will remain up for that first day requirement). Or begin purchasing almost immediately the following day, provided it appears early on that this second day will be upward (there is no sell, off on the opening of the markets or in the first 30 minutes.) Investors will climb aboard after waiting for the assumed upward turn to commence. This tact accomplishes two things: it means you do not try and guess the bottom, "Catch a falling knife," and you are not purchasing until there is some proof (second day advancing) that the first day advance wasn't a false start upward. It is also sensible to consider if the trend might be changing. For example, if the sector had been very strong, then presumably a few down days might/should be all that's necessary to correct too much recent upward enthusiasm. If there were multiple consecutive down days—five, six, and seven and even more—with fairly significant loss of point movement, it might be a warning worth paying attention to—that a major trend change was taking place!

Example: after the extraordinary event of 9/11 Novellus (NVLS), a semiconductor fabrication company, endured a murderous 13-day straight decline, finally ending at a low price of about 25 with a 17-day RSI of 21. Had one the nerve, timing, knowledge, and been blessed with some fortune, and purchased their call options one stage out-of-the-money, the 30 series, and allowed for time, thus having chose, a November series, the near final tally on November 8th with the stock hovering at 39 with still a week left before options expiration, would have looked like this:

| | | |
|---|---|---|
| With the stock at 25 | : | November 30 Call Option Price $1.06 |
| With the stock at 39 | : | November 30 Call Option Price $9.50 |

Nine times and 800 percent appreciation in the ensuing seven weeks during an enduring NASDAQ bullish intermediate advance. But the learned investor would have had to first heed the above and patiently wait until the falling price finally stopped…falling. Only then moving to purchase with fingers crossed. Imagine that a $10,000 "investment" would have grown to about one half of a "Lamborghini," or $100,000.

After a protracted down period for the market and when the RSI and chart formations look very close to a bottom, a torrid one day upward rebound does not mean a bottom is in place. It might, but it also might not. Demand to witness many days of upward pricing before assuming an all clear signal. After false starts—big one day moves which do not carry through—any positions that may have been put on, should be sold. A very oversold market, really worth being in, should be able to sustain itself for several days at minimum.

We should never need more ammunition to plainly accept the precept that in weak market periods *you do not* run after weak stocks—they are not bargains. And if you played those weak odds nevertheless over many years, there might be a time when the weakest stock ran in an upward barrage. Yet all that might have been made, that one time, will be given back many other times by continuing losses in trying to tap the bargains out of weak stocks! Weak is weak for a reason—don't waste your money trying for the home run which might occur once in ten outings. A simple way to avoid this is to only purchase the strongest relative stocks—those that fell the least during the rout. After the bloodletting subsides, they are apt to retain their relative bullish strength and move forward quicker. Just accept the obvious: weak stocks are in "weak seller's hands!" Why assume coincident with our purchase when everybody then reverses course? *Simple sense suggests if the stock is truly worth buying right now it wouldn't be that easy to purchase at such "bargain pricing." Bad stock trends can pick up speed. The real issue is where the bottom price is, and not that there is great potential in very oversold equities. A purchased "bargain" at 40 (relative to a high of 120) is ultimately no bargain if the eventual rally begins at 20!! Since a move of 100 percent—a double to a 40 price—earns this investor nothing!*

Near, intermediate bottoms, a good purchase time is early in a day—after 10:00 a.m. The first half hour plays the emotional side and sellers try to beat each other out the exit door. Amidst the early selling, any intraday attempts at an oversold rally have time to be played out, and naturally it takes constant selling to keep oversold stocks down during a day when the low may have been reached hours earlier. At minimum, you can play for an intraday attempt at an upward bounce with five plus hours maybe in front of you. An in-fact intermediate bottom may not be put in, but profit potential from even an intraday oversold bounce can be rewarding, since investors often bet heavily, and very quickly, on the long side when sensing a bottom might be forming.

As has been mentioned before, downward market bias is never perpetual. There are always people opening up IRAs and 401k plans looking for equities to purchase. No one initiates security research to find stocks going bankrupt. Investors and market tipsters are logically looking to buy something—not short something. The point here is after significant declines, keep focused on buying opportunities. Even being premature and then having to wait a few weeks is not a significant surrender to interest on otherwise earned money market interest on portfolio cash. *Of course, waiting too long or having expected purchases then turn into still further downside price action is to be avoided.*

By now it should be a given, but any rallies against a primary downward trend are apt to be short with the downward bias soon to follow. The exact opposite of bull market primary trends.

### *Intraday Price Movement*
When you sell intraday be prepared to also buy it back intraday or go elsewhere with the sale proceeds. This is because your sale doesn't put a cap on price; it isn't likely to stay below your sales price for any extended time. This phenomena of intraday overbought and oversold trending price action is common and expected price behavior—call it the natural rhythm of price movement—stocks go up and stocks go down. They never trade in on an eight range. The securities process is a dynamic one, not static.

The early daily direction of an intraday trend cannot be known on the basis of a few minutes. So be careful in acting too hastily when trying to ascertain direction. Unless you have witnessed a good portion of the day from which a more informed decision can be made, you are guessing and lowering your probabilities.

There is no difference when buying into an oversold market if the stock moves intraday or closes up, since we are only looking for a short-term move. A stock 4 points below its prior close, which then rallies to being down just minus one, *still yields us 3 net points contrasted to a stock down 1 point, which then closes at plus .5 for the day. If we want point movement for short-term plays, the former is preferred and any type of points movement is value.*

### *The "7 Percent Intraday Range Rule" for Normal Market Periods*
Over an approximate 125,000 daily observations completed in March 2001 on mostly the Russell 1000, sample stocks moved on <u>average 3.4 percent</u> up or down from their prior price close. Thus, approximately 90 percent of the time, the maximum intraday range of movement was just about 7 percent from the prior closing price. (However, the most volatile individual security—and this security trait is easily measurable—will move well <u>beyond</u> the 7 percent expectation.)

In weak sector intermediate periods, there is the quiet tact of remaining on the sidelines until an established reversal is under way. This eliminates excellent short-term intraday opportunities. For short-term traders, stocks having been very weak aren't going to be falling 5 points day after day after day. (Use the 3.4 percent rule—the usual maximum daily percent a stock will drop or advance from its prior close.) If an assumed market low is reached early in a day, it might easily become the low for that day, and any later recovery played for a few points, since <u>daily</u> money counts too! Do not become dissuaded from just buying and selling intraday. (Yet this type of short-term trading shouldn't be your sole investment ambition.)

Since the range of normalcy for average equities daily <u>maximum</u> range of intraday movement is approximately 7 percent from the prior close, movement far outside these figures might suggest there is something else at work. For the Dow, it is closer to 2 or 2.5 percent, because there are 30 stocks that have to be in directional agreement! (Nor is the 7 percent rule applicable during severe abnormal times—stocks advancing after long and bitter declining periods or when owning highly volatile equities.)

Intraday pricing is just as important as closing price for profitability. Too many times, investors are waiting for a stock to have a down day before purchase. To a fault, they'll miss intraday movement, stuck on wanting an up or down closing price. directionally through to the close. The point is: you can make money over a few hours or by day's end had you bought intraday. What the closing price might become should have less importance than what any intraday price might offer. There will usually be several implicitly profitable trades intraday; there is only one closing price.

Most of intraday movement is derived from the broad market effect, so it is important to focus there first.

Hints as to future intraday movement can also be seen when prices tend to cluster at the same intraday highs and lows. This means prices tend to find buyers at their daily lows or some lower type price level, and sellers at either their daily highs or same higher price level. Repetitive buying and selling at these price areas can often be done many times intraday. It's simple intraday support and resistance price levels, as well as,double bottoms and tops.

Sudden intraday moves are always non-continuous. There are always price "spurts" which advance/decline, then retrace, retest, etc. Multiple daily waves of two to five minutes, even 30-second spurts of movements coincident with the market and or sectors, or without—it's the normal cadence of stock price action. Once again, being patient might reward you with the price you just missed. Simple lesson here: don't rush into a fast wave of pricing.

Sudden rapid movement in the Dow or S&P 500 can be from buy or sell programming from hedge funds that are playing momentum. When their effect is over, the market often returns to its prior intraday direction just as rapidly. <u>Instant</u> chasing here isn't a wise idea.

Relative strength and weakness tends to hold throughout even a day. This can mean that a stock bucks a downward trend early in the morning, and as that trend becomes weaker still, the stock will tend to retain its relative strength, even though it might turn negative on the day. To no surprise, when they start out relatively weaker, they tend to remain relatively weaker. This is a day-to-day relative phenomenon. This also means the stock that starts out weak with everything around it going up, will tend to retain its relatively weaker state. *(And the psychological reasoning probably is that investors wanting to buy, but not seeing any upward movement, don't get induced or seduced into a purchase—since "nothing is happening." With many watching and not buying, demand can remain tepid. Bottom line: laggards tend to remain behind; those strong in the morning tend to remain strong into the final bell.)*

Initiating a strategy before the market closes means you retain the result of your strategy into the next morning, before investors have time to review that day's market news. *If you purchase a half hour before the close and if you are proven correct the following morning, you can reap the reward since you didn't allow time for others to assess what you acted on. Two caveats: one is to be proven correct—or being first won't matter; two, see caveat one.*

Example: ABRA Inc. (ARBA), during a diving NASDAQ in early November 2000 had support at about 100. On November 19th, the stock had hit an intraday high of 114 and toward the close sank to its mid-July 2000 support level of 100. An investor mindful of the support area might have assumed it would hold, bought in, and not allowed the after market review of that fact to affect the potential profit of having been first in line. The following morning, the stock opened up and quickly rose to 108. Even a 100 share purchase the prior afternoon yielded about $800; for 500, $4000. The support at 100 that an investor knew of, and acted on, created a wonderful profit.

Hyperbolic intraday up or down movement is often seen and should be handled in the same manner as if holding positions for long-term—act!

### Options Price Movement

Options pricing cannot get overbought/sold, only their underlying stocks can. No option price can ever go up too much. It reacts only to its "parent" stock movement. The lesson here: never sell an option on its price basis alone or think "I made enough already." *(The 1 in 100 chance that an options movement is based on an intended takeover might be the lone exception.)*

If the options are not moving as they should, watch out. It usually means the stock move isn't lasting or, more likely, that its volatility perception has changed and was already built into the option.

Watching the CBOE Market Volatility Index as a contrarian's measure of market expectation has been an excellent "fortune teller" over many years. Levels above 35 usually signal a market turn is due.

OEX is the symbol for the Standard & Poors largest 100 companies and <u>changes</u>

in its "Open Interest" for both calls and puts in the nearest month's hints as to future market direction. *(Open Interest changes are newly added purchases and indicate the anticipated market direction according to the actions of the options purchaser.)* To determine, divide open put interest by open call interest. Normally this ratio should be higher for puts—maybe up to 1.20. Too much of a change in pessimism is bullish.

When a stock's option volume is light, it does not mean a potential position is not warranted. Options specialists will adjust the bid/ask spread, even if only they are active on either end. *(Ideally, trying to trade options on equities whose options trade on multiple exchanges, means no single exchange can monopolize price and the competition across exchanges allows for "beating the spread" and enjoying fairer pricing. This is very easy to accomplish, since coincident bid/ask change doesn't occur and a fast-moving trader can advantage. This assumes that the exchange to which you directed the order will honor its own spread—at times, they "walk away"—refuse to accept your trade and, since all the other exchanges have adjusted their pricing and they haven't. Provided the spreads are not more than 1/8 away they may still get honored. Yet "walking away" is very illegal and against NASD policy—but it's often done!)*

Be aware when out-of-the-money calls and puts are equal in price. This is bullish. Puts should be higher in value to compensate for fast declines. This indicator is one of contrary variety. During extremes of pessimism when the above puts are three and four times higher in price than calls, this suggests too much market worry; a bullish implication.

Option prices tend to be higher in the morning; time decay is evident even over any single day. *This means if the stock price is not higher or lower at day's end, its options will still have fallen some. Consequently, waiting until the end of a day can prove advantageous to the buyer, and early selling favors the seller. (Big generalizations for sure, but they are theoretically accurate.)*

Real-world options pricing models which automatically set real-world options bid and ask levels, can be overridden manually by the specialist. This means they do not get lost within the model's estimation.

It sounds too simple, but if all things are equal, purchase options on stocks with the highest price. Not only do they move much easier and far greater in reaction to stimulus, their investors are less apt to limit price when bidding for stock ownership of these high price issues. This passes its way down to options pricing. *They are less likely to try and save an eighth or quarter point if the stock costs $150 and accept the "why bother, just buy it" mentality.*

When options volume in a security is light, bet that the options specialist, alone, is determining pricing. It means they'll run the ask price of call-ups during "hot" periods and drop the bid price very fast during heavy selling. The lesson: be careful and do not chase price, since price is being <u>artificially</u> set. *It is more often true than not, that other than activity in the most popular stocks, almost all options pricing is being set by spe-*

*cialists or floor brokers, professionals, and not by the governance of a free market between active buy and sell demand. Expect no price breaks for being the hope-they-treat-me-fair "uninformed investor;" it's been said most would beat their mother for an extra quarter.*

Never purchase an option on a stock with very low volatility unless you buy at-the-money or in-the-money, or if you expect an immediate dynamic move. Out-of-the-money low volatility options work! Don't waste your time or hand over your money with these ideas, since there are too many other alternatives.

Referring to the concept of implied volatility with options, an anticipated company news event will often carry an excess volatility premium, and after release a quick retracement to normal options pricing. Here be wise and defer purchases; maybe sell options just prior to a news release, etc., and capture the implied volatility premiums.

Whenever you receive a too-good, and too-quick options price—e.g., you are trying to purchase on the bid and get filled instantly—be wary. No specialist is giving away their money. Bet your side of the trade will be very quickly reversed. You might just turn around and liquidate the position. Or if you just sold and get a higher price than you should have, wait and see how long it takes for that same price to become advanced further. It confounds how often it happens. *They just don't seem to produce errors that advantage the customer, nor should they. Investment is about money. It's serious business and it's their livelihood.*

*For example: holding call options with a bid across four exchanges at about 1.40 to 1.45 and having one exchange at 1.55 seemed out of whack. Still a quick sale at the 1.55 price was "honored" by that exchange. Within 30 minutes, the same bid price on the same call option had risen to the 1.60 to 1.70 area. As usual, the 1.55 price wasn't really any gift—it never is! The option pros are not imbeciles.*

## News Dissemination

Good news should advance a healthy stock or market, and vice versa. If it doesn't, a reversal may be coming. *(Remember this does not have to happen in the same day. Example: after a long painful correction, just-released poor fundamental news will often not push a stock lower. Here, the stock is likely "washed out" and a bottom is forming.*

Be careful when reacting to news and the timing of it. Ask the question: Is the news really significant and worth *reacting* to? Company-specific will have more lasting impact on its stock; industry-related will likely have a temporary effect, since it tends to be a broad brush opinion.

The timing of news will affect stock pricing. Generally the news effect will completely occur within a few hours —almost always within a full day. This means when negative industry news is reported, it might be best to wait through hours to allow the emotional reaction to be absorbed. (Since immediate selling, coincident with everybody trying to exit with their collective negative mindset, is not the wisest approach. Of course this is generally the rule at all times.)

The market's current handling of news, particularly negative, is vital to watch. If poor news doesn't impact a company's stock price negatively and that appears to be the current pattern—maybe because the market is in a buying phase—it's likely any non-calamitous news won't affect the next company either. Hence don't be too quick to exit in these periods.

The investment press will be first in line to reason price movement with a slant and often talk up its continuance with their reporting fervor, maybe unknowingly slanting objectivity. Try to remain level-headed. The press had no more future insight into a lasting rally or a decline than the day before. They won't after the next market move either. Words don't make for price movement.

Be sensitive to the timing of news. Bad news that hits in the morning and causes selling on the market averages or an individual issue, might be easily absorbed later throughout the day, and rallies can ensue. The effect of news only can last so long.

There is an ancient Wall Street proverb that tells us, "Buy on the rumor; sell on the news." This suggests that stocks advance in anticipation of the event, then sell off. When companies report their earnings, note to see how Wall Street reacts and you will gain a clue as to how your stock might react. Additionally, watch the stock itself prior to the report. If it advances well into the news release, it might be set up to sell off. If it was fairly tame, it might not, since no positive effect had been seen with the presumed forthcoming positive news.

Because it is so stock-specific, investor response to an intraday news event will vary. The more institutionally held, generally the slower the response and vice versa. This means trying to pick up a quick bargain on a large well-known company suffering a negative press announcement might mean waiting until some price stability appears; most of the selling having then being completed. The effect of a news announcement after closing should be felt almost immediately the following morning during the first few minutes of trading, since there are so many stockholders and they will have had time to consider effect.

When Wall Street recommends a stock, its impact generally will tend to give the stock a few days of strength—most often in a good healthy stock market period. Partly because of the announcement and made, awareness, and because investor sentiment is always bullish longer-term. Downgrades carry less weight since, again, the investing public is generally bullish, and would rarely start an aggressive put or short sale purchase strategy. The overall climate has much to do with painting investor reaction anyway to recommendations. If it is bullish, negative press won't matter much.

Even though full-time market players have the first shot at news doesn't mean the full effect of that news will be <u>instant</u>, since many other affected investors may yet react upon hearing same. So again…be patient! Let the effect get spread. The significance of the news will affect the time it takes to react.

Reacting to expected news first—with seemingly an edge—won't automatically work if the news or tip was anticipated; only <u>unexpected</u> news acted upon quickly and correctly helps.

Accuracy in forecasting the event or news, is always *less important* than in predicting how investors will react to it. Have they already assumed the event? Is it in the pricing? So save your effort—not for what the news will be—but for figuring out how investors might react. You earn zero accurately predicting news events.

Consider the context, or the market's psychology, just before anticipated important news. If the prior days had been bearish, it is less likely that even significant negative news will impact investments again, and vice versa.

There is an important distinction between newsworthy worrying—like if the company's CEO goes before the SEC, or the CEO was indicted, etc.—and news that you can't foresee coming...neurosis isn't healthy. Example: worrying that the space shuttle will land on your house or events that blind side your investments that you couldn't have foreseen will occur; nothing can be done to avert it, and don't punish yourself for it.

If watching CNBC or any large viewer medium, and you react quickly enough, you can often capture very short-term gains. But if the news you reacted to first isn't that significant, a quick turn-around can occur, and having been "first in line," "being, quick on the trigger," might not help at all. Word to the wise in those situations: get the advantage and then sell it just as quick upon sensing any weakness to your position.

The impact on the investment community from news, be it favorable or not, lasts only for a brief period. Do not expect that good—or bad—news will affect the entire market for more than maybe a week. If the government were to declare that no tax would be due on any investment gain, you would hardly expect even that type of exceptional news to stimulate great excess demand beyond a week. How long would investors be expected to wait before buying? Six months? Hardly. The fact: the investment effect from news gets absorbed by our markets generally fairly quickly and particularly with large companies, where many eyes are continually absorbing any news release. Compare this to small cap stocks where news travels slower and can thus be advantaged over a longer period of time—not so with large cap, where news is almost instantly factored into price.

When companies hold news conferences to reassure the public because of unfavorable news, it is almost universally bullish short-term—at least that day. Rare are managements that don't contain or put a favorable spin on news; their damage control almost always works for a brief period.

231

## Earnings

During earnings reporting periods and surely during weak earnings periods or weak market periods, if it is possible, avoid initiating positions in companies not yet reporting, since Wall Street's reaction to earnings is highly unpredictable. *If you need to purchase, invest after the report.* Because while the short-term offers very little control, at least in more mundane periods, securities can be watched carefully and appropriate action taken. An unexpected EPS reaction, or downgrade, can bring instant pain—and much of it—and carry through the next day or two, as Wall Street allows us to remember during each and every sour earnings reporting period. *(As an alternative, buy the market in this period if it's trending higher, since it rarely will be altered for more than a single day from a single company's poor earnings or news release.)*

In recent work, *2001: The Death Of Fundamentals,* from the well-respected Lazelo Birinyi, earnings and stock price should be coincident movers, yet over several decades this relationship hasn't held. He reasons, *"Our view is that market dynamics and the restructuring of the capital markets, including globalization, have created a mentality in which classic fundamental approaches are not sufficient."* To which can be added, it may never have been the best singular approach irrespective of whenever it might have become accepted principle. Fundamental analysis, even if it now appears as limiting, isn't an end all to investment glory—we need more.

Be very cognizant during earnings periods of <u>leading</u> companies within their various market sectors reporting. A very good—even expectedly good—quarter can mean the entire sector will advance and an assumption can be made that they, too, will report a good quarter. It can work in reverse, as one might guess. *The trick is to make certain that any press pre-announcement of earnings is coming from a very reliable source, then try and capture the advantage.*

Generally negative earnings will be pre-announced prior to the normal reporting periods. For example, if a company will have less-than-expected results for its second quarter, they might announce it in mid-June before most other companies will report. Therefore, and generally, if a company does not pre-announce, they probably will hit their number—a big probably, but it usually works out this way. *In fact, any company dumb enough—or perhaps we might say sufficiently lacking in marketing acumen in an era of miss-the-number-get-slaughtered releases—to not have firmly guided Wall Street, probably deserves to fall in price.*

Wall Street analysts changing their opinions as to company earnings generally yields only temporary impact to the stock—one way or the other. Within a day or so, the "new direction" is forgotten and the stock does what it would have anyway.

Our Wall Street friends habitually announce earnings changes well after major price moves have occurred. Earnings are much more independent of price movement than most believe. In addition, it is commonplace for companies to have experienced no downward price, yet then announce a poor earnings release.

232

*For example, a stock might be down 40 percent and Wall Street analysts will slash the earnings estimates, thus offering its faithful followers—what? Did they need to be told after being 40 percent poorer that the earnings are going to be presumed less? Maybe Wall Street will be wrong again on this company, since they were before, hence why would they be expected to listen now? Wall Street has the insight which assumes earnings and price are almost one-to-one correlated. They aren't—don't be fooled! There is some relief in being told that the company you have invested in and that you are partners with, is going to earn a magnificent sum in the next 12 months, and based on historic observation, within the stock P/E formula, you expect to be every bit the richer. If price doesn't follow—did it matter? A good reason to watch price!*

Contrary to expectation, a company's expected EPS cannot be forecast from its most recent price activity. Good price actions frequently are followed by poor EPS results or warnings, etc.

Companies missing earnings targets tend to continue to miss; conversely, beating EPS expectations portends future earnings ahead of expectations.

When a major brokerage firm upgrades a <u>few</u> issues within an industry, almost the entire industry will advance regardless—it works in reverse as well.

# Technical Analysis

## Price Pattern, Technical Helpers

During broad market one-direction intermediate movement, 80 to 90 percent of equities will ultimately follow the prevailing trend. It means that being in something quickly is an odds-on advantage.

Generally, if the market is strong enough it will force a stock thorough its resistance; weak enough, to beneath its support. The outcome of this "test" is best handled by either taking a small position and participating in some manner, or patiently waiting for the proof to emerge one way or another over a few days.

In technical analysis, there is an accepted percentage of retracement of prior trend moves generally in 1/3, 1/2 and 2/3 increments. If a stock rose 30 points in, say, two months, an accepted retracement of 1/3 or 10 points, then 1/2 or 15 points, and finally 2/3 or 20 points or thereabouts, would not violate the yet primary trend in place. *These are some <u>possible</u> support levels were a decline to take hold—but not overly used.*

Gaps in price charts tend to suggest where the next directional move will be.

The significance that Wall Street attaches to a specific price target for a bellweather company is easily forgotten after its occurrence. Take, for example, October 2000: if Cisco Systems (CSCO) dropped below 50, the feeling was that all of NASDAQ would suffer, the break of 50 portending lower prices in mass. Upon CSCO's break to 47 and subsequent rally back above 50, then again below 50, NASDAQ offered no reaction the second time—proof that what was once thought as price significant, upon occurrence, gets forgotten quite quickly. The same initial reaction and later market's "yawn" occurred with IBM breaking the "all-important 100 price level" in the fall of 2000. There was initial reaction for sure, then, subsequently—nothing. Wall Street really does forget.

When an individual stock gets hit with an almost immediate 25 to 50 percent downward spike, and especially from specific company concern, any rally reaction—the "funeral bounce"—will almost always be short-lived and should be sold into. Waiting too long after the first upward bounce can result in losing a fast "one-time" profit. Take the quick gain and run! *It takes at least a few months for investor confidence to return and the fear of further loss to be alleviated, and that really does make sense. The "street" calls this phenomenon the "base building" period, or call it the "confidence building period"—just don't call it the "bargain period." The base building period that follows is an excellent time to sell covered call options just a few points above the stock price—or just out-of-the-money—with almost zero likelihood of having the stock called away.*

When stocks fall even intraday, it is so typical for them to find support—albeit perhaps temporary—at important prior technical support levels, such as 200 DMA and longer-term trendline support levels.

Trends reversals are usually not initiated from a one-day occurrence. *(This usually takes the form of a trend in one direction with a sizable countertrend move and a concern as to whether it will last. A single day isn't proof and it won't alter the prevailing trend by itself—it takes more time and evidence.)*

The worst market declines bring everything down and prices plummet only so much before common sense and trader/investor confidence reappears. These periods exhibit terrific turn-around opportunities. Examples where people sense bargain hunting and easy money, rush in without fear and in a frenzied state to "get aboard." Their opposite tact displays at tops.

Experience has taught us that Wall Street analysts will sometimes make a fundamental recommendation with a falling stock near its support level. *More reason to be very aware when large undervalued companies—the types analysts review—have fallen near their 200-day moving average. They suddenly may get a quick rush without too much effort. There have been at least as many times, when overall recommendations were being made with NO apparent <u>technical</u> attention paid—and that is very wrong!*

Very often after a severe or long lasting declining phase appears to be complete and an equity price low is made, investors will demand "proof" that the low is not going to be violated—a lower price to occur. The proof they need is whether after another declining period, the stock's prior low "held" and thus was "tested" successfully; expectation that a "second low" will be not appreciably lower than the first. Yet there are many times that this testing does not take place and the stock, or in the case of the broad markets, simply advances and doesn't look back. *Do not wait for the test before participating if an advance appears to be continuous. There is no rule that a retest must be made.*

At suspected times of very overbought/sold status and a potential reversal, a very sudden abnormal intraday price range might suggest capitulation (investors simply acting on the price momentum regardless of thought.) This might mean a trend reversal.

One obvious reason why placing a position the day before the opening price is that on the opening there isn't anywhere near the degree of shares optimism or pessimism to hold back price. The number of shares to be absorbed isn't watered down with normal buy and sell decisions until later. Being positioned early can mean price moves faster and can prove to be easy money.

The phenomenon of options premium decay is evident even intraday. To take advantage of this  and it is a big generalization—buy late and sell early. (Prices tend to recede during a day where all else is equal; for the same magnitude of price, the same options series will cost less.)

### Live Charting

The evidence appears that either a one-or five-minute frequency bar chart is best for charting stock intraday movement. Ten, but certainly 15 minutes and even longer periods, are just too infrequent—too much can happen in between these measuring periods.

Volume spikes intraday at assumed low or high points don't appear to have much predictive value. Moves start and end without heavy relative volume, contrary to what we might expect

Pricing having a hyperbolic look—up or down—will not last too long; they don't run straight up or down toward 90 degrees even intraday for very long. *Take an opposite position when appearing—this is now old advice!*

The period to measure for price movement from prior peaks and troughs is not just a single day but two or five days back on a one or five minute basis. It offers an excellent comparison for support and resistance.

## Sectors

When entire industry sectors move, it is important to determine what is temporary and what isn't. Example: when the brokerage industry in mass falls, it is coming back…the financial industry is too an important part of the U.S. economy to fail. This may not be the case for "hot" new market sectors.

There is significant co-movement within market sectors/industries. Great earnings from Ford will likely advance all the auto companies, etc. Ditto with a biotech takeover rumor—some biotech stocks in a like area will advance in sympathy. The effect of a takeover within an industry can continue to advance other stocks within that industry for several days. *(Investors assuming others will get snapped as well in the next few days are 99.99 percent wrong, but the underlying stocks move, nonetheless.)*

If a stock is down, check to see if its industry is as well. Often its surprise fall is based on industry weakness and nothing else. In these cases, grab a phone, call the individual company you own or might wish to, and get their spin. They may not be affected, and an overreacting lower price might be an opportunistic purchase—or, as always, vice versa.

Since an industry's companies will move together when a rally starts, initiate a strategy for one industry company, not two, since any one should rise. The purchase of two decreases the possibility of placing capital in another sector which may become stronger. If the industry does not follow an advancing overall trend and, worse yet, two industry members had been purchased, there is less money which can be placed into other more deserving sectors.

Short-term sector-significant movement might be based on fundamental changes or price momentum. The key question is, which is it? The answer might tip us as to a trend change! If no news accompanies the movement, it can mean the momentum crowd is leaving or entering the party. Unfortunately, you learn this after the "music" stops—after the momentum has changed. It is usually best to consider exit. If the price change is from news, the importance you deem to it should depend upon its source, credibility, etc. If it's not too meaningful, the odds favor resumption of the sector trend. To no surprise, investor reaction will be telling very swiftly. If movement is from general broad, unspecific as to a company news, then it should also be interpreted that no one company is having or being hurt by the unannounced news—or, that nothing is fundamentally wrong.

*In late July through early August 2000, the semiconductor industry had been under severe selling pressure from a single source that the economic cycle that they move in might be slowing or reversing. This caused almost all semis from Intel to the smallest to tank. It probably also meant that no one company during this sell-off was fundamentally any worse than the entire industry, in the absence of released specific-company news.*

Almost any news, even non-financial, can impact a company (or companies) in related and unrelated industries. *A breach of Internet security can hurt the downed site's stock price, but advance a company elsewhere engaged in e-commerce security, etc. a commercial plane crash hurts the manufacturer and aids the companies designed to prevent a similar occurrence. An increasing yield curve aids government mortgage issuers, Fannie Mae and Freddie Mac. The World Trade Center catastrophe caused defense and security stocks as well as teleconferencing companies prices to rise, with airlines and leisure stocks plummeting. The list is endless...*opportunities abound daily from news events*. Falling interest rates favor all financials (banks, brokers and mortgage companies) as well as the housing industry. Rising oil prices generally aide the oil industry, hurt airlines and some utilities who utilize oil as a fuel source. It's laborious, but setting up a grid as to what types of news event might affect which industries can make for handsome opportunities.*

Wall Street loves to follow and invest with industry leaders. If a sector gets hot, it is more likely than not that its leader will advance first and more continuously than might smaller untried companies. So invest in the leader in the hot sector. It has the "brand" name and is the easy—no brainier—for institutional investment where big dollars and their investment muscle is found to push out buy recommendations.

Generally, during periods of rising interest rates, interest rate sensitive industries, home builders, banks, etc. tend to begin to peak and the opposite is usually true as well. Yet late in 2000 through 2001, in a falling rate environment, stocks fell. But bond pricing still reacted very normally. As rates fall, bond prices rise and provide excellent price appreciation. They can make up for an unpleasant equity environment.

The valuation that Wall Street accords to an industry tends to be constant. This means if they are not willing to pay a greater level for earnings—a P/E ratio—it is not likely to have been overlooked and is not going to change. *In the 2002 through 2003 period, housing was red hot, yet the P/E for the industry was far less than for others. In practical terms, this meant buying a housing stock and assuming the industry would be granted a much greater valuation measure would prove disappointing.*

Although it will involve a lot of digging for information, determining which public companies are another's largest customers can provide easy return from the "piggybacking" effect. If a company in the health sector care announces dismal results and its price plummets, its largest public company customer would be apt to fall in price in sympathy...and quickly as well. (This information is not as public as most but can be found by knowing your companies.)

## General Information

Information explosion: the great advantage is that if you can get ahead of the curve—be invested prior to a takeoff. In today's environment, you can make more money in three months than what used to take years to replicate. According to previously mentioned author Robert Shiller, "The incessant exchange of information is a fundamental characteristic of our species"...investment ideas get spread out quickly.

Markets today are indeed like track meets, yet if you do arrive first, and are right, instant and significant gratification can be had. The briskness of reactions and telling-all, is your advantage...but be correct!! Understand that raw information per se, now almost commoditized and instantly accessible to all, is not necessarily useful unless the user of that information knows what, and how, it might affect <u>investment</u>.

*We are now computerized worldwide decision-makers with hundreds of billions of available money being capable of being put to work on little more than a mouse click, hence being fast and first will be advantageous if the trade is not just very short-term natured. So here, some form of market timing can lead to big advantage. Those very proficient in this area can now become very rich and very quickly! (The bearish NASDAQ trends in 2000 and 2001 were the first example of a bearish trend in the new information age. The first bear market we have been through with trading technology and the information flow so advanced, where trades are executed and decisions made in fractions of seconds. This phenomenon and the resulting index carnage portends that trends may have a far quicker effect, and leave devastating impact, than ever before in market history—since we all now can know if we choose to and thus react.)*

Stocks added to the S&P 500 will advance on the day of inclusion and usually the day after.

The S&P 500 futures are the telling index as to where stocks are headed minute to minute. *They have to, since if they didn't, arbitrage situations would allow for riskless trades—free money—to be made. It's another investment in quotes information services, but probably well worth it.*

Remember there is a NASDAQ effect on the OEX—the 100 approximate largest companies of the S&P 500. For each Dow 20 point move, the OEX will change one point or about a 20-to-1 ratio. *A 10 point OEX move requires a 200 Dow move;* NASDAQ point movement is 5 times its DOW equivalent.

IPOs (Initial Public Offerings) can have their P/Es go to the moon (as well as, separately, their price), since there isn't sufficient investor knowledge as to what the company does or what EPS is expected, what historic P/E might be considered normal, etc. Over time, IPOs are made to conform. But don't think a quick IPO sale is ever necessary based strictly on fundamentals; on price action, for sure.

The NYSE indicator of "Trin" moving toward .40 or less, is the time to buy!! The Dow Jones indicator "Tiki" at +25 to +30 means very short-term and the Dow will retreat. A -25 to -30 means it will advance. If a Dow stock is delayed on the opening, but is likely to open much higher or lower, then purchasing an option on the OEX in anticipation of that stock's effect on the Dow when it does open can lead to an almost riskless trade when all of the Dow does open.

It is better to pile in the money and worry about the tax effect afterwards unless there is favorable tax relief within a very short period. *Liken this to being offered a huge pay rise—you don't say no.*

Mutual funds cash percent is a long-believed indicator of their ability to sustain or initiate a market rally—it probably still has merit, but existing price trend is far more influential.

Since our markets are time sensitive and often require complete attention, it's best deferring all other tasks that can be completed, until after hours. This discipline means your required attention and temperament isn't being compromised and you thus think clearly. Prioritizing your time is the advice.

During hectic periods, it is very coincidental to have technological problems— *quotes go off line, phone rings, info you need gets misplaced*—and to allow yourself to get distracted, etc. Not unlike Murphy's Law playing out! If a sound strategy has been planned for, put it on. Don't use the distractions along with the normal anxiety that accompanies placing an investment as the excuse to delay taking definitive investment action. *This may be a time when huge money can be made—don't cheat yourself out of that opportunity.*

A falling dollar, as in 2003, benefits U.S. multi-national companies since our goods are then cheaper for the rest of the world to purchase.

# A Few Specific Strategies

### Earning Your Share of Wall Street's Monthly "Gift Giving"

(The various exchanges that trade options, as well as any firm that allows its customers to initiate options trading, will provide—free of charge—a small pamphlet entitled, "Characteristics and Risks of Standardized Options." It is a short but excellent introduction into options and well-recommended. Libraries will have many standard financial texts explaining in great detail the ramifications and theory of options as investments. Author Bernie Schaffer's options text, *The Option Advisor,* is one read not to be missed to explain the fundamentals of options.)

In the securities industry "a free lunch," or something close, is a rarity, and when one is available, it should command your interest. The concept of selling options on stock positions you own is almost 30 years old. Shame on all of us for not utilizing this aspect of investment more.

Selling call options on stock positions you hold, which gives a call option buyer the right to purchase your shares at a price you select (the strike price), and from the action of which, you get paid for shifting the investment risk elsewhere, is analogous to almost "free money." Any stock holder is in the enviable posture of having someone else willing to hand them $1, $2, $3 and maybe more points of options premium, every month of every year, and their stock doesn't even have to rise. With about 4,500 stocks trading options, the likelihood is you can now participate in options, or buy the stocks that do. Or—*and it's far less risky, since broad markets almost cannot get blindsided by one significant news item—sell calls against your portfolio's position's equity by writing options, selling call options, on the major indices: OEX (the S&P 100), S&P 500, etc. This type of activity in investment parlance is known as "portfolio insurance."*

When you sell the right to purchase stock, that right will have value only if the stock price remains above the strike price you sold, through option expiration. For instance, were you to sell a 50 call option, and the stock price never gets above 50 prior to expiration, the buyer of your call option—the owner of the right to purchase your shares at the exercise price of 50—has nothing of value.

If the stock price is under 50, let's say at 48, any right to buy at 50—is worthless. A desired purchase can take place in any quantity at the 48 market price! In this example, you keep the stock and you always keep the premium—the price of the option (here calls) that you were initially given when you first sold the option. You have managed to permanently capture, albeit small, portions of your original cost basis, which become realized and permanent additions for your having continued to own the stock.

239

You have made a portion of the day-to-day *unrealized* gains and losses continuum, now realized. This was wise—and won't work out to be. It always works if you were inclined to hold long-term through thick and thin, or in qualified investment plans.

Under ideal conditions, you would want the price of your shares to close on the day of expiration, at precisely the strike price you sold the call premiums at. The option would then have no exercise value. *(The owner of the call with the right to buy at your 50 strike price from above would have nothing of value if the stock were beneath 50, or exactly at 50.)* When under 50, your sold covered call option provided its buyer nothing of value. Here you win twice. You keep premium income, and you retain the shares at your maximum profitable point.

With the goal being to keep the stock and enjoy the premium received, we next determine which strike price is the preferred one to sell and when might the timing to offer our shares be most opportune. Remembering that the owner of the stock—the seller of the call option—does not participate in price action above the strike price sold, we ideally sell a strike price high enough so as not to receive an exercise notice to sell our shares, yet still be an upside stock price participant—yet also low enough to receive maximum premium. Fortunately, there is a general "probabilities" methodology to find out.

A stock price in the 50s will have at least 5 point strike price increments and above 100 at 10 point increments. Currently, these are 10 percent increment changes. In the example we have been using, if the stock was selling at 50, the first out-of-the-money, the first stage, call option would be a 55 series and is 10 percent above the current 50 price. If we decide to sell the 55 series calls, we are betting that the stock cannot gain more than 10 percent or surpass 55. Were it to, we would no longer participate. *(Again, a 55 exercise notice means that we are given $55 for our shares by a buyer—someone owning a 55 call option—and for each call option sold $5,500 (100 shares times a $55 exercise price. There may be a very minor commission to the one being exercised; and there is a more normal commission for the call option owner, now desiring—actually owning—shares by exercising their optionable right.)*

What's the then probability that our or any stock can move 10 percent? "A sure thing" might be the answer if we were talking about 24 months out. But what about six months out? Or maybe two months? How about two, maybe three, weeks?

There is strong likelihood in having shares called away—that is exercised—if the option expiration date we might choose expired in 24 months. Granted, we would receive an initial high commensurate call option premium, but the odds are we would have to give up ownership and maybe wouldn't receive enough compensation from the call option premium. Yet if we sell perhaps two or three weeks prior to expiration—10 to 15 trading days of time—the probabilities of retaining our shares remain overwhelmingly with us.

The odds of the average stock choice consistently moving 10 percent in 10 to 15 trading sessions is an investment impossibility—for that would suggest <u>constant</u> astronomical <u>annual</u> percent returns.

This is an alternative way of saying, you must "win" selling covered calls on a repeat basis with underlying stock positions. (We define win here as keeping the stock and earning occasional profits on the stock position...we always keep the options premium.)

The long-term appreciation for equities is about 10 percent <u>annually</u>! Even with the standard deviation of return around this figure being factored, the odds on selling calls with a few weeks remaining and having shares called away, is very small. If done on a consistent monthly basis, perhaps but once per year, you might receive an exercise notice. Remember most investors who buy call options don't have the interest and probably the capital to exercise anyway. Most options owners simply sell the options outright if in-the-money, and all out-of-the-money call options expire worthless if the stock didn't exceed its exercise price. Again, the *probabilities* of price movement don't allow for <u>consistent</u> 10 percent advances over two or more weekly periods.

If permissible, writing options within qualified accounts, IRAs or 401ks, where there is no taxable consequence, mutes any long-term capital gains advantage that one might be forgoing under an exercise notice; again, taxation then isn't relevant. Options writing must be an allowable investment action within your qualified account, to have the right to sell covered call options. Since stocks are being held for long-term periods, why not get paid monthly for holding your portfolio and shifting purchase risk! Can you think of any disadvantage intending to hold long-term and receiving monthly checks?

### Case A: Stock Looks Strong; You Are Very Bullish: Wish to Keep the Stock

Action: do not sell call options. It would limit upside profit potential far too much. If the desire for premium is that great, sell calls 15 or 20 percent out-of-the-money, and/or on more volatile stocks; you still acquire desired premium and still leave ample room for profit participation with price advance.

### Case B: Mildly Bullish; Want to Retain Stock, Earn Premium Income

Action: sell calls one stage out of the money—at a strike price about 10 percent above current price.

Ideal Scenario: stock ends on the strike price on expiration date; keeping all premiums plus profit, you earn maximum profit without stock forfeit.

Advantages: participate in any upside to the strike price and premium capture.

Disadvantages: lose value on each point drop beneath premium received.

### Case C: Mildly Bearish Market Short-Term: Earn Premium Income

Action: sell calls one stage in the money—slightly beneath the stock's price for calls.

Ideal scenario: stock ends at strike price on expiration; keep stock and large premium income.

Advantages: insurance protection for a fall back to strike price and then some; earn large premium—paid almost as having sold.

Disadvantages: if stock doesn't fall you lose it; no upside participation.

### Case D: Stock Looks Very Weak; You Are Bearish

Action: sell It! Remember, when you sell call options you are still the owner of record and the continuing "lucky" loser on each lower point value were the stock to sink. You are a stockholder first. Your immediate obligation is not to allow a *potential obligation* to deliver shares to impede your immediate want to sell, wherever and whenever appropriate! You will never, and you can never, receive—in options premium—protection sufficient to completely protect against a protracted downside slide. When you sell options, the initial premium sold is the *maximum* protection you enjoy.

## Just How Lucrative Are Selling Calls on a Monthly Consistent Basis?

The early portion of this segment touched upon the almost free nature of selling call options on a stock or stocks that make up one's portfolio. This can invite a continual and substantial income stream. Note the following examples.

Assume a stock is 33 with two weeks prior to expiration. The 35 series call option is at 1. We decide to purchase 500 shares of stock and then sell five of the 35 series calls.

Our cost to purchase stock: 500 shares times $33 market price = $16,500.

Our return selling 5 options at $150 (1) = $750.

If we make no more that month than just the $750, our percent return using all cash equals (750/16500) or 4.5 percent. All right you aren't thrilled but this is 4.5 percent for one month. It is more than likely you will be able to realize some comparable return, six to nine times each year!

Recognize the above return is with all of <u>your</u> cash, yet using your broker's—buying the stock on margin—that translates to about 9 percent even minus a few dollars for brokerage interest.

Let's now assume the stock drives above, or to, the 35 strike price on the day of expiration. (Remember we participate in any stock appreciation up to our sold strike price.) Our cost to purchase remains at $16,500 with all of our cash used, and $8,250 using 50 percent margin. Our return from premium income remains at $750...but the return from the stock having gone to at least 35—all of 2 points—is very great. Five hundred shares with a 2 point move from 33 to the 35 exercise price—thus we are active participants in 2 points of appreciation—equals $1,000.

Hence, our return becomes $1,000 from appreciation plus $750 from premium income, or a total of $1,750. $1,750 divided by our cost to have initiated the strategy, $16,500, equals 10.6 percent for that month! *(More than 20 percent if done on margin.)*

Lastly assume we had a $50,000 stock portfolio of perhaps 1,000 shares on five positions. What if we sell calls on each of the five stocks on a monthly or at least bimonthly basis? Why not? $50,000 even bimonthly at 4 to 5 percent equates to an added 25 to 30 percent return each year!

It isn't terribly imaginative to see just how resourceful options selling can become. It is excellent, conservative, investment strategy!

### Important Second Chances with Stock or Options

There can be times when being too early or usually too impatient with a trend can still result in sizeable profits. The trick is not to allow the "too early position" to affect other opportunities or to immobilize you.

Maybe you have found a stock exhibiting all the technical characteristics of overbought, maybe even hyperbolic. If the market environment suddenly becomes weak, it makes sense to place the position and not wait any longer. But let's assume you buy put options before the stock actually starts downward; in other words, you assumed a short-term trend change from bullish to short-term bearish (something you should try not doing) and the market continues to advance. If the stock marches upward and likely with the market wind at its back, and you are still convinced it will drop, you can merely buy the next higher series of puts if the stock starts downward. If you are right, and the stock starts the expected downward move, you will be amply rewarded.

Example: on October 2, 2001, 99 Cent Stores (NDN) had been up four straight days with a five-day RSI of 96 and a chart pattern that had the look of short-term hyperbolic. Assuming a top might be in place, a put purchase order could have been placed at 1.10 for their October 35 option series with the stock then about 35 or just slightly out-of-the-money. *(Their 40 series puts were 4 3/4 and unnecessary with the 35 series and stock, but 1/2 point out-of-the-money.)*

On October 3, 2001, the stock continued upward hitting an intraday high of 39, coincident with the overall market continuing to rally. The 35 puts were valued at about .45 or a loss of over 60 percent. But the 40 option put series, then the only in-the-money series, could be purchased for about the same 1.10. The stock shortly began a drop to 36.40 and those same puts increased in value to a shade under 4.00, despite the market's still-upward movement. *(As previously noted, any stock can move opposite the market for a day or two, depending upon how overbought/sold it might have been.)*

This is nearly four times appreciation, and intraday, if you were skilled and "brave" enough to go back in and buy puts, or patient enough to have waited until the stock started down to have initially bought. If you had invested $5,000 in the 40 series of put options you would have yielded almost $20,000 intraday! (And the original 35 puts climbed back to just about even after the drop, yet a four factor intraday is always better.)

Within three more days, on October 8th, they marched to almost 7 1/2, a striking 650 percent move from purchase ...seven times one's money. By October 19th, the same puts, with the stock now at 30 were valued at 10—then 900 percent more than when they might have been bought all of eight trading days earlier.

Another of the fabled lessons: fresh in mind from the October 3rd experience, patience was the optimal word the next time a hyperbolic situation developed.

October 15, 2001: Genzyme (GENZ) had the hyperbolic posture in a market environment itself a bit overextended and ripe for a retreat. The stock alone began its descent, intraday, at about 53, with their October options set for expiration just four days later. *(Thus, while time is no ally here, it is no expensive partner either, since only four days remain in the options life.)* This time, the stock only heads lower, hour by hour, and having too much patience in allowance for a rally, and purchase, would prove useless.

The stock managed to fall to 46.98 about noon on Tuesday October 16. The October 50 put series priced originally at about .70 runs out to 3.30...a magical 4 3/4 times one's investment in about six trading hours! The following day the price hits 44.17 and the 50 put brings 6.20—about nine times one's original investment—now in 14 hours! If this is work, we should all make this our employment.

The learned lessons:

**Do not give up too soon on a strategy that at worst has you neutral— and always watch for a second opportunity. Why? Because markets never have to behave exactly when we demand.**

**Be a bit patient when attempting to enter hyperbolic type positions... but absolutely do get in after pricing starts downward in any apparent sustained price action. It is ultimately destined to be much lower— and very soon!**

# Executing the
# Opening Transaction

## Preview

This primary reason for this section's inclusion is to capture the best possible price at the specific instant a securities transaction is being originated. This is accomplished either through very savvy specific price placement or the timing for the order placement. Consistently receiving the best price or superior pricing to what "market orders" offers, over many years, builds a worthwhile monetary advantage.

When securities are trading, their "market"—their price to buy is called a "bid," and their price to sell is termed "ask" (often termed its "offer price")—is made available throughout the investment community through electronic quotes. The difference between the bid and ask is known as its "spread." The highest bid and lowest ask make up the "<u>inside market</u>," and that which is most quoted throughout the investment community. This inside market offers the best pricing for both the buyer and seller— that is, the highest bid to sell to, and the lowest asking price to buy from. Along with this inside market, is the size quote in hundreds of shares of the intended buying and selling interest.

For example: 59.700, 59.800; 10 x 20. Interpretation: 1,000 shares bid for purchase at 59.700; 2,000 shares are being offered for sale at 59.800; the spread is .100 dollar, or one dime.

In late 2000 and into 2001, the decimalization of quoted security prices further reduced spreads, since buyers and sellers can opt to place their orders at as low as one cent above and below last trades, so it has become somewhat common for spreads in active issues to be as little as one cent. In these instances, waiting to save a penny or two per share is a fool's wish—pay it and move on. Nonetheless, where the spread is still high, trying to minimize it always adds value.

## The Preferable Order Type

Contrary to a market order, where you will receive an execution on the next trade, a "Limit Order" is exactly what you might think. You purchase and sell at your set price or your limit. You pay nothing greater for a purchase (and you might pay less), and receive nothing less for a sale (and you could get more). So in an example, if you were interested in buying 500 shares of a stock and not paying 50 (the highest bid price) and deployed the patience to wait, a limit order to purchase at a 50 1/8 purchase price might be enjoyed. *Incredible as it seems, prices do fluctuate! The "perfect" time to have been buying might not be so in a few minutes or hours—let alone days. Granted, a 1/8 savings on 500 shares amounts to about a "$60 bill," but on options, using the example of 10, it doubles to $120. You can play out the numbers over years and years of transactions.*

You might have also placed your order at a lower bid price of $50. If a sale transaction had been entered at about the same time—either a market order, or a limit order of 50—you might have enjoyed an execution at your set limit price—thereby saving the entire 1/4 point. And were the trading in NASDAQ issues, with all bids and asks (offers) displayed, you might try to transact with a specific market maker who might be capable of providing an instant fill at your limit price.

The obvious risk if your limit price is away from the current trades is that you may not get an immediate execution. This means it may be more costly for you to purchase if the stock moved upward, or you might get a shade less for a sale transaction if prices were to fall.

We also add one more important item with our transaction Limit Order, AON, meaning "All Or None." This means we will only accept on execution for all of our intended shares, or none will be transacted. This simple add-on prohibits partial orders, which always cost more in commissions and can foul-up strategies. (If you had planned on a 500 share purchase, you might not want a 157 share lot.)

Another order type which can be used but can be manipulated is a GTC or "Good Till Canceled." Generally it is best used only when you cannot monitor investments intraday. As an example, it could lead to an options specialist purposely setting bids—where you might wish to sell—lower than they might otherwise, in an advancing stock, knowing that doing so means your GTC sell price won't get executed—at least not then. The specialist, thus, is betting the stock turns down or you relent and sell at the market value.

On the NASDAQ, leaving very large block shares of 10,000 or 20,000 or more via a GTC order to sell on their Level II quote screen provides an easy reason for Level II buyers to pause, and for market makers to skirt the selling price on any given day.

It is better to place an order on the day you believe it is appropriate to execute your particular strategy. Try not giving the pros the advantage of "tipping" your hand with a GTC order.

One further recommendation when placing orders: all things being equal, try to open an account with an online broker that has "direct access" capability. This means for our purpose, your ability to place a trade where you want, on any specific exchange, with all their spreads appearing. After an actual execution, you know it immediately. This literally means seconds. (Once upon a time, clients would wait hours and often until the next day to know for sure if their orders had been executed. That seems incomprehensible today, but it was the norm 20 years ago.)

## Timing the Order Entry

If everything necessary to set the transaction in motion has been completed, the sequential order considerations are as follows:

### *Is Now the Preferred Time to Execute?*

By fable, the pros buy late and the amateurs buy early. Minus real proof, it's probably because pros have learned to match their ideas with trend as well as becoming more proficient the more times they experience a trade execution. If stocks go out strong late in the day, that strength will likely carry over into the early morning...why not then buy toward the close, and sell into presumed strength in the early minutes the following day, which will be provided from the "rookies" too eager to patiently wait—those who just "have to buy as soon as possible to get in before everyone else and the investment starts soaring." *(Naturally coincident with their placement of the buy order.)* Advantaging those less knowledgeable sounds good on paper, and it can be practiced frequently.

There are times when buying late in the day and anticipating a correct stock direction on the subsequent market opening offers uncontested (the proper word is really instant) profit, since stocks will be open before most investors can react. Swift dollars cannot melt away if you guessed right the night before, since the opening will be instantaneous. And the lack of pre-market liquidity means opening pricing can be more dramatic by setting that first price. You could sell into price strength and remove your rewards for having guessed right! Well before more sanguine thought might come into play, which otherwise could have harmed profits. So free and easy money? Not always. Wall Street is rarely that easy.

Yet, it would be true if an investor assumes a bloodbath cannot continue into the next morning because time soothes and reason should dominate after a long evening's pondering. A purchase completed at the close of the prior day, and a stock pop on the opening, means champagne! Here is taking advantage of the amateurs at work if the assumed price direction was, in fact, directional. But this is more geared toward short-term thinking and, other than a provision for instant reward, isn't much different than buying in anticipation and being ultimately right. The results are exactly the same.

Being right on the opening can provide an entire day's worth of movement in minutes, even seconds! Just be right. Pick your spots infrequently, since it's still a fast chance. Do it when large sectors are in mass being hurt, or the overall market overreacts. Remember, one stock can be brutally punished for long periods, but entire market sectors/industries usually won't, because the momentum crowd can too easily pick up on the broadening, overreacting carnage and hunt for fast bargains. It is a much tougher effort to "group react," when only one isolated company is "bleeding." It can escape the "bargain tag." But if perhaps all of the financials are being lambasted, that won't go unnoticed for long. The vultures will soon show.

There have been many hints already discussed which give rise to appropriate timing, but since short-term pricing is so random, it would be virtually impossible to know if price is always better at various <u>hours</u> of a trading day. We know, for example, that placing trades at difficult price levels is more likely to get execution during normally more active periods—those prior to, and after, the mid-day lunch period (11:00 a.m. to 1:00 p.m.).

Lastly, if you are attempting to purchase options in their final week of monthly expiration, time can't be your partner if you run the risk of being right on the strategy, but lose nonetheless, since the position didn't play out before expiration. In these cases, always buy in-the-money positions and exit almost within the same day, unless profitable. Or assuming you can risk losing most of a small bet for the large payoff if proven correct in a sizeable way, purchase a partial position. If you wait too long you would lose most of that money, but it would be a mild loss. If you're correct—an in-the-money play could bring rapid price appreciation.

The non-option alternative is to purchase, or short stock—on margin for leverage—and avoid time becoming your enemy. *(If you find strategies are not working and timing is a hindrance, you might be better applying your ideas with stock positions, where time is generally not an issue. Timing is always a concern when behind and losing, since holding long—falling stock—brings no applause.)*

### The "Watching Pricing First before Transacting" Approach

There is a difficult consideration as to whether first watching the price change of the intended security just before entering an order can provide anything of value. But we all do it.

The first time during a day we intend to place the transaction might be the best and worst price for the next several hours because minute-to-minute price is so random. We will know for fact—after the fact. We are assuming that the price will remain biased toward where we ultimately expect *(this means consistent with the directional trend)*. But the price can move adverse or coincident, immediately after placement. We don't know and control none of it. Consequently, if no extreme market movement, or industry—all external effects or individual security—specific effect, has just come into play, which might wisely cause us to delay and ascertain any effects, simply place the transaction. And why not?

If the initial transaction were a purchase, is there anything to be gained just watching the price march upward—here we appeared right! While we sit through the lost anxiety and hope for another chance for a short downward move for a second chance buy, but which might suggest with a falling price we might be now wrong for a want to purchase. But, with the new hope—through <u>further</u> price observation— that naturally we could get in at a price still less than we might have originally, since we didn't buy when we could have? Huh? Sounds convoluted? Buying into a planned directionally trend as it's developing isn't flawed.

Too many times in trying to save, say, the 1/8 or a 1/16 over a 10 to 15 minute wait, the price moves further away—in actuality confirming our prescience—and we allow the position to be forgotten? We give up on the strategy because "we didn't get our way," our price, at that particular instant. Hello!

### If the entirety of the planning process in time, commitment, and ultimate payoff, can be dismissed because it now costs us +1/8 more, are we being practical? Are we breathing?

If the position works out, the added 1/8 of a point isn't any issue; if the position doesn't work out, the extra cost of the eighth isn't any issue either! Doubtless, the investment potential exceeds the extra cost, so don't allow *"placement trade anxiety" to get you sidetracked.*

If the price goes immediately away from where we expected after our executed transaction, and we had done all of the homework prior to this, then we might accept that this time the balance of the buy/sell equation simply ripped against us at an unfortunate moment. Because there couldn't be any other reason, at the point we were ready to execute, that would have made us pause. If we couldn't know, we do not take blame. Unless the trade was intended for very short-term option on a great number of contracts, it might not ultimately matter.

If the price immediately advances the way we deemed it should have, it only means, for at least that short period, that we took the bait that research and our information was telling us—and we look good—and it may be the trend in place will continue to continue. That's all it tells us for the first few minutes or next hour. Nothing prevents a retreat later in the day which might our former, "Got the low entry (purchase) price for the day" seems more like, "Got stuck with the high price for today." We simply won't know.

The conclusion: watching the price first offers no provable benefit without eventful specific news, relevant to out transaction, or a fast market action having just come about. If there wasn't any reason not to....

**Relax, place the transaction—the odds are really with you.**

The only exception to the above is placement on the opening of business when prices can be somewhat "artificial." This can be from unsophisticated investors driving price on emotional "tips," buying and selling without solid thought, or so the theory goes. When trying to initiate on, or very near, the opening, must mean you do so sans emotional reaction to the first few price movements which may be passing very soon and where a more genuine price pattern might shortly emerge. In simple English, opening prices can be very artificial.

### *Always Enter Positions—Only with the Trend "At Your Back"*

Buying call options or outright stock demands you only initiate the decision to buy when price starts upward, which, if continuing, means a higher position price and profit. Buying "long" as price is falling would mean the "bargain" you thought you were getting isn't to be had until, and if, time goes by and the price recovers back to where you first bought. Under this scenario, a long later advance might provide you with nothing but a long wait.

Buying puts or shorting stock demands you enter orders as the stock price starts moving downward and you invest consistently with a downward continuing trend.

Word to the informed: buying too early can be as bad as selling too late. Enter positions only when the shortest of price trend is moving in the direction you expect.

# How Much of a Position Is Enough—And When?

The ideal for the intended amount of dollars invested is fraught with so many variables, a one-size-fits-all answer might be impossible. If it worked—you couldn't *have* had enough. It is similar to the example of having a one stock portfolio—placing all your eggs in a single basket—and then praying they don't all crack. It might be as simple as that amount that does not cause any large degree of anxiety, but still makes having been correct very satisfying. And it certainly would seem 1,000 shares or 10 options represents a good maximum start. Yet investment wealth is relative, and if you are comfortable holding larger positions, then do so, since the market will act on your transaction in exactly the same manner, whether it be a single share or 10,000. The market has no sense of obligation if yours is a small fortune or a get-your-feet-wet trade.

*It just confounds why so many investors buy and sell everything, all at once—either being 100 percent exposed or completely sideline-bound. The timing of a buy and a sell is estimated, being input at an opportune moment, but history has taught that even the shrewdest planning won't coincide with exact tops and bottoms—save those rare and lucky times. So why not get "two shots" at your price? Merely spread out the buying a little bit.*

It would also seem prudent to be more inclined to invest in stages when investing over longer periods, intermediate- or pure long-term. Yet looking for a fast short-term move would warrant a probable total placement of a position—certainly within the same day—since the strategy might play out before a total commitment had been positioned.

Since the immediate movement after a transaction is entered is quite random, it makes sense to purchase a <u>portion</u> of the strategy and retain the balance to be utilized *only after* being proven correct by the price action. In this manner, we are "averaging up" consistent with our expected price direction. Additionally, we are not exposing 100 percent of money unless we have been proven initially correct regarding the anticipated strategy.

*Yet if we were correct and an instant profit appears on both transactions, while not to the extent that had the <u>entirety</u> of the planned invested monies been invested immediately, a good feeling results nonetheless.*

*If proven instantly wrong, only a portion of money is suffering and anxiety is less than otherwise and there are still monies on the sidelines that can be utilized if the position warrants a second chance.*

*And if the idea later appears to have been <u>incorrect</u>, the proportional balance remains safe and liquid, and continues earning some interest.*

*This system almost has the feeling of multiple wins.*

*(And this proportionate idea is <u>strongly</u> advised when dealing with short-term expectations, mainly in options.)*

The proportionate amount should mean no less than 50 percent of the entire ultimately intended position and probably no greater than 70 to 75 percent. For an ultimate 1,000 share holding, directing a 500 to 700 share lot on the first purchase with the balance being invested only after being assured the strategy is working by the telling from price. You have at least a marginal profit on the initial portion. You are also "averaging up," or increasing your break-even price level, and with the trend in your corner. *("Averaging down" can mean you are averaging to zero! Be careful—Polaroid and Global Crossing situations still do occur.)* While this necessitates two transaction commissions, their costs are so small with the seasoned discount brokers that it is not an issue. And remember, use the AON add-on to your order when you can, since some firms do not permit the attachment because it complicates their execution and might mean all their efforts are for nothing.

Regarding the issue of when the second portion should be placed would depend upon whether the stock is above our initial price entrance by a fair percent—maybe five to 10 percent—and with perhaps a period, days of "aging," so as to prove the initial profit was no fluke.

If we buy 50 percent of our intended amount and the stock races ahead 2 points and remains profitable three to four days afterward probably permits the 50 percent remainder to be placed. The 2 point initial gain further provides one point of downside relief if the stock were then to fall 1 point, or where we would then be even.

251

Say we buy 500 shares at 50 and watch the stock rise to 51 a few hours later. If we then buy the balance—perhaps 500 more shares—and the stock drops, we would be in a losing position on one lot and maybe both. It would have been better to have waited a few days or had a 2 to 3 point profit, to at least briefly "ensure" that our initial profit on the first buy wasn't keyed to a one-day-only buying spree urged on by a recommendation and sector market move, etc. In this manner, we also enjoy at least the chance of removing profit from our initial purchase were we fast enough to recognize a swift downturn.

If we attempted to initiate the second lot at a price several points lower than our initial price point during a continuing falling price direction, we would be "averaging down" (lowering our breakeven point) but buying more with more trending risk away from us.

It would be wiser to limit exposure until one clear profit is being enjoyed or after a clear bottom and advancing trend has restarted.

In fairness, what prevents the security from advancing after the second purchase and then declining, creating losses on both ends? Of course, nothing. But it would be more intelligent to have witnessed one, and possible two, paper profits, and had at least the *chance* to try and liquidate prior to a price reversal. This option cannot exist as readily if you are always averaging down. Stocks do price themselves to nothing, at which point their dying shareholders will be thrilled to take any money you wish to bury!

When investing under a bearish forecast, one would not invest the second portion unless the first buying was profitable—investing with the trend, not fighting it; something investors always should want to do.

## At What Entry Price Do We Set for the Transaction?

Isn't the size of the order relevant to price? If thousands of shares are being executed—absolutely. But what if the transaction is 200 shares? Is it worth trying to gain 1/8, which saves but $25? Each individual investor must make that call.

If there is a specific reason to buy now, place the proportional transaction price with a limit order at the lowest prevailing asking price for a purchase transaction—and for a selling transaction or shorting stock at the highest prevailing bid price. With multiple choices *(many market makers or several options exchanges)* several pricing choices can be had; with the stock exchanges, just one. If you do not receive an execution, then use a market order.

If there isn't an urgent need to initiate the strategy, we should always try and attempt to obtain a price advantage with our limit order, especially if the issue is very actively traded.

Assume we wish to purchase with the "inside" market (the highest bid and lowest offer) for a stock, 30 Bid 30. Ask, 10,000 by 5,000. We know we can purchase enough intended shares at the current asking price of 30 , yet without any immediate need, why not allow what we have learned, and the kind hand of fate, to maybe, this time, work to benefit us. The market maker and or specialist must be willing to sell to us at 30. The unknown seller wanting to liquidate shares with a market order, and coincident with our wanting to purchase at 30, might still sell with our receiving their shares net at 30. This happens if we are the first party to match their 30 ask/offer for their shares. If the pros are doing it by the book, they should not compete with our 30 bid to buy. If they are, a way around this is to "step in front of them" by bidding 30 1/16, or higher than their 30 bid price, with ours then becoming the high bidder. The next market order for a sale of shares with our high bid, at 30 1/16, would go to us. So we see by trying to buy either at the bid—where there is certainly some competition—or when raising our bid where there is no competition at the moment— places us in front, next in line to receive shares from a selling investor using a market order or with a matching limit order.

If we were trying to purchase a NASDAQ issue and had access to Level II quotes, we would know how many shares are being bid beneath our bid price. This tells us if we were wrong about the price direction, and the stock to drop, and how much stock still wants to be purchased—this is similar to an insurance hedge. The other point however, is that the size of the inside market, just like the buy/sell dynamic, changes very quickly.

What happens if our price isn't met? The attempt at securing a better price, and then perhaps having to change the order, might take a few seconds when done electronically. It is worth the effort to try—since why just give in automatically? With respect to options pricing, always check all of the exchanges that are trading your security to locate the "best" price. In fact, if you are inclined to participate in options, it usually pays to note which exchange leads or trails price change for a particular stock. There tends to be repeat patterns where, for example, the American Stock Exchange might be first to raise their market in calls as one of its stocks advances, and maybe the Pacific is last to drag its pricing upward. This pattern tends to persist for some time—and it's primarily because of the update frequency of the spreads—some are much faster than others.

One also finds times when a stock gets hot and volume is thin and where the specialists seem to delay on bringing upward their bid pricing, but have no trouble in increasing their asking prices. This allows them to sell to willing buyers at their set-high pricing and buy at low pricing—at the then bid—from those resigned to selling. They buy 'em low and sell 'em high, and if they control options pricing in periods of little interest, they'll do it every day. These options facets are worth watching—being observant is key.

If the position you wish to place trades on only one exchange—some proof of illiquidity—you are probably trading against the specialist alone...and they rarely will concede on price. You can expect to have large spreads, games played with price, and the pricing response to the underlying stock adverse to investors. When possible, try and avoid trading stock whose options trade on only one exchange.

There will almost always be some price difference between exchanges, but it must be very small, since options price competition drives execution, and therefore no exchange will allow its pricing to get too far away from the others. *(If it did, you could buy low on one exchange and sell high at another—it won't work. Freebies are not had for long in our securities markets.)* In whose pocket is money better laid, in yours or the other guys? At least try for better executions.

Example: we are trying to purchase <u>call</u> options on Eastman Kodak, EK, and we site the four principal exchanges—and we now have a fifth, ISE—for their pricing. And as you might expect, the more active options will have much smaller spreads.

| American | CBOE | Philadelphia | Pacific |
|----------|------|--------------|---------|
| 2 1/16 - 2 3/8 | 2 - 2 5/16 | 1 15/16 - 2 3/8 | 2 - 2 5/16 |

We want to purchase now, but naturally as low as possible. The lowest asking price is the same across two exchanges at 2 5/16. Hence, it may not matter which exchange we use. What if the volume on the Pacific Exchange is quite strong? Maybe with all that activity we can place our order at 2 and perhaps get an execution. It costs nothing to try—at least for a few moments.

It is also worth reiterating that if the volume (the activity) is low, the options exchange specialists and/or market makers will manipulate the individual bid/ask spread components more slowly, and to their liking, since they will have far more control in pricing than when the public's participation is brisk. This means options prices will lag the stock price changes and therefore your experience in placing a trade may—and I emphasize the word may—assist in better purchase execution pricing. It also clearly means that the "fictitious" delta relationship will change for declines as compared to advances or, in some cases, the opposite. (The delta relationship should be stable regardless of upward or downward movement.) For example: during fast stock declines, the bid side of call options will often move downward faster and greater than they move up during advancing stock price. Why should this occur?

Because specialists/market makers make money on the spread—they control the game. If they can drop bid prices faster than offer prices during a stock slide, the want-to-be <u>sellers</u> will have to sell at their artificially depressed bid price to exit. Since want-to-be <u>buyers</u> will have to pay the more normal ask price, the spread between these two having just increased will favor the specialists. It works in reverse during very bullish stock moves. The call's asking price runs upward almost instantly with the bid pricing slowly increasing, if at all. Both the calls bid and ask prices should rise in an equal proportion during an underlying stock spurt if the game is fair. They usually won't, since in most cases the spread is being set, not by demand and supply forces, but rather by greedy professionals.

An option's value at a moment is a <u>two-part</u> component: the bid price and the ask price. The spread between each should not change—fatten nor shrink—during any stock movement. If a call is more valuable as the stock makes a fast rise, then logic tells us that each <u>part</u> of that same call—the bid as well as the ask portions—are equally more valuable instantly, not four minutes later, after the pros have made a quick kill. (They would argue that it's all about the public's desire to purchase/sell and that they don't unilaterally set pricing spread to benefit themselves—of course not. And the Easter Bunny arrives in November.)

If the spread had been 10 cents prior to the advance, why should it widen in the absence of great order flow toward the buy side? Of course it shouldn't, nor is it fair. It certainly isn't moral—but It Is reality. And a way to handle the sale of a call in these situations is to place an addition to any sell order at the bid price by the amount the offer side was raised.

*Example: if the spread was $1.00 to $1.20 and the offer side suddenly becomes $1.35—as the stock starts to quickly advance—add .15 to the likely still $1.00 bid price, and limit order the sale at $1.15. This retains the original .20 spread, which it magically will get to soon anyway, but let it not be at your expense right now. (The reason why it would eventually rise to where it belongs is that the competition for business from the other options exchanges forces it up. Or is there a delta relationship for both the bid side and the ask side? No. Therefore, the entire option should move up or down almost equally with the spread remaining roughly stable.)*

Perhaps we might become less hasty and prefer to try and buy at bid price, or at least close to it. We know we can always buy at the asking price. So we curtail our desire a little and place our order at the low bid, here on the Philadelphia Exchange at 1 15/16. Maybe if a coincident sale has just been placed on that exchange at, or below our bid, and the specialist does not compete against us (once more, don't bet on it), we might get lucky and get a "fill." Or, as with the stock purchase, we might add to our bid to be ahead of the specialist and bid at $2. Don't forget: the greater the spread and the more options you may wish to transact, the more room you should have to place a trade at your price—somewhat analogous to "quantity discounts."

*Example: the spread is $2.00 to $2.40. For inactive options this isn't too far out of whack. Rather than purchase 10 options at the specialist's $2.40 price, try and buy at $2.30 and then $2.35 if unsuccessful. The specialist community isn't stupid. A 40 cent spread is great if they can get it. They may well accept your $2.35 price, reducing their profit to 35 cents on 10 options or $350. Greed can only go so far. They might just reason some profit is better than no profit. And trying to lower their profits is your right and function as a savvy investor. (Trade 50 options here, and the spread costs a staggering $2,000!)*

*For those who may not immediately cite the extreme monetary effect in the above, note the following: a purchase of 10 options at $2.40 requires a $2,400 investment. If two minutes later, a sale were to take place at the bid of $2.00, our investor would part with $2,000. This is a $400 loss on just the spread, and what a 40 cent spread means on the* *equivalent of 1,000 shares or what ten options contracts represents. Be smart. Try to get the spread down, or either walk away. Or utilize stock in these instances (a 10-15 cent spread is normal.)*

## In Conclusion

Any price execution, however sanguine at any point in time, can look bad even minutes later—certainly days and weeks. Nonetheless, if an execution is necessary, a better attempted price first with a carefully crafted limit order is still superior to market orders. Remember, your cost basis is always a one-time stagnant, not dynamic, figure. Trying to acquire your positions as price beneficial as practical. If you fail, and the investment starts to move in your expected direction and nothing noteworthy has surfaced to cause you to rethink your intent, buy the position with confidence, since it would appear to be headed where you expected and the added price for waiting should be absorbed if you are proven correct.

# Executing Closing
# Transactions...
# After Allowance for an
# Explosive Return

## Preview

When exit involves the extent of profitability, not how we might minimize losing, selling techniques usually change. Profits are wins. Whether we depart with 100 percent of all that was available, in at the bottom, out at the top—you know, the boastful cocktail party story repeat—or only 50 percent of what might have been. In the abstract, profits should be judged as good transactions. In relative terms, you can be saddened you didn't capture more, but have faith, for that tune will be sung for all the years you ever invest. Need any investor ever forget: you are dealing with both many unknowns and with no ability to foresee absolute future price perfection.

## When?

The timing for an execution of a securities sale other than for a purposeful immediate monetary need, is a series of any three events, with a final common sense resolve.

### Evident Technical Price Deterioration

First, and primarily, is the further likelihood of potential technical price deterioration from witnessed proof of your security, the extent of numerical allowance dependent upon your initial strategy and the potential potency of any trend already in place. Stocks reaching hyperbolic stages should be sold in any downturn while those reaching more serene toppish price action should be given more downside latitude. There is nothing smart in the assumption of a price top and sale. Demand to see price evidence—then react.

*Example: investor A purchases 1,000 shares of his well-researched stock at $30 and within several months it has risen to $35. Sporting a $5,000 profit, Investor A assumes the $35 area as a top and sells. The end result is of course a $5,000 profit.*

*Investor B purchases the same 1,000 shares at $30—having first patiently read and re-read the material within this book—and also finds the stock price at $35. Assuming nothing apparent in a price retreat, Investor B continues to monitor the upward trend and is delighted as it reaches $40. He or she now watches a slow decline begin but has assigned a $5,000 "stop loss" as the most he or she can tolerate. As the stock sinks toward $35, it is sold.*

Now in both cases the end result is the same—each has earned $5,000. In a quick review, it might be assumed both investors handled their respective investments equally well…it wasn't close!

Investor B did not assume a price top which could have run its course out at 50, 60 or higher. You can't know beforehand, and you want to still remain an owner! Investor B planned for a loss of value at not more than $5,000. Thus, had the stock reached $60, or yielding a $30,000 profit, only Investor B could have profited from the happy event. Only Investor B would have had the chance to sell out close to that temporary high at $55, thus earning a comfortable $25,000 more than the assumptive Investor A.

Investor B did two things superior to Investor A and over a lifetime of investment decisions would have faired much better. Investor B did not assume the end of a price trend; and Investor B controlled the selling price at his discretion.

When technical factors appear to be signaling your intended direction for the security, and time horizon is ending, and <u>actual price erosion away from your intent is underway</u>, and/or the market sector your security is part of is tumbling, it is time to start your exit positioning, since price movement is reality. You are being financially prudent to *start selling*.

The technical skills you might master are based on many thousands of observations of others and eventually will become personal experiences which you must allow to guide your actions. Always abandon the idea that this time might be different. It might, but more likely it will play out as your experiences and knowledge suggest it will. It's the way these become "rules" or investment "laws."

Don't pre-judge your multiple experiences and securities education in the improbable assumption that this time it will be different and you go against long-held proven rules. In doing so, you might be reducing your probabilities to "50/50" bets. *If that is the case, have your gambling urge pacified in Vegas; at least you'll have entertainment.*

Any one single transaction will prove a lasting nothing without multiple similar experiences which then start to form the new "rules." Even if the stock move plays out against the norm this one time, it sets no precedence for a next time; for then you might have but two contra proofs. Your multiple learned technical skills and price observation skills are far more influencing than being right but twice.

Listen to your knowledge and your experiences and don't use hope as your ultimate fate—the former is what you base decisions on, not prayer.

## Liquidation Checklist with Obvious Technical Deterioration

*Are you being too quick from the standpoint of time held?*

A one or two day holding isn't sufficient time for much of the strategy to play out. You designed a strategy to earn a fair return. Have you come close to witnessing if you are correct? You should not expect a large payoff in 48 hours. One-and two-day holding periods are symbolic of roulette!

*Is there sufficient money already made to justify selling to protect it?*

If a small amount of profit appears, is it worth the risk to protect it, to exit and forgo greater gains if ultimately proven correct? Unless a worthy amount of pre-planned profit is achieved, selling might be worse than forgoing it and chancing the strategy for a while longer.

*Suppose you think $500 is a minimum profit per transaction. You may have already experienced several prior gains in the hundreds ($300, $250, etc.), totaling across 5 positions, to equal $1,500, all of which were eventually lost in some degree, since no one gain exceeded your $500 limit! Yet the single position that works in a sizeable way might easily make up for the opportunities that became worthless.*

*Has the current market affect been scrutinized for effect?*

In what context might the market affect your position's movement? If you are intending a declining bias, a strong continuing market should affect you. However, for a few days your position can do its own thing.

*Are you selling into an emotional period or under an emotional reaction?*

The early portion of a day, for example, can have investors reacting without thought. Reaction to a news event can have cross currents. Emotional response is often premature and usually not necessary. Eventually, the trend will play out to an investor's benefit—just be aligned with it.

*Has the position's current owners had sufficient time to react to stimuli?*

This is a very telling area. If you watch the markets all day, you assume that the effect upon a stock will be felt almost as fast as you view it. In other words, you may assume if the external event, news, etc., is negative, or a stock is hyperbolic in price pattern, but doesn't drop or fall enough, then it won't. If the effect has played out for <u>many</u> hours or over days, then its effect will be absorbed by most of its owners who would have ultimately reacted, and price will react accordingly—therefore the effect is realized. If the event occurred last evening, you should not expect an accurate picture in the following first two hours—especially if the stock is thinly traded.

### Preplanned Exits: The Stop Loss...Really, the "Stop Losing Valuation" Order

A second reason to sell is by way of any preplanned decision, were the security investment to lose more than some maximum dollar amount, or percentage, from its prior level—commonly referred to as "stop losses."

For reasons peculiar to investors, too many have a narrow belief that preventing only initial capital losses are target goals, and that allowing of profits to melt away is less of a "loss." The flow of money—your money—away from you, is always value damage.

Any loss of asset value is a loss. Whether it's from initial capital or from unrealized gains, it is in either, losing money from some level a starting point or a high point. It is losing asset valuation that you would have been allowed to retain with prior planning. *There should little consolation if, in losing 20 to 30 to 40 percent of your potential profits, you still retain their original starting monies. That is suggestive of an acceptable roller-coaster ride through the making, giving back, making and taking away market cycle.*

The pivotal question is the uncontrolled balancing between not selling too soon (thus making some allowance for some retracement of profits, since the position might bring about larger valuation), and standing frozen with a "Gee I hope it doesn't..." and permitting far too much value to evaporate. This issue is central to investment: how much allowance should an investor make for the normal day-to-day and week-to-week gyrations in price before accepting that a trend change, and corresponding valuation change, might be starting, and thus exit? A scant more latitude should be given for retracements—stop loss pricing—*if the overall intermediate trend is still strongly with you; and much less latitude, if it isn't!*

These pre-planned levels, while individual and based upon our comfort in having sums of money "transact" up and down, should be religiously followed, and not second-guessed when they are about to occur! *(Otherwise, shrewd preventative loss levels are pointless!)*

Determine the amount of money you are prepared to part with in a corrective type price move, and then compute what percent figure of your portfolio that equates to, and use that percent as your price target sell point. *(You wish to do this because a simple percentage number in the abstract has no meaning; only when connected to a dollar figure does it have relevance—i.e., losing "12 percent." The 12 percent figure means nothing until compared to the dollars it represents.)*

*Example: the investor who owns 500 shares of a $70 stock and who felt that his tolerance for "giving up" value was 10 percent, but cringes at $2,000 daily changes. The investor is now in conflict were the above stock to drop 4 points to $66, or about 6 percent. This is well within his 10 percent threshold, but now he is at his $2,000 anxiety level (4* *points on a 500 share holding). You have to account for what dollar amount any innocent percent stop loss really represents.*

The dollar degree to which you may tolerate exposure to losing valuation is really individualistic, and it should be determined prior to transactions, or preordained if you will. "I sell whenever the valuation in my security(s) drops to 90 percent of where it had been." *(This is an approximate 10 percent automatic exit or "stop loss" order—and "stop loss" here is a misnomer, it should be termed a "stop decreasing valuation order." Others might raise their tolerance to 15 percent, or whatever a 15 percent valuation slide would equal in dollars. Some might go to 20 percent, yet going higher than that percent is simply too forgiving and defeating in purpose.)*

The percent level at which you sell is in ceaseless motion—it is never static. As portfolio valuation rises, so too does the "valuation stop" level.

*Example: if an account is worth $50,000, the 15 percent downside protection means that at about $42,000 the entire portfolio is taken out, sold, vamoose. If the account had first risen to $75,000, the 15 percent protection level, or here at about $64,000, is where complete liquidation should take place to retain 85 percent of the value of the investment assets at any point in time. The "stop losing valuation order" has risen; it is a dynamic level that isn't meant to be stationary.*

### A Sterling Alternative Investment Is Found

The third and final sell determinant is when you have very strong reason to believe an alternative investment can reward you greater than the one you are in, *and* you might have to liquidate the current holding to purchase funds for the alternative. It should be apparent that the "new" idea needs to have far more net potential after consideration of all commissions and perhaps tax liability before parting with the original idea.

Remaining married to positions that are not performing as expected is never wise. A replacement strategy can easily become the right substitute for monies either that were lost or below anticipation in the initial strategy. Why not allow a new alternative to create the wealth?

Lastly, elementary common sense *really* tells us when to sell. If we are in a long-term type bullish uptrend with the broad major markets making new highs every calendar quarter or two, and our stock choice(s) aren't advancing in the same proportion, this should be a subtle invitation to become very price focused...and fast. When the market's trend is becoming bearish and our portfolio is not yet losing ground, why, with the further possibility of price deterioration in a continuing bear trend, would you not become concerned? The broad market's bias should rarely be ignored.

### Added Exit Hints

It cannot be stated more forcefully, that selling, albeit profitably, too early during a strong intermediate trending move will result in far less than what might have been. Where we are intending to hold investments for any normal two and three month average intermediate duration and enjoy as much upside as that trend and position might produce, a little more latitude for retracements should be allowed. Although still, it may never be great, perhaps not beyond 15 percent (at very most 20 percent) price retracements. Selling too late within short-term strategies will mean giving away very large portions of value. Here your tolerance for giving up anything should be very small.

Your timing trigger with exit intention should be based upon the extent you are allowing for calendar time passage in your strategy. The longer the planned holding, the more tolerant of price retracement away from your expectations. The shorter the planned holding, you will exhibit less patience, and your exit will be faster.

Adopt the attitude: "I'm not going to allow only fate to play itself out to my advantage. I would rather take corrective action." This active, rather than passive, tact means you can somewhat control the degree away from your profitable expectations prices gravitate; the market or luck doesn't dictate price to you. You are selling under your set of exit parameters and when you want. And it creates more emotional peace this way as well.

### An Options Caveat

*The prior three exit determinants are the same with stock positions as with options, with one option exception. Since even small options price movement can cause drastic percentage loss—and in fairness gains as well—to protect against watching unexpected stock price action trample your options values, agree to liquidate positions at either losses of 50 percent of original capital or after one full-day, but before the close of day two of your having originated the position. Why?*

*Fast percentage options deterioration can occur. By limiting yourself to no more than a 50 percent parting of monies, you retain at least sufficient money to make a second run at another time. By remaining with a position that is working against you no more than two days, you are following the best short-term advice experience has taught: that stocks may not work the way their trend suggests or the market suggests every day for short-term prognostication, but they certainly better by the end of the next full day for short-term strategies. If they cannot, it just means they won't, and the strategy you employed will ultimately fail. A poor "waiting hero" you needn't desire to become.*

## Split the Exit Process—At Least When Selling Losers

Selling positions will almost always mean either a profit or a loss. The practical exit technique for each should be somewhat different.

Losses generate frustration that can be potentially lessened by selling in stages. In other words, sell a substantial portion, possibly 70 percent on a first sale after price evidence, and liquidate the remainder of the position two days later. It makes <u>little</u> <u>sense</u> to sell the entire second portion within hours. Remember, the reason we retain a small portion is to participate in a furtherance of equity. Selling within an hour or two doesn't provide us participation to any degree. Wait a short while, and in this way you "bracket" the sale around days and can enjoy the advantage if price moves your way in later days. This proportionate selling accomplished three things:

> • First, it moves most of the asset value, when a sale is warranted, into cash and away from presumed further harm.
>
> • Second, we can be wrong just as easily as being correct over very short-term periods. Retaining enough of a small portion allows for the possibility of some recovery and minimization of overall downside loss.
>
> • Third, the stigma of an assumed further loss of the held position isn't usually heightened, if even selling that remainder at a lower price, since lost money has already been accepted.

No one knows where price is headed over the next two hours or two days. You aren't likely going to be the exception! The main reason: the next price isn't intellectual. As an investor, you have to come to accept this securities fact. Play price momentum—not cerebral forecasting.

Exit technique when transacting out at profit can be in the same split manner, since the 25 to 30 percent "reserve" might still return more dollars, and that percentage degree of continued price participation is somewhat meaningful. Or it might just mean a 100 percent exit, since some happiness surely results, despite not "getting it all" if the investment were to continue to become even more profitable with you on the sidelines. If pressed, adopt the 70/30 split. It often surprises that as we exit, price invariably moves on to more profitably and, if so, it's nice to have at least a 30 percent participation share left. Once again, wait through the next day or two before selling the second lot.

It is trying to drive the fine line between removing yourself from harm's way if the pricing were to go against you, and having outright sold everything, and having nothing left to participate with.

## Exit Timing to Minimize Tax

If a profitable investment were made in just a few weeks, or certainly days, before attainment of long-term capital gains status, wherein profits are taxed at much less than ordinary income, probable sale deferral is required until that status is enjoyed. It doesn't make sense selling 12 days before long-term status, only to have to pay maybe 30 percent or more in federal income taxes because of impatience, or being foolishly unaware of your own security's ownership duration.

Secondly, there is a somewhat statistically simple formula to determine whether a complete exit is correct, if our existing position is short-term and some significant downside is expected.

Let's assume we have held a stock position for five or six months and felt it was ripe for a major move down. How can we know whether selling now and paying perhaps 25 to 30 percent in taxes as ordinary income is superior to waiting to see what develops? If we can anticipate our tax liability percent on ordinary income for this particular year, then we can know how far down the stock can approximately fall before the tax payment is greater than the potential loss.

*As an example, say we bought 500 shares of the stock at 40, and it's now at 100, six months later. It's still short-term. Assume that we still foresee a major sell-off (from having witnessed price evidence, technical price concerns, etc.) and must decide if selling now and paying Uncle Sam is better than chancing a 40 to 50 percent downward spike. Here's how you can do it.*

Our cost base for the investment is 40, selling now at 100, resulting in 60 profitable points or a proud 150 percent profit. The bad news is that it is subject to tax at our estimated 30 percent ordinary income tax bracket. This accounts for 18 points of the profit (60 profitable points times 30 percent). Selling today, even accounting for the tax liability, "protects us" down to a market price of 82, or about 18 points. If the stock were to drop much below 82 (more than -18 percent from current price) then our having sold short-term, and paying Uncle Sam now, was the better choice. (Had we retained the stock and had it fallen to 70, a 35 percent plunge, we would be far worse off having paid nothing in taxes and retaining our far less valuable shares. Selling out at a net 82 has us infinitely better positioned to buy back in, earn some interest, and seek another idea.)

The general formula: Current Market Price minus (the # of profitable points since purchase times the estimated tax bracket percent) compared to an Estimated Price After the Presumed Drop.

In the actual example:

100 – (60 x 30 percent) or 82 compared to (what?) price after the estimated drop.

A quick alternative is to utilize the assumed ordinary tax bracket you will be at in the year you sell, as the extent of percentage downside that you could entertain, before selling would have been an incorrect strategy.

Using the above as an example, if we decide to sell at 100 and we have a 30 percent probable ordinary tax rate this year, this means that only if the stock drops beneath 70 (100 minus 30 percent) are we better off having sold. (Had we sold and paid 30 percent of the gain in tax, and the stock meekly dropped to 90, we would have paid more in tax than the value of our shares at 90, had we simply retained the position.)

One further point: the idea that one can adeptly enter, exit, re-enter the markets and account for Uncle Sam's share per tax impact, on a short-term continuing basis, is next to impossible. The short-term tax impact alone accounts for generally 25 percent of any profits that might have been made. Add in a demand to "catch" the top and bottom makes the idea of quick enter and exit strategies nearly impossible to repeatedly master profitably. It may be worth the chance strategy if <u>huge price swings</u> can be anticipated, yet normally short-term profitable exit ideas coupled with paying away 25 percent and more in federal tax, is a tough impediment to overcome.

The bottom line here is the tax impact even when correct, and must be factored in as much as a loss of potential profits if the price moved away from expectations.

Selling positions is not as leisurely an exercise as the act of purchase, since the former must be done at some point in the future. The instant we sell might be bringing us the high price for the day, for the next week or even several weeks, but seldom will it be the high over any long period of time. Long term general upward security price bias almost makes this a certainty.

One last tip: to engage in efficient usage of sales monies, always place the sales proceeds immediately in cash money markets, taxable or not, or as quickly as "good funds" allow, until a reasoned alternative becomes apparent. Most broker software does this automatically, but it is always best to check.

## Order Placement

Just as with pacing purchase orders, attaining even small incremental price advantages always helps.

When placing sell orders, use limit orders which, excepting immediate exits, are the preferred approach. As already outlined, initially try to sell to the ask or offer side. It is at least worth the effort. (There will be a minority of times you will transact at the offer price and therefore save on the entire spread. This is especially possible when trading in stocks with great investor interest and heavy volume.) If this fails, or you have to close the position right away, enter your price at the highest then bid price.

The stock volume leaders will have a reported transaction about every five to ten seconds and during heavy activity, as is very common near the opening, nearly every two to three seconds. You may have anywhere from five to 15, even 20 trades per minute adding up to 800 to 1,200 per hour. This frequency through a full six or more hour trading day, might amount to more than 5,000 crossed specific transactions. We now see that the likelihood of not having any chance to execute where we want throughout most days isn't very great.

And it is usually the exception when stocks don't make two and three attempts near intraday high/low prices. Word to the prudent: patience might bring your price, although not exactly when you wanted.

# Epilogue

*It is an undeserved belief that if the authors of any financial text really had much of value to say, why would they provide it so relatively inexpensively in a book, and chance harming their own personal investments potential? In effect, why "tip" the public?*

*First, worthy books generate profit if accepted in the marketplace; both author and publisher—more the latter—can earn handsomely. Secondly, it is suspect that everyone who readily reads, then really learns, and ultimately translates that knowledge to habit—i.e., practices what they discover. Thus, being eased out of investment potential by even reacting readers isn't, practically speaking, going to impact authors. Third, the investment climate is so rich with ideas and opportunities that being left with none—their having been "stolen" or "used up" by one's readers—is rather irrational. Lastly, sometimes it's just worthwhile helping someone with the knowledge or experience you have acquired.*

*To those readers who have paid their money for this book, you should reap a payback many hundreds—but I sincerely believe—many thousands of times its cost. To that end, I would feel I have made a worthwhile contribution to each of you. This is partly because the acquired knowledge from almost all the learning experiences herein have been mercifully paid for by many prior personal, client and storied experiences…the real painful kind. Thus, herein, is a very expensive practical education given to each of you, for but the cost of a single financial text.*

*Practice and repeat, what you already know and what you will ultimately learn are correct actions for investment success. For all the time you may spend learning and planning is of no use—none to zero—if you do not discipline yourself to put into reality that*

267

*which you have learned, to be more likely than not, probable successful actions. Try not to assume anything outside your sphere of learning. It's one thing to have acquired long-earned education; it's the ultimate of immaturity in its fullest to repeatedly abandon that wisdom and the investment lessons thereof for the presumption that "this time will be different." The lessons from investment experiences, are almost priceless assets unto themselves. But also accept this fact: perfection in this unscientific profession isn't even close to attainment. You can't win in this arena with the best quadratic equation. Yet hard disciplined effort to paint the probabilities you learn do work, is over time is very amply rewarded.*

*As investors, we control almost nothing. Expect not that the marketplace will affirm our investment strategies consistently, for that is an impossibility. Without final control to dictate our investment future, even 80 percent successes don't occur for anybody. You will lose money. Strategies will bomb. Short-term price moves will turn you inside and out. This is typical. Just get positioned on the right side of most major trends and you will do very, very well!*

*Best of good fortune, and please allow the education of the material herein and your own real-world experiences to be your guide—not second guesses. Repeat enough successful actions and you may find our markets really do share their secrets…as well as their fortunes. For success on Wall Street is far less of a cerebral achievement than it is a disciplined effort to follow the repetition of what simply and repeatedly works, and that is learned from experience—yours, mine, and from others.*

*Learn the street's "rules"—then only practice what <u>works</u>. We're not polarizing neutrons!*

*Lastly, never, ever, underestimate the price trend. It is the dominant variable for investment performance. Respect its authority—its directional force. Do not assume what is not price evident. No one can ever know how far, or fast, urgent investors will move price.*

*Make the prevailing price trend your prime inspiration. Partner with your successful experiences, for they are the educational principles which will yield your future reward…go make some deserved money!!*

# Intermediate- & Longer-Term Investment Summary Outline

### Is There at Present an Obvious Market Trend In Place?
*It's in evidence if trending upward or downward over a reasonably aged calendar time frame; neutral, bottoming, and toppish price patterns are not forceful directional trends.*

### Is There Sufficient Time Left to Participate?
*Running after an <u>intermediate</u> trend having already moved 40 percent isn't good probability—nor is it proof we were even awake. If 15 to 20 percent moves won't motivate an initial participation, wait for another opportunity.*

### Is the Industry or Sector of the Specific Intended Investment in a Trend Parallel to the Market, or at Worst Neutral?
*Price trends in opposite direction to the broad market are to be avoided.*

### Is the Specific Intended Investment In Coincident Price Direction with the Market and Industry, or at Worst Neutral?
*Demand a parallel trend with the market and industry sector; if either is opposite, do not invest in that individual security instrument!*

### Does the Specific Investments Technical Condition Favor Right NOW?
*Check everything technically relevant! Everything!*

### Have You Checked if There Is Specific Company or Very Eventful Market News Imminent?
*Avoid being unpleasantly surprised—exposing your money.*

## Is the Period You Are in a "Normal" One?

*If not, the normal expectations may not work and all efforts to rely on these past experiences and the knowledge learned therefrom, might not help. Abnormal times are few in number but very important to discern.*

*If You Have 7 "Yes" Answers, Move To Initiate Action with Either of* Step 8:

**Buy or Short Stock with Cash or Transact on Margin**

**Open an Options Call or Puts Position, Preferably in-the-Money**

# *Short-Term Investment Summary Outline*

*As has been repeated, if the intention is to transact with a short-term perspective, it will be far more urgent to be extremely disciplined prior to a strategy. There won't be time to correct mistakes.*

### Only Invest in the Short-Term Directional Trend in Place
*It's up or it's down—there won't be time otherwise.*

### Consider the Stock's and/or Industry's/Market's Five-Day RSI
*One of the better short-term overbought/sold indicators at extremes.*

### Redo Time Tested Strategies You Know Work
*There may not be time for new ideas or lukewarm strategies to play out profitably.*

### Devote Total Time & Attention
*The random short-term nature of price demands that one be a total witness to all that might affect price movement until the position is closed out.*

### Pass on Hitting Financial Home Runs—There Isn't Sufficient Time
*Holding out for too much is a fool's wish; yet quick substantive profits should invite an exit.*

### Buy Larger Positions and/or on More Volatile Issues
*The reason being that even small correct price movement will yield far more worthwhile profitability.*

### Try & Acquire Real-Time Graphics

*Seeing where price has been and potentially headed intraday provides invaluable insight.*

### If Purchasing Options, Utilize In-the-Money as Priority One

*In-the-money options are preferred, since the correlation between stock and their trailing options. Price movement tends to be almost one-to-one. If you are correct regarding your equity price assessment, you want the option investment to completely reflect it in exactly that manner.*

### Focus on the Broad Markets and Their Intraday Trends

*There is almost no more dominant effect over the very short-term than the broad market your investment is part of. Accurate assessment of its direction, even intraday, is a prime reason short-term ideas play out successfully. Never be adverse to its short-term direction for more than a day or two at most.*

### Understand Your Investment's Price Volatility

*In doing so you, prepare yourself for the approximate extent of price reactions, and tend not to panic out of fast price action.*

### Accept the Probability That Trending Stocks Are Likely to Continue

*Despite the intuitive belief that they can't, short-term, consecutive price trends are at least a 50/50 bet to continue many consecutive days.*

### Sell Out of Unprofitable Positions No More Than Two Points Adverse to Your Entry Point

*We do not invest to part with monies. If loss is inevitable, as is common with short-term efforts, make it less and soon, rather than more and later.*

### Ignore Any 50/50 "Bets"

*If the near-term fate of strategies is premised upon a hit-or-miss piece of news or event, pass on the strategy. Insist the probabilities always be substantially in your favor…or wait for another day.*

### Accept Some Element of Front-Running Price Is Probably Necessary

*Waiting for certainty prior to initiating strategic involvement is an assurance to minimizing profitability. Some short-term price guesswork is prudent and essential to maximize short-term ideas.*

### Design an Exit Strategy before the Commencement of the Position… Exit if Met

*Short-term efficiency will not allow for too much price witnessing. Design an exit plan with fairly tight price points and if "hit," exit immediately. Only in this way, do you control price to a limited degree, rather than being inactive, hopeful, passive, and subordinate to the fate of random price action.*

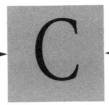

# What Really Caused the Late Fall 2001 Rally Post 9/11

*December 2001*

*As the main portion of this manuscript was being completed, the markets were driving to three month highs and even offering some evidence that a new bull market was prepared and being served. Only time will tell, but exploring the why is interesting and consistent with what we have already learned.*

*If we return to mid-spring 2001, our markets were in another dramatic sell-off, with the usual fundamental reasons to explain the drop. The markets managed to remain solvent through the late summer with an up and down bias, but with a continuing meek economic engine despite the Federal Reserve pumping help through lower interest rates and Congressional stimulus.*

*As fall began and September 11th tore through us, the markets expectedly dove again to new lows in late September, with new worries which continue. But the markets thereafter began a steady rise not unlike their country, and which continues as this is being written. Still, nothing of real significant and positive economic change has taken place since that spring. A weak economy, a bleak corporate profit outlook, occasional company debacles, Enron, etc., but what would point to logic-based explanation for the markets running? There isn't one.*

*The truth is that a selling dynamic simply always ends, and buyers eventually emerge. Wall Street is a true follow-the-leader world, that leader being the broad markets. At some point, there simply won't exist an overabundance of sellers. And on that day, in that period, despite the reason of logic, the markets will tip to the buy side with a blowing wind at their back from too many now eager to buy, with really nothing left to sell. Call it this time patriotic buying after "treasonous" selling—short and some purposefully long; but in fact, a trend's start really doesn't change over the decades, since price action begins from wherever and why it wants. The price trend is what it really remains ultimately all about.*

*Peace to those who left us.*

# *Index*

# About TEXERE

Texere, a progressive and authoritative voice in business publishing, brings to the global business community the expertise and insights of leading thinkers. Our books educate, enlighten, and entertain, and provide an intersection where our authors and our readers share cutting edge ideas, practices, and innovative solutions. Texere seeks to cultivate, enhance, and disseminate information that illuminates the global business landscape.

## www.thomson.com/learning/texere

# About the typeface

This book was set in 10 point Adobe Garamond. Adobe Garamond was created in the sixteenth century by Claude Garamond, a French printer and publisher. This typeface is known for its versatile and elegant design, which has made it a standard among book designers and printers for four centuries.

# Library of Congress Cataloging-in-Publication Data

Dussault, Thomas L.
  Price trends & investment probabilities / Thomas L. Dussault.
    p. cm.
  Includes index.
  ISBN 0-324-27150-6 (hardcover : alk. paper)
  1. Portfolio managment. 2. Investment analysis. 3. Stocks--Prices. l.
Title: Price trends and investment probabilities. ll. Title.
  HG4529.5.D87 2006
  332.63'222--dc22

                              2005025553